Workers of All Colors Unite

THE WORKING CLASS IN AMERICAN HISTORY

A list of books in the series appears at the end of this book.

Workers of All Colors Unite

Race and the Origins of American Socialism

LORENZO COSTAGUTA

UNIVERSITY OF ILLINOIS PRESS
Urbana, Chicago, and Springfield

Manufactured in the United States of America
1 2 3 4 5 C P 5 4 3 2 1
♾ This book is printed on acid-free paper.

Library of Congress Cataloging-in-Publication Data
Names: Costaguta, Lorenzo, author.
Title: Workers of all colors unite : race and the origins of American socialism / Lorenzo Costaguta.
Description: Urbana : University of Illinois Press, [2023] | Series: The working class in American history | Includes bibliographical references and index.
Identifiers: LCCN 2022034886 (print) | LCCN 2022034887 (ebook) | ISBN 9780252044922 (hardback ; alk. paper) | ISBN 9780252087073 (paperback ; alk. paper) | ISBN 9780252054082 (ebook)
Subjects: LCSH: Socialism—United States—History. | Working class—United States—History. | Equality—United States—History. | Race discrimination—United States—History. | Multiculturalism—United States—History.
Classification: LCC HX83 .C648 2023 (print) | LCC HX83 (ebook) | DDC 335.00973—dc23/eng/20220914
LC record available at https://lccn.loc.gov/2022034886
LC ebook record available at https://lccn.loc.gov/2022034887

To my family, for their love, care, and patience

Contents

Acknowledgments

The Socialist Labor Party entered my life more than a decade ago, when I was an MA student at the University of Turin in Italy, and I decided to write a dissertation on its leader Daniel De Leon. At the end of my very first research trip to the International Institute of Social History in Amsterdam, I thanked my uncle—Francesco Puppo, a militant historian and long-term member of the Italian Marxist-Leninist group *Lotta Comunista*—who had come with me and offered supervision and guidance in the archive. His response remained with me: "I am glad I joined you in what will be the first of many trips in your career." I thanked him without conviction, unpersuaded by his optimism about my career perspective.

I write these acknowledgements with a deep sense of gratitude toward the many who, like my uncle, have shown trust and faith in my capacity to pursue a career as a professional historian and to bring this book project to completion. I moved my first steps in the professional academic world (and in the literature on U.S. labor and socialism) following the advice of Nando Fasce. His staggering knowledge and intelligence gave me a model to aspire to. Christopher Phelps and Robin Vandome, my Ph.D. advisors, taught me the craft of the historian and gave me the confidence to pursue my own ideas. Their steering was crucial to this project and beyond. Brian Kelly and Bevan Sewell examined my thesis and provided me with more feedback than I could ever hope for. James R. Barrett and Angela Zimmermann read the entire manuscript and offered their comments on several versions of it. They were piecemeal, meticulous, and always supportive. I could not have hoped for better readers. My project set off with James Engelhardt at the helm of the Working Class in American History series at the University of

Illinois Press and ended under Alison Syring's watch. Their caring, enthusiastic, and patient guidance has been invaluable. To them and to the rest of the publication team at UIP goes my heartfelt gratitude.

Many colleagues and friends deserve a mention for the multiple ways in which they offered their support along the way. Charles Postel and Michael Strange did so much for this book. Charles offered trust and academic guidance. Michael was a tireless and meticulous proofreader of the final manuscript. Their extraordinary generosity and kindness toward me (and Marta) is a source of inspiration. Nikki M. Taylor, David R. Roediger, Mark A. Lause, and George N. Green were kind enough to share research findings with me. You will find their names mentioned in the relevant parts of this work, but I want to add a collective thank you here for their trust and generosity. I discussed my research and received support and insight from Tom Alter, Raffaella Baritono, Matteo Battistini, Tom Bender, Jakub Beneš, Tiziano Bonazzi, Paul Buhle, Mario Del Pero, Andrew Hartman, Mischa Honeck, Marco Mariano, Tony Michels, Matteo Pretelli, David R. Roediger, Arnaldo Testi, and Elisabetta Vezzosi—to all of them go my thanks. I drew inspiration and useful advice from the audiences of numerous conferences, workshops, and events in Europe and the United States where I presented my work. The 2015 HCA Spring Academy remains one of my fondest memories, not only for the feedback received on my work but also for the spirit of support and collegiality encountered. At the conferences of the Labor and Working-Class History Association, I found a community of like-minded labor historians that became a benchmark of academic quality and a constant source of admiration and inspiration. The RACEs reading group at the University of Birmingham kept me focused on my goal when I most needed it. The Modern History research cluster at the University of Bristol infused me with the enthusiasm and confidence to bring the revision of the manuscript to completion.

Many institutions provided vital financial support to this project. My gratitude goes to the Santander Mobility Fund, the British American Nineteenth Century Historians (BrANCH), the European Association for American Studies, the Eccles Centre at the British Library, the Department of American and Canadian Studies, the School of Cultures, Languages and Area Studies and the Graduate School of the University of Nottingham, and the School of History and Cultures at the University of Birmingham for their generous support. Moreover, a number of librarians and archivists guided me through the process of gathering the primary sources on which this research is based. I benefited from the kind and benevolent assistance of the staff of the Hallward Library in Nottingham, the British Library in

London, the Tamiment Library in New York City, the New York Public Library, the Wisconsin Historical Society, the Cincinnati History Library and Archives, the Dolph Briscoe Center for American History in Austin, the San Antonio Public Library, the St. Louis Central Library, the State Historical Society of Missouri, the International Institute of Social History in Amsterdam, the YIVO Institute for Jewish Research in New York City, the Harlan Hatcher Graduate Library in Ann Arbor, the Joseph A. Labadie Collection in Ann Arbor, and the Bancroft Library in Berkeley. Finally, I would like to thank the editors of the *Journal of the Gilded Age and Progressive Era* and *Contemporanea: Rivista di storia dell'800 e del '900* for the permission to publish in this book revised versions of material that was first published in their journals.

As a born and bred Italian who is based in the United Kingdom and travels the United States for work, I have come to embrace a certain confusion in my social, political, and cultural life. I rely on people to anchor my identity to something stable, and in the writing of this book, I have been blessed with the support and love of many. I have been traveling between the U.K. and Italy for more than a decade now—I owe to my Italian friends the capacity to bring me back in time whenever I am at home. Nottingham provided me with a beloved cohort of kindred souls—now scattered in the four corners of the world—that made my Ph.D. years as pleasant as they could ever be. The collegiality of Birmingham's "Team America" helped me through one of the hardest work periods of my life. At Bristol, I found an incredibly welcoming and rich human environment. I look forward to offering my contribution to what seems the ideal place to pursue my academic goals. I wrap up this section with a special mention to my book pals, Alex Bryne and Tom Bishop, who have waited far too long to add my book next to theirs.

This book is dedicated to my family. To my parents, Carla and Matteo, who made me the person I am and stood on my side at every turn of the road, ready to offer their help; to my siblings, Chiara and Giovanni, and their families, for the way in which we managed to hold together, despite the distance and the many bumps along the way; and to my partner of a life, Marta, source of endless care, love, and support. As you always say, the best is yet to come.

Workers of All Colors Unite

INTRODUCTION

A Racialized History of the Origins of American Socialism

On July 26, 1877, during a crowded meeting organized by the Amalgamated Trade Unions in New York City, the leader of the socialist Workingmen's Party of the United States (WPUS), Joseph P. McDonnell, took the platform to express his enthusiasm for the events of the previous week. Just days before, an impromptu strike by the workers of the Baltimore and Ohio Railroad had catalyzed the most widespread labor upheaval in the history of the country. As McDonnell addressed the crowd in Cooper Union's Great Hall, workers at the main railroad junctions in Pennsylvania, Maryland, Missouri, and Illinois were on strike for better working conditions.[1] One specific feature of the protest amazed the socialist leader: its interracial and internationalist nature. "It was a grand sight to see in West Virginia, white and colored men standing together, men of all nationalities in one supreme contest for the common rights of workingmen." McDonnell, an Irish immigrant, could not believe how events had apparently overcome national and racial divisions among workers. "The barriers of ignorance and prejudice were fast falling before the growing intelligence of the masses. Hereafter there shall be no north, no south, no east, no west, only one land of labor and the workingmen must own and possess it."[2]

If the strike confirmed to McDonnell the viability of a multiethnic and multiracial strategy for the organization of the American labor movement, socialists in other parts of the country were not so sure. In St. Louis, just two months after the strike, the German-language paper of the WPUS, *Volksstimme des Westens,* published an article titled "Die Indianer, Neger und Chinesen in Nord-Amerika." In it, the party militant R. Mills reversed McDonnell's perspective and identified the WPUS as the defender of the interests of white workers in America.[3] For McDonnell, the strike had moved the American working class one step closer to obliterating the "barriers of ignorance and prejudice." For Mills, clashes between racial groups were inevitable—the product of "ethnographic laws." The article used ostensibly scientific theories to demonstrate that the "Negro" and the "Indian" races were destined to become extinct, while the Chinese were at present the clearest threat to the white working class. "The Chinese [worker] does any kind of job, perhaps with the exception of the skilled ones" and "is the worst consumer there is." He "works for any cost" and "his stamina and skillfulness make him a rival for white workers."[4] This heavily racialized reading of American working-class relations closed with an openly white supremacist call based on socialist rhetoric: If workers wanted to defend themselves against Chinese immigrants, they should join the WPUS at once, the only party that would prioritize the defense of white workers against the Chinese menace.

McDonnell and Mills wrote during a moment of profound crisis for the United States. Each of their radically different opinions found a way in socialism to respond to the problems created by Gilded Age industrialization. Despite the political compromise between the Democratic and the Republican Parties brought about by the election of Rutherford B. Hayes to the White House in 1877, the country was going through changes that the political system was hardly able to control. Workers were struggling to reconcile with the seismic shift of American capitalism away from a proprietary-based structure to a corporate-based one. They found themselves confronting uncontrolled urbanization, weakened democratic structures, and a discarded agrarian culture and set of values.[5]

Socialist discourse attested to important transformations occurring in the very structure of American capitalism: the racialization of the relations of production. The abolition of chattel slavery in 1865 and the sudden transformation of four million formerly enslaved people into wage workers, sharecroppers, and convict laborers was followed by a rapid increase in immigration from Europe and Asia. This added new disparities to a society that was already characterized by the presence of Native American enclaves in the Midwest and West, Mexican American communities in the southwestern territories, and African American workers everywhere.[6] The American working class became internationalized, multiracial, and multiethnic. McDonnell, with his appeal to interracial and interethnic solidarity on the one hand, and Mills, with his white supremacy on the other, furnished answers to a key dilemma faced by American workers active in labor associations, trade unions, and parties during the Gilded Age: To what extent were racial solidarity and class solidarity compatible with each other?

How did American socialists address the racialization of capitalist relations of production during the years when the United States was in the process of transforming into an industrial superpower? The end of Reconstruction coincided with the foundation of the first national party in the United States that had a socialist program. Socialist activists convened in Philadelphia in 1876 and fused four different socialist groups into the Workingmen's Party of the United States, a name that was changed to the Socialist Labor Party (SLP) one year later.[7] Despite ups and downs in its political presence, the SLP was one of the few labor organizations to remain active throughout the Gilded Age, a period characterized by political volatility. With a strong presence in industrial centers like New York, Chicago, Cincinnati, and St. Louis, and with various outposts in the South and West, the SLP laid the foundations for the American Left in the twentieth century.

Within the ranks of the SLP, American socialists embarked on an unprecedented attempt to use socialist principles to understand, explain, and ultimately change the circumstances created by racial and ethnic divisions in post-Reconstruction United States. They did this from a perspective different and apart from what David Montgomery has described as the "mainstream of the post-Civil War labor movement."[8] During Reconstruction, the American labor movement formulated its own conception of American freedom. Tapping into abolitionist language, American unions denounced rising industrialization as a system of "wage slavery" and vocally campaigned for its abolition. Institutions like the Knights of Labor based their activism on "labor republicanism," an unstable mix of cooperativism and individualism.[9] American socialists only partly adhered to this producerist outlook. While sharing rhetorical attacks on wage slavery, they opted for class struggle as their main analytical framework.[10] Precisely for this reason, socialist ideas on race and class were unique among Gilded Age radicals. Unlike the many labor and farmers' organizations active in the period, from the Greenback Labor Party to the Knights of Labor and the populists, socialists cultivated an understanding of race relations that was intertwined with their class-focused ideology.

It was not just class issues that distinguished socialist opinions of the time. Even a cursory glance at the first SLP members lists reveals that ethnicity was another decisive feature shaping socialist thought during the Gilded Age.[11] In the period under consideration, American socialism was thought, spoken, and written almost entirely in German. Between 1876 and 1890, 80–90 percent of SLP members had German origins, a situation that changed only after the mid-1890s, when German American socialists more markedly oriented themselves toward trade unionism while English-speaking activists took control of the organization.[12] German American socialists drew heavily on their German background to understand and tackle issues of racial and ethnic diversity in the United States. They applied "imported" intellectual categories to the problems of paramount importance at the time, such as Chinese immigration and U.S.–Native American relations on the frontier. In so doing, they produced conversations characteristic of the highly internationalized, multicultural, and multilingual public sphere of late nineteenth-century United States.

Socialists in the large German American communities of the Northeast and Midwest trusted the thriving scene of radical local newspapers to faithfully reproduce their opinions on the multiple questions of the time—the "Chinese question," the "Negro question," the "Indian question," and the most important of all, the labor question.[13] The columns of official and non-official SLP publications, such as the *Labor Standard*, the *Socialist*, the *Vorbote*, and the *Arbeiter Stimme*, provide an extensive and prolonged discussion on socialism and race that took place between 1876 and 1899. The sheer number of articles in the socialist press dedicated to African Americans, Native Americans, Chinese immigrants, and immigration more generally, contradicts the argument that early socialists were not interested in race.[14] The nature of the material explored, however, also tells us that socialists rarely produced analyses of the racial problem, including racism and its impact, in the same outspoken way as contemporaneous intellectuals and politicians like T. Thomas Fortune and Ida B. Wells.[15] What we observe among American socialists is a wide variety of opinions on the multiple ways race was discussed in the late nineteenth century. Discussions on race explored the cultural, natural, and social compatibility between different racial and ethnic groups. They tested the limit and flexibility of conceptions of American citizenship and democracy. They envisioned the future of the country in a way that was compatible with socialist ideology.

Modern racial science, from geographic determinism to Darwinism and anthropology, provided the most common scaffolding to socialist understanding of racial difference. In the Gilded Age, conversation on scientific racial theories was by no means limited to the elite but was a constant feature of everyday life. For socialists, tackling racial equality in the context of a burgeoning capitalist economy meant envisioning a path toward industrial modernity and progress where class and racial equality went alongside. The use of scientific racialism by socialists was not an expedient to justify and rationalize economic advantages based on race. It stemmed from a genuine intellectual concern and curiosity. In a moment when imperial expansion was on the agenda of every European power (with the United States soon to join at the end of the century), colonization of large swathes of Africa and

Asia took place, and mass migration to the United States was at its peak, theories of race became the means through which both domestic and global hierarchies of power and control were articulated. A movement like socialism that described itself as "scientific" was in need of clarification on these debates. Socialists *had* to deal with modern scientific racialism if they were going to become a credible and acceptable alternative to the republican and/or corporate liberal mainstream.[16]

In this context, there were two main ways in which socialists approached racial diversity that reflected their overall position on class organization—the scientific racialist viewpoint of Mills and the internationalist stance of McDonnell. Scientific racialists agreed with Mills that modern natural and human sciences provided enough evidence to suggest that humankind was divided into different groups ("races" or "cultures"), that some groups were inferior to others, and that socialism, in order to be considered as a truly modern intellectual doctrine, needed to accommodate this evidence. In this perspective, equality as a value was not abandoned. But more often than not, its defense came with racial undertones: In contemporary America, only members of certain racial groups could aspire to it. By contrast, internationalists joined with Joseph P. McDonnell to fundamentally reject the idea that racial and ethnic division had anything to do with economic relations between employers and employees. Rather, they held that class rather than race should be the heart of the matter when tackling the problems of American workers.

The following pages chronicle the clash between these two points of view in the American socialist movement during the Gilded Age, arguing that a major shift occurred. Balancing intellectual and institutional history, *Workers of All Colors Unite* establishes the path through which scientific racialism was abandoned and an internationalist, class-focused, and racial-conscious socialism became the most common method to approach the question of race in the American socialist movement during the twentieth century and beyond. Against a backdrop that dismisses Gilded Age socialism as "un-American," politically irrelevant, and uninterested in race, I trace the peculiar origins of a movement that relied on its immigrant nature to carve an original path toward a racial-conscious, class-focused, and world-oriented socialist ideology.

• • •

Published more than a hundred years ago, Werner Sombart's essay *Why Is There No Socialism in the United States?* has retained an enduring influence in the historiography of American socialism. Sombart voiced the heartfelt concern of European socialists: How was it possible that a structured socialist movement, by definition the by-product of capitalist economic development, was not taking root in the country that, more than any other in the Western world, was subsuming a capitalist economic structure? Although Sombart's argument was rapidly abandoned in favor of more informed and detailed points of view, the question he put forward continued to haunt scholars of the American Left for generations. While a full analysis of the significance of Sombart's pamphlet is not relevant in this context, a description of how it has shaped the historiographical landscape on socialism in the United States helps to introduce the key themes this book seeks to investigate.

Since the publication of Sombart's essay in 1906, scholars of American socialism have been animated by one of two goals.[17] Either they explain the ultimate reason why socialism failed to thrive in the U.S., or they make the case that, in one form or another, socialism actually did shape the history of the country in some significant way. Works in the first group begin with Sombart's essay and include undertakings by Selig Perlman, Seymour Martin Lipset, Gary Marks, Mike Davis, Robin Archer, and Kim Moody, among others.[18] This branch of historiography has produced more and more sophisticated versions of American exceptionalism. Initially, Sombart suggested that American workers did not join socialist parties because the booming American economy made them better off than their European counterparts. Perlman later complicated the matter by suggesting that American workers were *job*-conscious rather than *class*-conscious. Scholars including Lipset, Marks, and Archer introduced other elements, such as the exceptional narrow-mindedness and sectarianism of American socialist movements and the impact of ethnic and racial divisions on the organization of the American working class. For all these scholars, the bottom-line argument remained the same: Given the exceptional social, economic, and political features of the country, socialism simply could not develop in the United States.

Scholars in the second group have followed two paths. The first has been to loosen the definition of "socialism" and include the many ways left-minded radicals, activists, and intellectuals, often working outside socialist parties, contributed to making change in the country.[19] Alternatively, scholars have made the point that, despite first impressions to the contrary, America *did* have a genuine socialist tradition of its own, whose history has been neglected. This group includes scholars as diverse as the socialist leader Morris Hillquit and the American historian Timothy Messer-Kruse. Nevertheless, their work is united by reclaiming the existence and impact of an indigenous and distinctively American socialist movement.[20]

While Sombart's dilemma has contributed to explorations in the history of American socialism, the repetitive focus of his argument has created problems. As suggested by Eric Foner and Leon Fink, with its Marxist premise—that it was inevitable that the capitalist United States developed a class-conscious working class—Sombart's framing has invited a tendency toward ahistorical answers that fail to understand the significance of the American radical world, including the socialist, in its own terms and with its own features.[21] The very existence of questions on the political success of American socialism belies the obvious: American socialism was, and still is, a part of U.S. history. Exploring the specificity of socialism in the United States is more important than attempting to explain why it did not follow the trajectory that Sombart, or other Marxist thinkers, believed it should.[22]

Workers of All Colors Unite leaves aside the insistence with explaining the reasons for the failure of socialism in the United States and avoids the search for a "genuinely American" (read: non-immigrant) socialist movement. On the contrary, it adopts race and ethnicity as the two privileged lenses to understand the early history of socialism, in the conviction that it was precisely the multiethnic and multiracial nature of the American working class that shaped the way in which American socialism developed. There is an abundance of literature detailing how race and ethnicity played a crucial role in shaping the American social fabric and how racism has been an unfailing ideological construct used to shape and stabilize relations of power. In the words of James R. Barrett and David R. Roediger, "Americanization . . . was never just about nation but always about race and nation."[23] Through "race and nation," the history of the origins of American socialism acquires new meaning.

Works of leftist movements inspired by the multicultural turn show two paths to follow.[24] The first is found in the numerous histories of specific ethnic groups dealing with their social, economic, and political contributions to the development of the country. In *The Spirit of 1848*, a political history of the antebellum German American community, historian Bruce Levine wrote that his work "rejects the 'either/or' approach to studying ethnicity and class."[25] By adopting an analytical framework that accommodates the fluid relationship between these two concepts, Levine shed light on the ways in which German Americans contributed to building the Republican Party and shaping the abolitionist movement in the 1850s. In this way, Levine opens a path for the many scholars who have come after him.[26] The second tendency is characterized by historians who pay special attention to the combined effects of political development and ethnically based dynamics. A case in point is Paul Buhle's *Marxism in the United States*, a history of left-wing movements that focuses on the multiethnic nature of American radicalism.[27]

In a parallel development, the studies of "whiteness" that proliferated in the early 1990s have both complicated and refined existing views on the relationship between race, ethnicity, and radicalism. Kathleen Cleaver has written that David R. Roediger's *The Wages of Whiteness* starts with a vital premise, "that the race problem is a white problem." Her assessment can easily be extended to many foundational works on the question of whiteness.[28] This innovation—studying white ideologies of race—undertaken by scholars of whiteness racialized extensive areas of inquiry, ways of conceptualizing, and methods of analysis that had previously been untouched.[29] In labor history, one concept that has undergone renovation thanks to whiteness studies is labor republicanism. In the words of James R. Barrett, "Labor republicanism, long an organizing principle for so much nineteenth-century labor history, will never quite be the same."[30] To effect this change, historians have focused on language and the development of labor ideologies, explaining the racist implications of labor republicanism as a concept created by white workers in opposition to enslaved Black labor.

In ethnic and immigration studies, whiteness studies have had a key role in what Anna Pegler-Gordon has called the "racial turn" in the discipline.[31] In 1999, George J. Sanchez lamented the inability of immigration historians to acknowledge "the centrality of race in the United States," especially in regard to the experience of Asian Americans and Latinos.[32] In the past two decades, as noted by John J. Bukowczyk, ethnic and immigration studies have moved in the direction signaled by Sanchez. "Academic openings in European immigration and ethnic history have become scarce, while Asian American and Latino research has flourished."[33] Whiteness scholars, studying European immigrants as racialized subjects, started a trend that, in turn, has caused barriers between racial and ethnic studies to fall.

Workers of All Colors Unite sits at the intersection where scholarship on socialism in the United States meets ethnic and racial studies. It leaves aside the obsession with explaining the reasons for the failure of socialism in the United States and avoids the search for a "genuinely American" socialist movement, which have ensnared previous generations of historians. Instead, by following the path opened by scholars of whiteness, race, and ethnicity, this book explores the profound political significance of race and ethnicity in the history of the American socialist movement. As scholars have rearticulated the conceptions of ethnicity and labor republicanism in racial terms, it is now time to explain the origins of American socialism through the lens of race. *Workers of All Colors Unite* achieves this not only by using the malleable concept of ethnicity adopted by whiteness and ethnic studies and showing how the German origins of socialists affected their understandings of race but also by putting debates on race center stage and reconstructing the early history of American socialism through that perspective.

Political scientist Michael C. Dawson has contended that in works on left-wing movements and the origins of Marxism in the United States, we see a "general absence of taking race seriously, as a historical phenomenon that has profoundly shaped American institutions, politics, and civil society, as well as individual preferences, norms, and ideologies."[34] This assessment is farfetched for periods such as the Progressive Era or the 1930s—decades to which historians have dedicated much attention—but it fully hits the mark for the literature on the Left and race during the Gilded Age.[35] By combining the focus on institutional history of existing scholarship on socialism with the innovative understandings of race and ethnicity which have developed in the last fifty years, *Workers of All Colors Unite* takes up Dawson's invitation to put race and ethnicity at the core of histories of the Left and conveys a new understanding of the role of the SLP in shaping ideas of socialism and race in the United States at the turn of the twentieth century.

• • •

A longstanding tenet of literature on socialism in the United States has been that Gilded Age and Progressive Era socialists were not interested in the "race question." According to this view, socialists rarely discussed race at all, and when they did, it was mostly to remind workers that they ought to be focused on class exploitation rather than race exploitation. Scholars, saying that socialists were being faithful to a rigid interpretation of Marx's historical materialism, have argued that socialists in the Gilded Age and Progressive Era dismissed race as belonging to the "superstructure" of human relations, whereas class shaped the structure. Furthermore, they have claimed that for socialists, racial divisions were a distraction, an artifice, used by capitalists to divide the working class. Taking it as a symbol of the time, scholars have pointed to Eugene V. Debs's infamous wording, that socialists "have nothing special to offer the Negro."[36]

In *Black Marxism*, political scientist Cedric J. Robinson identified the origins of the fraught relationship between socialism and race in Marx's and Engels's underestimation of the historic role of racism in structuring global capitalism. For Robinson, capitalism was "racial" from its very inception. Ideas of race already structured European relations since the Middle Ages.

They filtered through in the establishment of capitalism in the sixteenth century via the spread of slavery and imperialism. Robinson suggested that both Marx and Engels failed to adequately integrate the impact of racial ideologies in their historical materialist analysis—a shortcoming reflected in Marx and Engels's poor comprehension of nineteenth century nationalism. Only the advent of a Black radical tradition led by C. L. R. James and W. E. B. Du Bois in the twentieth century succeeded in restoring the correct place of race and racism in the historical materialist framework of analysis of contemporary capitalism.[37]

Interpreters of Marx's thought responded to Robinson by contending that Marx's works already provided the means to understand the functioning of racial capitalism. Kevin B. Anderson suggested that in the folders of Marx's writing on non-Western socialists, colonialism, and the American Civil War are the pieces to assemble a non-Western-centric, multilinear, historical materialist framework. It is a framework in which capitalism is already understood as a global phenomenon taking different routes in its unfolding in various continents; in which there is no established road toward socialism; in which multiple means through which workers can emancipate themselves are envisioned. Even if Marx's racial thinking—and his understanding of American racism in particular—remained limited, his works already provide the keys for a racial critique of global capitalism.[38]

Gilded Age socialist analyses of the racialization of American capitalism provide us with a perspective through which to explore the entangled relationship between Marxism, socialism, and race. The late nineteenth century is a generative and understudied period. In the decades that followed the death of Karl Marx in 1883—in the passage "from Marx to Marxism," as historian Geoff Eley aptly puts it—socialists across the world established the framework of a conversation on Marxism and race that would continue throughout the twentieth century and beyond.[39] American socialism hardly features in histories of global socialism of the period—yet another legacy of the long-held idea that socialism did not exist in the United States. The early racialization of American capitalism provides one more reason for making American socialism a pivotal chapter of the unfolding history of Marxian socialism across the world. When further contextualized in a global conversation on modernity, class and race, and colonialism and imperialism, the relevance of American socialist debates on race becomes even more evident.

For the period under scrutiny in this book, analyzing socialist debates on race requires delving deep into the intellectual climate of their time, and in particular, in debates on scientific racialism and evolutionism. This is because the Gilded Age is commonly identified as the epoch of the rise of "social Darwinism." Richard Hofstadter first articulated this concept—for long time an organizing principle of the period. Hofstadter maintained that during the Gilded Age, a moment of clarification and simplification occurred. In the late nineteenth century, long-existing trends of racism, imperialism, and laissez-faire economics were fused together into the all-conquering social Darwinist credo. Hofstadter maintained that through Herbert Spencer's and William Graham Sumner's popularized versions of Darwin's theories, the capitalists could further their conservative agenda by basing it on principles of economic and racial competition and the doctrine of the "survival of the fittest."[40]

Starting in the 1970s, scholars have dissembled Hofstadter's theory piece after piece. They have suggested that, while many of the tendencies described by Hofstadter effectively took root in the Gilded Age, the connection between that period and social Darwinism was more tenuous than Hofstadter has argued. With regard to ideas of race specifically, scholars revising Hofstadter have maintained that in the Gilded Age, the version of Darwinism supported by Spencer and Sumner was but one of many scientific accounts advanced to address evolution and human differences. The theories, which included scientific racialism, Lamarckism (the most widespread scientific exposition of geographic determinism), and Lewis H. Morgan's anthropology, were often mixed with one another and were drawn on inconsistently, in a variety of ways, and with an eye to developing political positions on racial and ethnic difference.[41] *Workers of All Colors Unite* situates the history of the SLP within this intellectual context, showing how waves of immigrants and the advancement of the party intertwined with an unfolding conversation on evolution, race and modernity.[42]

SLP politics, in particular the distinction between scientific racialism and internationalism, mapped onto transnational trends. Socialists across the world sought ways to link evolutionism, the analysis of racial differences, and anti-capitalist activism. The political contrasts in the SLP predated clashes that would structure contrasts over colonialism, imperialism, and race in the Second International at the beginning of the twentieth century.[43] As such, their significance transcends the American scenario. The first years of the SLP reveal that scientific racialism was a broad tent under which it was possible to forge unity between German immigrants of various generations and English-speaking members with different radical orientations. SLP German American members added components to the wealth of pseudoscientific approaches adopted by American intellectuals and politicians to confront differences among human groups. An early generation of socialist immigrants, born in the 1820s and 1830s and arriving in the United

States after the 1848 Springtime of the Peoples, coupled geographical determinism and Darwinism with German historical linguistics and Romantic naturalism. Conversely, a later generation of radical socialists, pushed to migration by Otto von Bismarck's 1878 anti-socialist laws, presented a rigid worldview in which Darwinism was an inescapable law of nature that governed social relationships as well as the evolution of humankind. While their ideas were very close to the worldview presented by Herbert Spencer in both the United Kingdom and United States, this group was influenced by Ernst Haeckel, the most important Darwinian in Germany.

In this context, characterized by a hegemony of scientific racialist approaches, internationalists were an exception. Structuring their worldview on a radically alternative set of principles—historical materialism—and rejecting any connection between their political doctrine and evolutionist theories, they placed themselves outside the mainstream intellectual conversation of the time while furnishing a point of view that defended workers with no distinction of race and nationality. Internationalists adopted an approach that was often incompatible with the social, economic, and political conditions that they encountered in the U.S. Still, their principled commitment to class equality helped forging innovative political pathways in a context where workers' solidarity was systematically undermined by racial and ethnic tensions.

Reconstructing the early politics of the SLP through a racial lens has the twofold effect of placing U.S. socialism within a global conversation and rescuing the American specificity against its European counterparts. The most detailed histories of the SLP, such as Perlman's and Foner's, dedicate much attention to the early socialist contrast between trade unionists and supporters of political action (usually defined as "Marxists" and "Lassalleans"). These are German labels that do not capture a situation that in the United States presented different social features.[44] If "Marxist" and "Lassallean" are abandoned and replaced with "internationalist" and "scientific racialist," this ideological distinction based on racial policies allows a better explanation of the origins of American socialism and the significance of race in it.

Political expediency in relation to race and ethnicity was the principle organizing socialist politics in the early Gilded Age, and this was reflected in the political behavior of the two factions that animated the party at its foundation. Electoral politics was far more compatible with scientific racialism than with internationalism. Internationalists like Friedrich A. Sorge and Joseph P. McDonnell aimed to campaign across racial and ethnic lines, an approach that rarely met electoral success. At the same time, they were not willing to support restrictive immigration norms (such as the 1882 Chinese Exclusion Act, for example), which were popular among white workers. Conversely, scientific racialism was more malleable and versatile. It allowed internal debates on multiple topics, from Chinese immigration to the Native American presence on the frontier, actively seeking to strike compromises that could guarantee electoral success and still be in line with socialist values and modern theories of race.

The SLP, founded on a compromise between scientific racialists and internationalists, struggled to find a balance between these two mismatching approaches. Just a couple of months after the 1876 founding convention, party sections broke the compromise upon which the party was founded and mounted SLP candidates in local elections. By the end of 1877, a sizable group of internationalists had left the socialist organization and founded a new trade organization, the International Labor Union. Other trade unionist groups remained in the SLP, but from that moment onward, internationalism became a minority position in the socialist party, with socialists of the SLP at ease with a scientific racialist ideology that controlled the organization. This circumstance had profound consequences for the 1880s American socialist movement. It was no coincidence that in this decade, many supporters of internationalism operated outside the organized Left—in the Knights of Labor, in the American Federation of Labor, in Henry George's and Edward Bellamy's movements, and so on—rather than within it. Pragmatic socialists who aimed to bring forward their ideals of working-class solidarity did not hesitate to join other organizations that gave them the opportunity to bring forward their internationalist message.

Meanwhile, in the 1880s, the SLP became a site of political and intellectual experimentation. Scholars have demonstrated how in the late nineteenth century, race and ethnicity regulated the access to American citizenship. Chinese immigrants were the first group whose right to enter and settle in the country was openly targeted through federal legislation. Native Americans had no chance to decide their destiny. Their ancestral lands were occupied by white colonizers and sliced by corporate capitalism. Debates on "civilization," "savagism," and "assimilation" rationalized this process for white public opinion. African Americans saw the advancements made during Reconstruction being dismantled bit after bit in the restoration of white supremacy in the South and consolidation of de facto segregation in the North.[45] It is in relation to these problems that American socialists of the 1870s and 1880s exercised their most original theoretical attempts. Confronted with a reality of stark inequality and convinced that such inequality was written in immutable scientific laws, socialists came up with highly inventive attempts to reinvent socialism in egalitarian terms. Rarely successful in either theory or practice, these opinions attest to the enduring influence of evolutionism in the Gilded Age.

The 1890s saw a decisive and, this book argues, definitive shift away from scientific racialism and in favor of working-class internationalism. Several factors contributed to this shift: With the intensification of labor conflicts and the worsening of economic conditions (especially after 1893), more workers were attracted to socialism. In turn, immigration brought in a wealth of non-American workers who found a home in radical movements, like the socialist and the anarchist. In the meantime, the German American grasp on the SLP weakened, with many German American socialists loosening the connection with organized socialism in favor of trade union activism. This ethnic and organizational reshuffle favored a clarification of the SLP's political strategy. Under the controversial leadership of Daniel De Leon, the SLP solved the tensions between internationalism and scientific racialism by embracing a socialist evolutionist approach strongly focused on class struggle and class equality. In the 1890s, the SLP replaced Darwin and Spencer with the anthropologist Lewis H. Morgan, adopting a very rigid platform that pushed for labor solidarity across the racial line based on common class interests. This is the position that many socialists adhered to when they abandoned the SLP and joined Eugene V. Debs in 1901 to found the Socialist Party of America (SPA).

An analysis of Gilded Age socialism helps us to better understand the reasons that pushed socialists in the direction of embracing a class-first (but not necessarily class-only) approach. It was precisely the idea of disentangling socialism from potentially damaging forms of racial essentialism, which characterized modern theories of race during the Gilded Age, that pushed socialists in the direction of class-first socialism as the official doctrine of the party in the 1890s. By the time this approach had become the position of the American movement, the eugenics craze was yet to start. Pseudoscientific theories that justified illiberal and genocidal policies against racial minorities were gaining momentum.[46] The rejection of Spencerism and other racist paradigms that underpinned the diffusion of eugenics and Jim Crow in the early twentieth century nurtured socialist convictions of the importance of a class-first point of view. Only *outside* that intrinsically racist conversation could socialists articulate a doctrine that was truly egalitarian in its approach to workers' relations. William P. Jones has convincingly argued that Eugene V. Debs's class-focused approach on race needs to be reassessed in light of Debs's egalitarian beliefs.[47] *Workers of All Colors Unite* pushes the case further. It suggests that an investigation of the origins of American socialism attests to the attempts of many socialists to create a class-focused and race-conscious stance, a position that Debs's outlook embodied perfectly.[48]

This attempt to deconstruct class-focused internationalism does not dismiss or obliterate the shortcomings of Gilded Age and Progressive Era socialists. In fact, an analysis of a class-first socialist point of view better exposes what made American socialism incapable of understanding race and its impact on the American social context. While clearly aimed at defending racial egalitarianism, socialists' adoption of a "colorblind" approach excluded them from the wider conversation on the role of race in shaping economic and social structures. Paradoxically, supporters of scientific racialism in the late 1870s and 1880s were actively in search of a version of socialism compatible with the multiracial and multiethnic composition of the American working class. Conversely, internationalists produced an approach as perfect in theory as it was inapplicable in practice.

American socialism entered the twentieth century equipped with a racial policy that carried within itself these contradictions. In 1901, the torch of harbinger of American socialism went from the SLP to the Socialist Party of America. Under the skilled leadership of Eugene V. Debs, the American socialist movement purged itself of its most sectarian attitudes to embrace its multiethnic and composite nature. While retaining in its folds the large immigrant communities that had animated the movement during the Gilded Age, the SPA further expanded across the country by picking up the legacy of the populist movement and leading the charge against the underregulated corporate capitalism of the Progressive Era, both at the local and at the federal level. Yet these changes were not sufficient to solve socialist contradictions on race. In the early twentieth century, white SPA members continued to insist that socialists should discard race to focus on class instead—a position that ignored the structurally racist nature of American capitalism.

Only a broader shift could break the impasse. In the 1920s, the hegemony of scientific racialism and eugenics over the global racial discourse—a hegemony that fit with the consolidation of Western empires across the world and whose tenets shaped the U.S.'s immigration policy in 1924—came under attack. The birth of the U.S.S.R., with its open challenge both to aristocratic authoritarianism and to liberal capitalism, sent shockwaves across the world. What is more, the Russian Revolution uprooted the relationship between race and working-class internationalism from its foundations. At the heart of this shift was Lenin's position on imperialism. By understanding imperialism as the "supreme phase of capitalism," Lenin turned the colonial masses—especially its working-class component—into the protagonists of an impending war that could take down capitalism and imperialism in one stroke. Under communist doctrine, race stopped being irrelevant to left-wing activists across the world. Instead, it became the privileged way to recognize the working-class frontline of the global war against capitalist imperialism.[49] In the 1930s, American communists embraced this approach and started an unprecedented period of working-class activism across racial lines in the American Left. This decade consolidated the United States as a territory of innovation and experimentation of the global Left when it came to addressing oppression along the lines of class and race. None in the Gilded Age socialist movement went close to achieving the theoretical and practical effectiveness of the communists in the 1930s. Yet in the Gilded Age victory of an internationalist, class-focused, racial egalitarian socialism over scientific racialism, the seeds were sown for the future of the Left to grow.[50]

• • •

The structure of this project reflects the mutually reinforcing imperatives of institutional and intellectual history. While the events described here cover the period from the early 1850s until the end of the century, the first twenty-six years of the SLP's political trajectory is given particular attention. In this period, there are two key chronological landmarks: the foundation of the party in 1876 and the 1899 split between De Leon's supporters and his political adversaries. In this interpretation, the 1899 split was the moment when the SLP lost its centrality in the American socialist movement and stopped influencing its political and intellectual inclinations. While the sources analyzed have been collected across various newspapers, and personal and institutional archives, the bulk of the analysis focuses on a group of leaders of the party, whose political trajectory is used to explain broader trend in the movement and the country as a whole.

Within these chronological and methodological limits, the first chapter reconstructs socialist ideas of race and ethnicity before and after the Civil War. It provides the intellectual background that informed later discussions of socialism and race. Chapter one takes the Civil War as a dividing line and argues that, whereas in the antebellum period socialists were part of the radical wing of the abolitionist movement, after 1865, these same socialists emerged from Reconstruction as one with the majority of American workers who believed that, once chattel slavery was abolished, it was time to solve the problem of wage slavery, leaving aside the question of race. The second chapter starts with the foundation of the SLP in 1876 and introduces the dichotomy between internationalists and scientific racialists within its membership. Most of the chapter is dedicated to demonstrating how different waves of German immigrants brought with them different approaches to the problem of racial diversity and how their differences impacted the history of the party.

Chapters three, four, and five have both chronological and thematic structures. Each of them covers the period between 1876 and 1890, variously discussing struggles within the SLP over the "Chinese question," the "Negro question," and the "Indian question," respectively. The focus of each chapter moves from single leaders of the party (such as Adolph Douai, Peter H. Clark, and Albert R. Parsons), to specific sections, to events that characterized the history of the party in that period. In this way, the chapters develop the multiplicity of voices that characterized the SLP in its early history. Finally, chapter six documents the party's shift in the 1890s. In this decade, the movement went from a small German American cradle to maturity as a nationally organized, English-speaking political party. It developed a clear political line, in part as a result of the invasive leadership of the controversial Marxist leader Daniel De Leon, abandoned its scientific racialist opinions, and embraced a rigidly class-first stance. The 1890s success of the SLP was based on a compromise between an English-speaking Marxist leadership and a multiethnic rank-and-file solidly rooted in the northern and midwestern industrial cities. By the end of the century, the too-rigid program of Americanization of the organization imposed by De Leon and his acolytes provoked a split in the party. While the SLP lost its centrality as a result of this split, internationalism remained the enduring legacy of this first phase of the history of American socialism.

CHAPTER 1

"Freedom for All"

German American Socialism and Race before 1876

From the general headquarters of the International Workingmen's Association (IWA), Karl Marx saluted the surprising victory of Abraham Lincoln in the 1864 presidential election with unprecedented enthusiasm. In a message to the president that the IWA Central Council unanimously approved, Marx praised "the single-minded son of the working class" Abraham Lincoln for his role in rescuing "an enchained race" and leading "the reconstruction of a social world." For Marx, the coming triumph of the North in the Civil War would open a new phase in global history, in which the "working classes" would finally be protagonist of their own emancipation. Already in early 1860, Marx was writing to Friedrich Engels that "the most momentous thing happening in the world today is the slave movement—on the one hand, in America, started by the death of Brown, and in Russia, on the other."[1] In 1867, he reiterated the concept by writing in *Das Kapital*, "Labour cannot emancipate itself in the white skin where in the black it is branded."[2] The freedom of Black workers was an indispensable precondition to open a new and more favorable phase for the advancement of working-class freedom on a global scale. In the message to Lincoln, Marx wrote that "the workingmen of Europe feel assured that, as the American War of Independence initiated a new era of ascendency for the middle class, so the American antislavery War will do for the working classes."[3] With slavery swiped off the country, the United States presented ideal social and economic conditions for the birth of a multiracial working-class movement whose impact would be felt beyond the North American continent. The American labor movement was on the verge of becoming the leader of the global struggle for socialism.[4]

Karl Marx's analysis reflected his own profound interest with American social and political conditions and the interconnectedness of the American and European radical world in the 1850s and 1860s. In the decade preceding the Civil War, a lively political community of German American radicals was forged under the leadership of a generation of German émigrés who had arrived in the United States after the failed revolts of 1848 and 1849. This group found its space in the American labor community and, in the process, redefined what it meant to be a socialist in America. Before their arrival, American socialism was associated with the utopian doctrines of Charles Fourier and Robert Owen. German immigrants, who had cut their teeth in the authoritarian political scenario of 1840s Europe, moved socialism away from the plains of Indiana and Iowa and brought it back to where they believed it belonged: the heart of the industrializing American cities in the North and the Midwest. The foundations of American socialist racial thought were forged in the debates of this transnational community.[5]

The struggle for the abolition of slavery defined German American socialist ideas of race in the antebellum period. In a political scenario charged with sectional tensions between the North and the South, the abolition of slavery became the landmark political objective through which German American socialists continued their campaign for freedom in their new country. As shown by Bruce Levine, Mischa Honeck, and Alison Clark Efford, by joining the abolitionist cause and later fighting in the Civil War in the Union army ranks, these socialists carved their own place in the social fabric of the United States.[6] At the same time, they also adapted their republican and radical values to a social context where racial and ethnic differences had an unprecedented importance. Through slavery, German American socialists came to understand the centrality of race and ethnicity in the American social context. "In the United States live English, Irish, Scandinavian, German, French Canadian, Spanish, Portuguese, Italian, Boehm, Slave [Slavic], Hungarian, Polish, Russian, Jewish workers," wrote German American Marxist Friedrich A. Sorge in 1897, and "distinctions based on skin color" further complicated "the task of the labor associations."[7] German American radicals understood through their own difficulties and struggles in the 1850s that uniting workers across racial and ethnic lines was a crucial premise to creating a strong labor movement in the United States. Karl Marx's hopes for the postbellum future of the United States were built off the convictions of these German American socialists.

But the dream of a multiracial working-class movement leading the fight for global emancipation soon appeared to be far off from the reality of Reconstruction America. The broad coalition for abolitionism in which socialists had so comfortably fit in during the antebellum period broke apart into a number of different single-issue movements after 1865. Socialists gathered into the IWA and tried to improve the conditions of American wage workers by forging a coalition with the newly born National Labor Union. But their efforts to organize across racial lines floundered before historical circumstances that seemed impossible to deal with. While organized labor toyed with the idea to create a labor party to defend their interests, African Americans had no other option but to keep supporting the Republican Party, the only political group that offered a realistic possibility to defend their newly acquired civil rights and work to extend their social and economic possibilities. Reconstruction socialists did not manage to go past this contradictory situation. While remaining committed to the value of racial equality, they never fruitfully reached out and built significant links with the African American working class.

Ultimately, German American socialists were builders, supporters, and finally victims of the illusion that the abolition of chattel slavery in the South could be a prelude to a new epoch of extended workers' rights. Before 1865, socialist militancy in the abolitionist movement allowed many German American radicals to learn the grammar of the American language of race, labor, and class. After 1865, this expertise did not translate into any tangible political advancement for the American socialist movement.

"Only in This Way Will We Be Germans": Transatlantic Socialism and the Abolition of Slavery in Antebellum America

In the Brussels office of Karl Marx, the temperature of the room was rapidly reaching a boiling point. At one end of the table, Karl Marx struggled to contain his disdain for the turn the meeting had taken. At the other end, Wilhelm Weitling continued, apparently undisturbed, with his tirade on his plans to spread socialism across Europe. That cold evening of March 1846 was the first occasion the two leaders of the Communist Correspondence Committee—an early attempt to coordinate operations among socialist leaders in several European nations—had the chance to sit around a table. While suspicious about the vagueness of the theoretical foundations of his socialism, Marx and Engels believed that Weitling's enormous popularity was well expendable for the cause. Weitling, a Christian populist who preached an evangelical version of sentimental communism, had a strong reputation in Paris and London.[8] He had moved to Brussels to strengthen the cooperation with Marx and Engels, ignited by the perspectives of a rising pan-European socialist movement. But he was failing the test. Questioned by Marx on his approach, the Prussian leader retorted with vague and imprecise justifications, to the point that Marx lost control of his temper. "Ignorance has never yet helped anyone!" shouted a furious Marx to an astonished Weitling—an exchange that put an abrupt end both to the meeting and to the political relationship between the two.[9]

After clashing with Marx, Weitling's life took an unexpected turn. Pushed by financial needs, Weitling accepted an invitation to become the editor of the German-language weekly *Volks-Tribun* in New York City. In America, Weitling crossed arms with Hermann Kriege, another protagonist of a famous political fight Karl Marx had picked up just months prior to Weitling's arrival in the United States. Kriege had moved to New York City in 1845 to escape arrest by Prussian authorities. Almost immediately, he had founded the *Volks-Tribun* and presented the paper as the American organ of the European socialist movement. In response, Marx published a circular in which he radically rejected his sentimental and unscientific approach. Of the eight socialist leaders who had met to discuss Marx's circular against Kriege, only one had voted against it: Wilhelm Weitling. Now Kriege and Weitling found themselves in the United States fighting together on a shared understanding of communism that markedly differed from Marx's.[10]

How crucial American connections were in the construction of a Western socialist movement is something that often goes unnoticed. Within this transatlantic radical community, the origins of American socialist racial thought were forged, and this came as a result of German American socialist interest in slavery. In September 1850, the approval of the Fugitive Slave Act had turned slavery into a daily concern for millions of white northern Americans. The new legislation had turned the entire North into an army of slave catchers: Whoever came across an escaped enslaved person and did not report them to the authority was committing a federal offense.[11] After 1850, suddenly being indifferent toward slavery became much harder. By debating slavery, antebellum German American socialists progressively came to terms with the significance of race in the American labor context. Yet there were many differences in the way early socialists responded to slavery. Through an analysis of these differences, it is possible to reconstruct not only the sources of socialist racial thought but also the role of socialists in promoting abolitionism within the burgeoning German American community.

Hermann Kriege ignored the growing significance of slavery as a source of division and conflict of the country. In his *Volks-Tribun*, slavery was clearly overshadowed by the issue of Free Soil and the defense of the interests of German immigrants. Right after his arrival in the United States, Kriege had married the cause of George Evans's National Reform Association (NRA). The NRA was a single-cause movement in support of Free Soil, an ideology preaching that a piece of land was the key to guarantee American workers a decent life for good.[12] Ignoring the contradiction between his support for Free Soil and the defense of the interest of slave holders, who wanted to expand slavery west, Kriege described abolitionism as an attack on individual property and a threat to the stability of the republic. In 1846, he wrote that "in slavery we see the issue of property; we would support the Abolitionist movement if our scope was to throw our republic in anarchy." Abolitionism, wrote Kriege, would have no real impact on the lives of "our black brothers," who would find themselves in a deadly competition with white workers. "For these reasons," he concluded, "we strongly declare ourselves against abolition."[13]

Weitling radically changed course on the subject.[14] Weitling's weekly *Republik der Arbeiter* was regularly published from 1850 to 1855, and since its inception, opposition to slavery featured as a prominent subject. Black enslaved people were identified as the individuals entitled to own the land they worked. In October 1850, the paper attacked the Fugitive Slave Act, sarcastically writing that "no one was born with inalienable rights . . . otherwise in the year of grace 1850 there would have been no need for a law regarding the delivery of non-refugee slaves. Or," the correspondent added, "is this law made to protect the inalienable human rights of Negroes?"[15] The paper clearly recognized Black enslaved people as part of a revolutionary class and campaigned for them to overtake southern lands. "The slaves, the black workers of the South, form an integral part of the social revolution in America . . . Anyone who has not become stupid because of the passion for his interest, who still has a spark of moral honor, must recognize that the one who works the land, in other words the black slave in the southern states, should be entitled to claim the enjoyment and possession of such land."[16] When slavery would be abolished, an event that the *Republik der Arbeiter* deemed as inevitable, southern states would have to be assigned to those who transformed them with their labor—the Black workers.

The significant variations in Kriege's and Weitling's opinions on slavery attested to the fluctuating importance attributed to the issue by German Americans in the 1840s and early 1850s. In August 1859, the Black abolitionist Frederick Douglass emphatically wrote that "a German has only to be German in order to be utterly opposed to slavery. In feeling, as well as in conviction and principle, they are antislavery."[17] Douglass captured the widespread support for abolitionism of the German American community, a community that would be crucial for Abraham Lincoln's election in 1860. But things had not always been that way. In the 1840s and early 1850s, slavery was hardly a priority for German immigrants. German American workers longed for a piece of land, and in so doing, they embraced the Free Soil cause; they looked for ways to defend themselves from the attack of the Know-Nothing Party, often finding shelter behind Democratic lines; they had to reject repeated attempts to police their lifestyle, especially from evangelical Protestants who preached the temperance gospel. In this difficult scenario, slavery rarely featured at all.

Several factors led to a change in this situation, but one in particular has been stressed as crucial: the mass migration of radicals from Europe that followed the failure of the 1848 Springtime of the Peoples. This younger generation of German immigrants brought radical ideas of freedom and emancipation along with them, nurtured in their fights against European authoritarianism. For many, throwing their support behind the newly born Republican Party was a way to find a socioeconomic positioning in the American society while at the same time reinvigorating their adhesion to the republican values of equality and freedom defended in Europe. The abolitionism of the "Forty-Eighters" was a patchwork of different political approaches, spanning from liberalism to republicanism to socialism, that before the Civil War found a way to cooperate for a common goal.[18]

As part of this wave came an activist who more than any other contributed to the development of American Marxism in antebellum America: Joseph Weydemeyer. A former general of the Prussian army, Weydemeyer was a die-hard republican who had fought during the 1848 Palatinate revolts. Wanted by the Prussian police after the end of the revolts, Weydemeyer permanently relocated to the United States in 1851, becoming Marx and Engels's most trusted contact in the country until his death in 1866.[19]

Joseph Weydemeyer's political and intellectual trajectory shows what type of contribution Marxian socialism offered to the forming German American abolitionist block. The Marxist militant had arrived in the United States with ambitious plans to organize the American working class. Weeks after landing in New York, Weydemeyer had set up his own weekly paper *Die Revolution*. Marx had contributed to Weydemeyer's attempt by sending a piece he had written on Louis-Napoléon Bonaparte's 1851 coup. The essay, serialized in Weydemeyer's paper, would later become Marx's pamphlet *The Eighteenth Brumaire of Louis Bonaparte*.[20] When *Die Revolution* failed for lack of subscribers, Weydemeyer turned to the *Turn-Zeitung*, the monthly

FIGURE 1. Portrait of Joseph Weydemeyer. Undated. SPD Collection, International Institute of Social History, Amsterdam.

bulletin of the Sozialistischer Turnerbund (Socialist Gymnastic Society). Modeled after German gymnastic societies, where people met to discuss, read, and exercise, in the United States, the Turnerbund moderately shifted away from their German model and took up a more clearly political vocation, including the adjective "socialist" in their title. The Turnerbund rapidly spread across the country in the early 1850s, reaching seventy-two clubs and around 4,500 members in the middle of the decade—numbers only partially representative of the thousands of immigrants who occasionally gathered at these facilities. The Turnerbund were the backbone of the German American working-class socialist community.[21]

Weydemeyer early showed an acute awareness of the significance of slavery for the future cohesion of the country. In an article published in September 1852 titled "Australian Cotton and American Slavery," Weydemeyer identified the fact that Australia was starting to produce cotton and therefore breaking the position of monopoly of the U.S. South as a sign of troubles ahead. "It is unlikely that this change in Southern reality will happen without provoking a strong reaction across the entire United States, because this fact will have inevitable repercussions in the North as well. The sectional tendencies of the South, its particular interests will not be tolerated for much longer. The division will sharpen and will define more clearly the entire country."[22] Already in 1852, well before Karl Marx and Friedrich Engels started writing more extensively on the topic, Weydemeyer foresaw the possibility of a sectional conflict, identifying slavery as the fundamental contradiction that would initiate the clash.[23]

Two years later, Weydemeyer was on the front line to protest the approval of the Kansas-Nebraska Act. As stressed by historian Bruce Levine, the act was the moment in which a clear generational divide in the German American community became evident.[24] Friedrich A. Sorge recalled that, at the approval of the bill, on one side, "Grays" of the old generation remained attached to their moderate pro-slavery attitude. On the other side, "Green" Forty-Eighters roundly rejected slavery and embraced the abolitionist cause. "When the Kansas-Nebraska Bill . . . was being debated in Congress," writes Sorge, "and the *New Yorker Volks-Zeitung* wrote in a friendly pro-slavery tone, the Greens on the newspaper broke out in solemn yowling—to the great distress of the Grays."[25] Weydemeyer led the protest against the bill from the ranks of the newly founded Amerikanischer Arbeiterbund. The Amerikanischer Arbeiterbund organized a demonstration against the Kansas-Nebraska Act, featuring him amongst its speakers. During the evening, the assembly passed a resolution declaring that American workers "have ever protested, now protest, and ever will protest all Slavery" and rejected a bill that "offer[ed] fresh advantages to the heavy capitalists and land jobbers of the country."[26]

Weydemeyer's opposition toward slavery built on an abolitionist sentiment that was growing in German American communities across the entire country. The shift toward abolitionism of the Sozialistischer Turnerbund clearly indicated how widespread the trend was. Gathered in Cincinnati in 1855 for their annual convention, members of the Turnerbund approved a clause that stated, "The Turners are opposed to slavery, and regard its institution as unworthy of a republic and not in accord with the principles of freedom."[27] In doing so, the Turnerbund positioned themselves well on the left of the forming Republican Party, whose vast majority of members were against the extension of slavery in the territories but would not dare to approve a document that so clearly attacked slavery as an institution in itself.[28]

At the end of the decade, Weydemeyer returned to his analysis of the southern economic system. In an article series published in the *Illinois Staats-Zeitung*, one of the most influential German-language papers in the Midwest, Weydemeyer set the terms of a problem that Marx-inspired scholars would discuss for decades to come: whether the South was a precapitalist economy or not and how this was impacting the industrial development of the United States as a whole. For Weydemeyer, these problems had a clear answer. "Slavery precludes any industrial development, like any scientific and industrial agriculture, and is solely dependent on the culture of stacked products that allow the use of human power in its rawest form, supported by the rawest tools." Instead of Australia, this time Weydemeyer mentioned India and Africa as the areas of the world whose cotton production would make the South obsolete (of Africa, he wrote that "we would be pleased with the irony of history, which threatens slave labor with the most dangerous competition from that same place from where the workforce to cultivate [cotton] had been violently dragged in"). Slavery and the slave system were weakening the American economy. The more the American economy maintained its sectional division, the more difficult it would be for the American workers to organize themselves.[29]

Weydemeyer would come back to the topic of interracial workers' organizing only after the Civil War. In the meantime, elsewhere in the country other German American activists offered a plethora of contributions to the articulation of a socialist anti-slavery position. In West Texas, Adolph Douai preached the abolitionist gospel. Like Weydemeyer, Douai belonged to the generation of the German American Forty-Eighters. However, he came from a different part of German-speaking Europe: Thuringia, miles away from the Prussian and Rhineland regions where the early socialist movement of Weydemeyer, Kriege, Weitling, Marx, and Engels was taking shape. Douai was a Ph.D. in philosophy, a teacher and a journalist, a social-democrat and a freethinker. Animated by a visceral antislavery sentiment, Douai represented another side of the composite abolitionist socialist front. Adolph Douai did not embrace Marxism until after the Civil War, but already in the 1850s, his ideas were influenced by a broad and insistent attention toward labor issues. After his early abolitionist militancy in West Texas, Douai would move north to become a key leader of the Gilded Age American socialist movement.

"Why did I want to go to Texas?" wondered Douai in his 1888 autobiography. "The principal reason was that I was tired of civilization, that I wanted to become a farmer and that I wanted to bring up my children as wholly free as individuals."[30] Despite his optimistic intentions, Douai could not have picked a worse location to try a new life in the United States. When he landed in Indianola in 1853, Texas was a wild region fraught with profound political, social, and economic tensions. Douai drove the group of German people who migrated with him to West Texas to the newly founded German colony of New Braunfels, thirty miles from San Antonio. He sought independence, freedom, and optimal living conditions. As a proud immigrant with a strong attachment to racial egalitarianism, what he found were intolerance, violence, and oppression.[31]

Before joining the United States in 1845, the population of Texas included around 13,000 enslaved African Americans. This number quadrupled by 1850 and boomed to 182,000 in 1860, when enslaved people represented more than 30 percent of the state population.[32] Although the number of German immigrants did not follow the same trajectory, by 1850, around 5 percent of the population was of German origin, forming a dense enclave that was mostly concentrated in the sparsely populated West Texas where Douai had settled with his community. The Lone Star State had won its independence after a long series of engagements with the Mexican army. Its foundational myths were rooted in a strongly anti-Mexican sentiment, an animosity that, in the decades following independence and eventual admission to the Union, was rapidly redirected toward Germans and African Americans. The Know-Nothing Party expanded significantly in the state because its nativist platform built on ideas already widespread among white Texans.[33]

Considering these circumstances, the appointment of Adolph Douai as editor of the first German-language newspaper in San Antonio in 1853 had the same effect as a bull in a china shop. In his autobiography, Douai wrote that in 1840 he was "irreligious and a democrat."[34] Later, he declared that in 1848, he was "still a pantheist, but already a social-democrat." By the time he arrived in the United States, he had developed a more coherent radical and nonreligious point of view. Douai was a freethinker and a republican who believed in political and social equality and held his home country in high esteem. After two years in the New Braunfels area trying to make ends meet as a primary school principal, cigar maker, and piano and singing teacher, Douai relocated to San Antonio and decided to accept the offer to edit the newly born *San Antonio Zeitung*.[35] The German American community was growing in wealth and influence, and it looked forward to the opportunity of having an independent forum of discussion for its political and cultural interests. Douai, a passionate and vocal expert in literature, philosophy, music, and the arts, seemed the perfect fit for the job. But the businessmen sponsoring the paper apparently turned a blind eye on Douai's radical beliefs, and this turned out to be a great mistake.

Under Douai's editorship, not only did the *San Antonio Zeitung* immediately start to attack the nativist activists of the Know-Nothing Party but it also published articles aimed at countering the spread of slavery in West Texas. According to Douai, aversion to slavery went hand in hand with defending the honor and respectability of German immigrants. Slavery was not only a moral wrong but also constituted a weak economic system. Additionally, continued immigration into the area was fundamental because it could provide Texas with the free workforce to colonize the South and make it prosperous. "Why should we not try to make at least West Texas free of slavery?" wrote Douai in his autobiography, offering a post facto explanation of his ambitious approach. "In the South, the Gulf; in the north, the desert; in back of us, the republic of Mexico, which was antislavery; and from the north to the south, a chain of German colonial settlements which could cooperate with one another." German Americans—with the support of Mexicans who lived in West Texas and were "antislavery and unfriendly to Americans" and with the help of "negroes [who] often escaped to us and then easily fled to Mexico"—could "roll back slavery to Louisiana and even further East."[36] This was the ambitious political platform that Douai defended during his time in Texas.

In the *San Antonio Zeitung*, Douai used moral and economic arguments to condemn slavery. An article published in 1853 clearly stated that slavery caused the moral degradation of human beings. Commenting on the lynching of a Black enslaved person accused of homicide in Missouri, Douai wrote that "this is again an example of the desolate depravation in which the white race is overthrown by negro slavery."[37] Under slavery, contended Douai, both slaveholders and the enslaved lost their capacity to distinguish between moral and immoral behavior, and violence inevitably proliferated. Douai was not silent on the issue of racism in the North, showing awareness on the fact that abolition would not have ended the problems of African Americans. In 1854, the *San Antonio Zeitung* published an article about the condition of Blacks in "non-slavery states," which was defined as a "purgatory," a halfway house between slavery and freedom, where African Americans experienced the fruition of some rights but also the persistence of racism.[38]

Yet Douai believed that the North was in a much better condition than the South. Several articles in the *San Antonio Zeitung* made this point through economic arguments. A piece on "free labor and slave labor," reprinted from Elihu Burritt's paper *Citizen of the World*, set moral arguments against economic arguments. The article started by declaring that, from a moral point of view, there were no consistent ways to defend slavery. But even if Southern slaveholders did not want to consider this side of the problem, they must recognize that slavery was not profitable from a mere economic point of view either: "Throwing aside every reference to the moral aspects of such a question, we doubt whether any intelligent southern planter can convince himself, on strictly commercial principles, that a property which must be inevitably valueless in 35 years, and may perish or disappear any day, can be legitimately estimated as so low a rate of 10 per cent for annual rent."[39] Slavery exposed investors to more risk and could not compete with the quality of the work guaranteed by German and Irish farmers. Therefore, a mass immigration of European farmers into the South would have stopped the moral shame of slavery and reversed its economic decline.

Douai was a republican who believed in the value of labor as a force of emancipation and fulfillment. Using Edward Gibbon's *The History of the Decline and Fall of the Roman Empire* and comparing the decaying Roman society to the Southern social system, Douai contended that the lack of a laboring middle class would soon throw the South into economic collapse: "Men cannot be happy but by laboring and enjoying the fruit of their toil. No man can be happy who does not labor, neither can anyone be happy who is deprived of a part or the whole of the fruits of his labor."[40] Only a sizable number of people who enjoyed the fruit of their labor could make Texas stronger and richer. In an analysis reminiscent of Weydemeyer's, Douai identified in the inner contradictions of the Southern economy the aspect that would lead to its collapse.

In Douai's rhetoric, the support for immigration and abolitionism reinforced each other: The more immigrants arrived in the United States, the more the cause of abolitionism would strengthen because Europeans, in Douai's mind, were by definition against slavery. The German American editor made this point clear in an article published at the peak of the *San Antonio Zeitung*'s popularity in 1854. First, Douai reprinted the famous letter from the "true Republican" Thomas Jefferson, in which the Founding Father had argued that "the hour of emancipation is advancing in the march of time."[41] Secondly, he referred to German history to prove the point that his fellow countrymen were abolitionist in principle: "Scarcely any German can be so stupid as not to understand the question of slave emancipation: they know it from their own or their fathers' experiences [in the form of serfdom]."[42] Finally, he targeted the Know-Nothing Party by asking, "Why censure Germans, if they in common with Jefferson and so many great and immortal Americans call slavery an evil, and honest in their convictions, merely differ with you in opinion . . . ?"[43] The German American editor was replying to the accusations of nativists who labeled as "un-American" the denunciation of slavery: Being abolitionist, as Germans were, was nothing more than practicing Jefferson's own teachings.

Douai could rely on a network of German American abolitionists to frame his message. In March 1854, the Forty-Eighter Karl Heinzen had gathered radical Germans from across the entire West to sign what came to be known as the "Louisville Platform." In it, the editor of the landmark German American paper *Pionier* offered a comprehensive political program for action for a new party led by free Germans. This program included the repeal of the Fugitive Slave Act, no further extension of slavery, and its gradual abolition wherever it existed.[44] The platform was followed by another one redacted with the help and support of the Society of Freemen, of which Adolph Douai was part and that had met in San Antonio in the early 1854. In the weeks following the San Antonio gathering, the *San Antonio Zeitung* offered long commentaries on what it called "The Platform of Free Men."[45]

Douai's political activism rapidly put the *San Antonio Zeitung* in jeopardy. Within a year of founding of the paper, Douai had already received lynching threats, his partner had left, and many advertisers were withdrawing their offers for fear of being associated with the "abolitionist paper." Eventually, by the summer of 1854, the pressure on the *San Antonio Zeitung* was so high that the stockholders who supported the paper decided to sell it. Douai, with no intention of abandoning his fight, raised among his friends the money necessary to buy the newspaper and continue publication. One of the donors was Frederick Law Olmsted, the New England architect, whom Douai had met in Texas during Olmsted's trip to the South in 1853.[46] Olmsted supported Douai's project of publishing some articles in English to reach a wider audience.

But after a couple of years of resistance, Douai caved in against the anti-immigrant and racist sentiments of the Texan public opinion. In 1855, he was forced to sell the *San Antonio Zeitung* and leave the state. He did not go quietly. In the closing issue of the paper, he shared his reasons to depart. Douai had early realized that a majority of Germans in Texas were in favor of slavery. Since then, he had worked to preserve his "freedom of speech" and the conservation of his press. That, too, had turned out to be impossible. "Because we do not think it worth living [in a place] where the sacred right of freedom of opinion is denied . . . we, and a number of our countrymen who agree with us in sentiment . . . have resolved upon emigrating from Texas, so that you will get rid of those troublesome Dutchmen at the earliest convenience."[47]

Having seen with his own eyes the effects of slavery, Douai continued to fight it with reinvigorated energy from Boston, where he moved with his family. In Texas, Douai had defended the cause of abolition using a selection of arguments that spanned from the moral to the economic. He embraced Free Soil with republican values. Coating all his ideas was a proud faith in the progressive attitude of the German immigrant community. Douai's analysis of the position and opportunities of the German American community was more a reflection of his own hopes than a fair assessment of the West Texan situation, but his relentless political activism shows the level of commitment that German American Forty-Eighters brought to the cause of abolition.

The mixture of republican, economic, and patriotic arguments used by Douai returned in the writings of August Willich, another Forty-Eighter whose contributions were crucial to shaping antebellum socialist abolitionism. Willich had impeccable radical credentials dating back to the 1840s. Born August von Willich in 1810 in East Prussia, Willich dropped his titles and became a radical supporter of republicanism during an early period spent as an officer of the Prussian army. After resigning in 1846, two years later, Willich took up a leading role in the Free Corps during the Baden-Palatine uprising. Here, he fought side by side with many other future leaders of the German community in America, including Franz Sigel and Carl Schurz. At the same time, Friedrich Engels served as his aide-de-camp. After the failure of the revolt in 1849, Willich continued to try to stir a popular uprising in Prussia. In 1853, when he arrived in New York, for some time he remained on the East Coast, ready to go back to Europe as soon as some concrete sign of revolt showed up.[48]

By 1858, Willich had resigned himself to the fact that the revolution in Prussia was not going to happen any time soon. After years spent in New York and Washington DC working for the Brooklyn Navy Yard and for the federal government, Willich decided to accept the offer of Judge John B. Stallo to relocate to Ohio and edit the *Cincinnati Republikaner*, the daily of the local Social Workingmen's Club.[49] Arriving in Cincinnati to take up his political career where he had left it in 1853, Willich rapidly understood that the abolition of slavery was what the fight against Prussian autocracy had been for him in Europe.

Willich was a socialist who understood abolitionism in the context of a broader struggle for labor rights. In a provoking article titled "Why

Should We Care about the Nigger? We Want to Start with Ourselves!" Willich openly mocked those white workers who could not see the connection between Black and white exploitation. "The slaveholders' party knows very well that slavery means not only the slavery of black workers but also of forced labor in general," wrote Willich. "It works purposely towards the formation of a two-class society as existed in the Greek republics: on the one hand, the class of the free, those engaged in science, art, and politics, on the other, the class of forced labor, irrespective of whether the worker be a colored or a white man."[50] Willich argued that chattel slavery and wage slavery were but two aspects of the same form of exploitation, and they should, therefore, be addressed together.

At the same time, Willich initially showed faith and trust in the American republican institutions. White wage workers had the opportunity to change their circumstances by using the franchise and civil liberties, a possibility that was denied to Black workers. "The white [worker] is formally free and has some chance to subvert his condition, i.e., to become the owner or co-owner of the shop where he works, whereas the black [worker] is quite involuntarily property of the capitalist." White workers had the chance to lead the fight. It was down to them to force the abolition of slavery and create a circumstance in which the "external political domination" was finished. Willich further added that only then would it be possible to enter "the real battleground of human rights" and fight for racial equality.[51]

John Brown's assault on Harpers Ferry contributed in a significant way to reorient Willich's approach. When Brown and his associates were condemned to death, the German American editor wrote, "The Rubicon has been crossed." That a court in the state of Virginia, in the full capabilities of its powers, could rule on the hanging of an activist for the human rights of African Americans was an intolerable act of abuse. "If the wrong and the crime become legal, if the wrong and the crime create their own courts, if these courts rule on humanity and human rights, if these courts pronounce their judgments in the name of the Law, then the life of the community and of the state are in danger." At this point, the fight against "legal crime" became a fight of "civilization against barbarism."[52] From this moment onwards, Willich added the phrase *enteweder-oder* ("either-or") to each article that dealt with slavery. Either with John Brown or against him. Either with civilization or against it. Either for freedom or for slavery. From this moment, there was no in-between.

Willich decided to organize a celebration in Brown's honor with the support of the Over-the-Rhine Social Workingmen's Club. The event took place on the 4th of December 1859 at the German Institute and was followed by a torchlit march in downtown Cincinnati. Moncure Conway, an abolitionist Unitarian clergyman, and Peter H. Clark, a Black teacher and activist (and later a member of the Socialist Labor Party) joined Willich on the stage. An interracial crowd attended the meeting. The speakers were cheered by unanimous applause which, Willich recalled later, described the "inner bond of humanity, [which] brought forth a harmonious melody sung by races and nationalities separated by nothing but outward appearance."[53]

In the chronicle of the events published on December 5 in the *Republikaner*, Willich refined his antislavery position with republican arguments: In Europe, a crime like John Brown's hanging would be comprehensible and explicable because authoritarian powers run the state. "But here in the Republic we make the law itself, there is no external despotic power here. We govern ourselves, and this self-government is written in the Constitution." The Constitution was based on the respect of "human rights," and slavery was incompatible with the words written by the Founding Fathers.[54]

Willich could not have expected that his fellow German countrymen would be guilty of a serious case of racial discrimination just twenty days after the demonstration in favor of John Brown. For Willich, antislavery politics and interracial equality went hand in hand; but such a duality of purpose was not necessarily obvious or desirable for other German Americans. On December 18, 1859, three Black people were refused access to the German Institute to attend a meeting. This fact was immediately denounced by the German editor, who initially thought that the teacher Peter H. Clark, who had given a much-appreciated speech during the John Brown demonstration, was among them. As noted by historian Mischa Honeck, Willich was particularly upset by the fact that German immigrants committed this act of racism.[55] His commentary on the events, titled "Are Colored People Humans or Not? The German, the American, the African," praised German attitudes toward minorities. German tolerance was demonstrated by the fact that the most mistreated people in Europe, the Jews, predominantly found homes in the German territories. In the United States, continued Willich, African Americans, Native Americans, and Mexicans knew that they could trust Germans. Germans were ready to abandon their language and traditions to mingle with Americans. For these reasons, the exclusion of Blacks from the German Institute was an abomination.

> We are and act as Germans only when we bring up the spirit of humanity . . . We proudly must not concede anything to the hate, the prejudice, the hypocritical contempt for the oppressed nationalities and races, in fact we need to make ourselves strong and fight it. Only in this way will we be faithful to our people, to our race. Only in this way will we be Germans.[56]

The echo of a strong national pride resounded in these words. Willich the socialist, republican, abolitionist, and supporter of human rights was also an ardent nationalist—a mix we have already seen in Douai's support for abolitionism.

Nationalism was one of the reasons why Willich abandoned the editorship of the *Cincinnati Republikaner* and enlisted in the Union army. The socialist recalled his German, American, antislavery and republican principles at the moment of taking service as colonel of the Thirty-Second Indiana: "This is the patriotic answer of the Germans of Indiana to the call of their government to take up arms to protect its republican institution . . . In this way the Germans will really prove that they are not foreigners, and that they know how to protect their new republican homeland against the aristocracy of the South."[57] Willich restated the same concepts in a speech given to his regiment in 1863, when he was asked to explain why he had decided to fight with the North. "I wanted to show everyone who believes that you can only be a worthy citizen of the republic if you are born here," argued Willich, "that we Germans are also republicans. I wanted to help the immigrant gain a right that they kept from him or sought to diminish."[58]

Willich was one of the thousands of German Americans that served in the Union army during the Civil War. In Missouri, Joseph Weydemeyer followed in his footsteps, becoming a technical aid of General John C. Frémont, commander of the west department of the Union army. After brief spells together in the Prussian army and in the revolutionary groups of the 1848 and 1849 revolts, the two found themselves shoulder to shoulder once again, fighting for the same cause: the abolition of slavery.[59]

By the end of the decade, the contacts between the other socialists scattered around the country became more regular and significant. Coming from the rather remote area of Thuringia, in the 1840s, Douai had never gotten in touch with the Prussia- and Rhineland-centered radical circles frequented by Marx, Engels, Weitling, Weydemeyer, and Willich. Once in the United States, however, Douai had rapidly thrown himself into the burgeoning world of radical German American socialism. Already in August 1853, the *San Antonio Zeitung* had published the platform of the Amerikanischer Arbeiterbund, founded by Weydemeyer in New York just one month before.[60] Once in the North, Douai forged new links with radicals in the area, especially Friedrich A. Sorge, a music teacher based in Hoboken who arrived in the United States in 1851.[61] In 1860, Douai and Weydemeyer attended the Republican National Convention that designated Abraham Lincoln as the party's presidential candidate. From Cincinnati, Willich wrote in the *Republikaner* that the nomination of such a moderate candidate was a "stunning blow" for the radical wing of the Republican Party, yet he decided to campaign for him "for free labor, against slavery." Weydemeyer and Douai also threw their support behind the moderate presidential candidate from Illinois. Before relocating west at the beginning of the war, Weydemeyer stayed in New York for a short time, where he actively cooperated with Douai in the Lincoln campaign within the New York German American community.[62]

By this point, the support of antebellum socialists for the cause of abolition was uniform, and in most cases, it went beyond the commitment to the cause expressed by the mainstream Republican Party itself. As the cases of Weydemeyer, Douai, and Willich testify, socialists used various arguments to oppose slavery. Weydemeyer focused on political economy and contended that slavery in the U.S. South was not meant to last. Douai applied to American slavery the categories he was familiar with: European serfdom and European authoritarianism. He thought that slavery was a moral abomination and a limitation on the southern economy. Willich saw in slavery a betrayal of American republicanism and a form of economic exploitation akin to that of wage workers. He fused radical republicanism and proud nationalism in a mix founded on the rejection of any sort of discrimination based on race and national belonging.

Despite their differences, German American socialists were crucially united by their use of class and economy as analytical lenses through which to understand the issue of chattel slavery. Precisely the fact of recognizing slavery as a form of economic exploitation in the first place was what differentiated them from Garrisonian abolitionists and from German American liberal Forty-Eighters. The focus on political economy did not prevent socialists from condemning discrimination based on race and ethnicity. In their writings, socialists stressed that racism and ethnic discrimination must be condemned and were incompatible with socialism. Through their analyses of slavery, antebellum socialism started to move the first steps in the articulation of a point of view that integrated race-based and class-based forms of economic exploitation together. Post-Civil War socialists would continue the task, even though they would have to face the complicated change of circumstances unleashed by Reconstruction.

Socialists after the Civil War: The First International and the Black Worker

A couple of months after Appomattox, Weydemeyer was hired as a correspondent for the St. Louis-based Republican *Westliche Post*. In the immediate aftermath of the war, his radical beliefs did not prevent him from becoming an opinion-maker in the important German American daily, an organ which, in 1867, was bought by Carl Schurz and became a landmark of Republican politics in the midwestern German American community.[63]

During the Civil War, St. Louis had started a transformation from the "imperial capital of the 'white man's country'" to a multiracial city hosting a significant community of free Blacks. Before the war, the only thing upon which Free Soil Republicans and proslavery Democrats agreed was denying entry to free African Americans. Circumstances changed with the war. Placed under martial law already in 1861, the city became a privileged destination for African Americans escaping war and white violence. Between 1860 and 1870, the Black population of St. Louis grew by 600 percent. Right in the middle of this process of transformation, the state discussed its new constitution—in particular, whether free Blacks should have the right to vote or not. This discussion anticipated many of the themes that would divide the country before the approval of the Fifteenth Amendment.[64]

In his *Westliche Post* articles, Weydemeyer connected the issue of Black suffrage with a wider analysis about the situation of African Americans in the South and the prospects for the American working class. He believed the outcome of the war had proved him right: Slavery had caused an irreversible conflict, and this conflict had forced the dismissal of an anachronistic economic system based on human bondage. But now the question on the ground was crucial: On what basis could the South be reconstructed? Weydemeyer tackled the problem from a stadial Marxist point of view: The spread of industrial capitalism was a required midway step toward socialism. But in that specific conjuncture, his questions were the same ones free labor liberal and progressive northerners were asking themselves. How could southern states reorganize their economic and social structures in order to follow the path of the industrial North?[65]

For Weydemeyer, the former class of slaveholder planters was useless to the task. Their objective was simply to find a way to restore the slave system, either by reintroducing Black slavery or by finding other social classes who could perform the same labor-intensive jobs for low or no pay. As of nonslaveholder whites, Weydemeyer defined the ignorance of this social group as "appalling" and "astonishing" and quickly concluded that these individuals lacked the skills and the spirit to support any kind of innovative form of economic organization.[66] "The much despised Negroes almost exclusively represent the working element in the South." It was down to them, "in addition to the white artisans of the cities," to lead the reconstruction of the South. Weydemeyer used the virtuous example of the Sea Islands in Georgia and South Carolina to make his case. Reporting the results of an investigation carried out by the *New Yorker World*, the socialist mentioned that in those areas, free African Americans were cultivating land and were depositing their profits in local banks. Weydemeyer contended that the successes of the Sea Islands should be replicated elsewhere by transferring to free African Americans the abandoned, confiscated, or forfeited lands scattered around the South. In this way, the South would flourish.[67]

Only at this point did Weydemeyer reintroduce the topic of Black suffrage, arguing that his project of economic reconstruction would work only insofar as "the new representatives of free labor" in the South were given the "political power" to defend their newly acquired rights. For Weydemeyer, democratic rights were a tool through which the improvements of African Americans could be harnessed. To those who thought that African Americans were too ignorant to exercise their voting rights, Weydemeyer replied with evidence coming from the post-Civil War South. "All reports reassure us with rare agreement about the Negroes' desire to learn; and their efforts to acquire the education earlier laws forcibly kept away from them distinguish them favorably from the 'poor whites' of the South, who have not yet even woken up to the need to escape from their ignorance." For Weydemeyer, African Americans were the pillars upon which the economic system of the South should be rebuilt, and granting them full political equality was necessary to guarantee the success of this plan.[68]

The full enfranchisement of African Americans was also the best way to avoid splits along racial lines in the American working class, and this was the last argument that Weydemeyer offered to convince his readership. He clearly articulated the concern that white workers might turn their backs on their Black colleagues. "On his [the white man's] shoulders lay the burden of the taxes," wrote Weydemeyer, "while the capitalists manage to flee to secure heights; and again he begins with jealous eyes to look at the 'eternal Negro,' who is still at the center of public interest." Feeling abandoned and despised, the white worker was "thrown back on the struggle for his own narrow interests, suddenly in opposition to those with whom he had shortly before made common front against a common enemy."[69] But the white worker must understand that it was the bourgeoisie, not the Black worker, that was the origin of their problems. By giving African Americans the right to vote, the white workers would find a new ally in the fight to change capitalism and ultimately improve their living conditions: "Where could he [the white worker] find these allies, if not among the workers who have a different skin color?" Only with an alliance with Black workers could the white working class stop the privileges of the capitalist class and the South be rebuilt on a newly industrialized model that respected the rights of workers across racial lines.[70]

Weydemeyer clearly foresaw the challenges that lay ahead of American socialists in post-Civil War United States, but he did not get a chance to exert his influence on the direction the movement would take. In August 1866, aged fifty-six, Weydemeyer suddenly died of cholera, leaving German American Marxism without one of its most acute observers. With Weydemeyer's death, the center of German American socialism moved east. New York was the epicenter of the nation's post-war growth, its financial capital, its leading port, and one of the major manufacturing centers of the country. What is more, New York's population was ideal for the proliferation of immigrant radicalism. In a nation that, in 1870, was still 86 percent native born, New York City was 44 percent immigrant, with the German-born population (16 percent) outnumbered only by the Irish (21 percent).[71]

From New York started an attempt led by German American Marxist Friedrich A. Sorge to fuse several experiences of radical activism flourishing together after the end of the Civil War. In 1866, leaders of a variety of American trade unions had gathered in Baltimore to found the National Labor Union (NLU). The NLU was the first trade union federation organizing workers from different crafts and skill levels. Its "Address of the National Labor Congress to the Workingmen of the United States" was a summary of the variety of resolutions approved by the assembly, but above everything stood the "all-absorbing subject of Eight-Hours."[72]

The popularity of the cause for a shorter workday found its roots in widely held republican values. Daniel T. Rodgers describes the tortuous way through which in the passage from an agricultural to an industrial economic system American workers retained a strong attachment to republican beliefs of civic and moral citizenship. These beliefs were embodied by the ideal of the "virtuous worker," a worker who had time to cultivate their independent interests, spend time with their family, and actively take part in local politics. In the famous slogan "eight hours for work, eight hours for recreation, rest, eight hours for sleep" rested the gist of what 1860s American workers were campaigning for: not just a reduction of working hours but the possibility to partake in active citizenship of their republic. After the Civil War, this approach had adopted markedly abolitionist undertones. For some, the abolition of slavery turned into the abolition of *wage* slavery, an interpretation of the "free labor" ideology that made evident how its meaning fractured along class lines after 1865.[73]

German American activists were drawn in by the flurry of organized labor activism. Building on the model of Weitling's Arbeiterbund and Weydemeyer's Amerikanischer Arbeiterbund, in 1865, members of German American trade unions joined forces into the Allgemeiner Deutscher

Arbeiter-Verein (General German Workers' Association). This group forged a brief alliance with the Communist Club, an eclectic group started by radicals of a variety of persuasions in 1857, and published a weekly, the *Arbeiter Union*, which between 1868 and 1870 was edited by Adolph Douai.[74] The Allgemeiner Deutscher Arbeiter-Verein found a solid anchorage in a transnational political grouping that in this period was laying its foundations in the United States: the International Workingmen's Association.

Generally described as Karl Marx's brainchild and a mostly European attempt of international labor cooperation, the IWA was definitely more than that. At its core, the IWA rested on a spirit of solidarity that the American Civil War had contributed to generate. As suggested by David R. Roediger, it was the "anti-Confederate working-class activism" that created "the confidence, organization, and ability to think beyond national boundaries" that underwrote the organization of the IWA.[75] The early history of the IWA continued to be somehow connected to the developments of the United States in the aftermath of the Civil War. In the IWA, the republicanism defended by British and American workers fused with different brands of continental socialism and radicalism in an organization whose declared aim was to defend the interest of working people across national boundaries. The IWA had solid roots in the British, French, and German working classes, but from the beginning, it sought to branch out to other countries. In the United States, the National Labor Union was the most obvious interlocutor.

Exchanges between the IWA and the NLU started in earnest. Peter Fox, the IWA's corresponding secretary for America, corresponded with various leaders of the NLU, including C. W. Gibson, William Sylvis, William Jessup, and J. C. C. Whaley. In August 1867, the NLU voted to send a delegate to the IWA congress of Lausanne, although the decision was taken too late to be enacted.[76] In parallel, Karl Marx activated his American acquaintances to plant IWA seeds in the American community. Siegfried Meyer and August Vogt were the two most trusted contacts at the time, and they became the first IWA German American agents. By 1869, the first North American branch of the IWA, Section 1, had received credentials.[77] The same group of German Americans was also registered as Section 5 of the NLU. Closely linked to the *Arbeiter Union* and its paper edited by Adolph Douai, it was this group that picked up the baton from Weydemeyer when it came to shaping German American socialist racial thought in the aftermath of the Civil War.[78]

From its inception, the IWA firmly linked its struggle for workers' rights to the defense of racial equality. Building on antebellum socialist abolitionism, the organization had no hesitation to endorse equality of rights across racial lines. The IWA followed in the footsteps of the Communist Club, which proclaimed in its statutes that it "recognized no distinction as to nationality or race, caste or status, color or sex."[79] It continued the tradition started by the Social Party of New York and Vicinity, a short-lived party founded by members of the Allgemeiner Deutscher Arbeiter-Verein that, in 1868, demanded the repeal of all discriminatory laws and favored the eligibility of "all citizens" for office.[80] In 1869, Siegfried Meyer offered the IWA's and *Arbeiter Union*'s unconditional support for the organization of a union for African American workers. Within a couple of months, the union had ninety members and had gained admittance into the New York Workingmen's Union.[81] The IWA did not send anyone to the founding meeting of the Colored National Labor Union; however, the *Arbeiter Union* saluted the event with great enthusiasm, writing that from now on, white workers would have "allies against all attacks of capital" if they wanted to move south.[82]

Yet this clear commitment toward racial equality clashed with strategic decisions that limited the capacity of the International to forge interracial alliances. Leading the influential group that shaped the IWA's response on race was Friedrich A. Sorge, a Forty-Eighter destined to leave a profound mark on the history of American socialism. A native of Bethau, Saxony, Sorge arrived in the United States in 1852, establishing himself in Hoboken, where he remained until his death in 1905. When he landed in the United States, Sorge was a radical atheist with no interest in Marxian socialism. In 1857, he was amongst the founders of New York City's Communist Club. Still, after the Civil War, Sorge was best described as a freethinker with little interest in labor issues. According to David Herreshoff, his priorities changed when the outcome of the Six Weeks War between Prussia and Austria made clear that the unification of Germany would not happen through popular revolt but under Otto von Bismarck's iron fist. At that point, Sorge resumed his activities in the Communist Club and started an unofficial attempt to link the organization with the IWA. In March 1867, Sorge sent a letter to Karl Marx asking for English-language correspondence to initiate a propaganda effort at once.[83]

Sorge had a rather unique political approach. In 1872, the Ukranian socialist Sergei Andreyevich Podolinsky described Sorge as "more Marxist than Marx,"[84] an accurate definition, especially when coupled with Marx's own famous saying, "If anything is certain, it is that I myself am not a Marxist."[85] Marx was a critic of liberal democracy. While consistently campaigning for the extension of the franchise, he also deemed liberal democracy

FIGURE 2. Portrait of Friedrich A. Sorge. Undated. SPD Collection, International Institute of Social History, Amsterdam.

as not sufficient to achieve workers' emancipation. Yet Marx's approach was mutable, evolving, and shaped on the basis of circumstances.[86] In the hands of Sorge, Marx's critical outlook toward the ballot box turned into an unmodifiable juggernaut. Time and time again, Sorge attacked the "Lassallean" idea that the franchise was the main road to achieve political power. According to Sorge, the American democratic system was rigged. Workers should avoid the ballot box and use trade unions to improve their living conditions and build up class consciousness. Until conditions were more mature, engaging in political action was only counterproductive.[87]

Operating in a country where voting rights were deemed to be the core feature of a civic republicanism that workers wanted to hold tight to, and formulating his political approach while the fight for Black voting rights was raging, Sorge adopted an approach that was hardly compatible with a successful interethnic and interracial class policy. During his time in charge of the International, Sorge relentlessly sought to enter existing trade unions and expand the IWA's membership among wage workers. One of the first things that he did after receiving credentials of the IWA was to travel to the NLU 1869 convention and seek to strengthen the connection between the two organizations.[88] In the internecine struggle that would characterize the early 1870s history of the International, Sorge even formalized the principle that only branches whose members were by two-third wage workers were invited to join the organization.[89] This insistence on organized labor and trade unionism was in line with the IWA's approach and with Marx's own belief that wage workers would be the agents of the revolution.[90] Yet in the American context, this approach exposed the IWA to two significant problems. First, it restricted the potential recruiting pool of the organization, cutting off enormous chunks of the American working class that still did not work in industries and for a wage. Second, it created an insurmountable barrier between the labor association and those sectors of the American working class that more would have needed its help: African Americans, in the first place, the quasi totality of whom in this period still lived in the South and had rural jobs as sharecroppers and farmers.[91]

This trade unionism- and wage worker-focused approach coupled with an ethnic policy that made the outlook of the International toward African Americans even more problematic. The end of the 1860s was the period when Karl Marx refined his theory on nationalism and ethnicity through an analysis of the "Irish question" in the British Isles. Closely following the anti-British struggle of Irish nationalists from his vantage point in London, Marx came to the conclusion that elites used ethnic hatred between Irish and English workers as a tool to retain power and keep the working class divided. In a letter to his NYC fellows Meyer and Vogt, Marx wrote that "the ordinary English worker hates the Irish worker as a competitor who forces down the standard of life . . . This antagonism is the secret of the powerlessness of the English working class, despite its organization. It is the secret of the capitalist class's maintenance of its power. And the latter is fully conscious of this." According to Marx, workers must stop this perverse mechanism. In an only apparent subversion of his internationalist outlook, Marx contended that the International should embrace the anti-colonial struggle of Irish nationalists, as Irish independence would have dealt a blow to England—the only country that was mature for a socialist revolution: "To hasten the social revolution in England is the most important object of the International Workingmen's Association. The sole means of doing so is to make Ireland independent. It is therefore the task of the International to bring the conflict between England and Ireland to the forefront everywhere, and to side with Ireland publicly everywhere."[92] It would have required an independent and original thinker, who knew the historical materialist approach inside out and had the confidence to use it creatively, to adapt Marx's England-centric analysis to the socioeconomic context of the United States. In the United States, the English immigrant community had a relatively minor presence in the industrial working class. Conversely, the two most important immigrant communities were the German and Irish, and they viscerally hated each other. Moreover, since colonial times, American working relations were shaped by racism and its consequences. The racial pact keeping African Americans in chains in the South had shaped working ideologies across the entire country. In his letter to his American comrades, Marx even used antebellum America to make his case, writing that "[the English worker's] attitude towards [the Irish] is roughly that of the poor whites to the *niggers* in the former slave states of the American Union."[93] Marx saw the analogy between the English-Irish rivalry he observed in the British Isles and the fracture along racial lines in the antebellum United States. However, he could not bring himself to elaborate on the obvious conclusion of his argument when applied to postbellum America: that in the United States, the fracture between Black and white workers still represented the key fissure to crack American capitalism wide open, in the same way as the Irish-English division would have done it for the British Empire.

Sorge saw the problem of racism. He showed awareness of the fact that race caused an extra layer of hatred against African Americans that emancipation had not dissipated. Writing in 1868 in a notebook dedicated to IWA Section 1's activities, Sorge wrote, "The truth is, the people generally hate the African color and race. Many of the Repub[lican] leaders would yield and be glad to yield the negro back in the hands of his masters and give the rebel states back to rebel. These are the leaders, sovereign over the whole party policy . . . they are the party and Grant is but the clay in the hand of a terrible pastor, Mr. Phillips himself being witness."[94] Sorge had no faith in the Republican Party; he thought that radical Republicans were too weak to impose their politics of racial equality. But neither he nor Douai from the columns of the *Arbeiter Union* got close to fully grasp the issues of African Americans in the context of Reconstruction-era United States.

When it came to understand the fundamentals of southern politics, for example, socialists showed a good dose of wishful thinking and scarce sense of objectivity. In the *Arbeiter Union*, Douai commented on the victory of "true Republican" Gilbert Carlton Walker against radical Republican H. H. Wells as a sign of the realignment of Southern politics along class lines. "The quarrel that previously ruled between the capitalists who owned their workers (in the south) and the capitalists who hired their workers (in the north) . . . has turned into a quarrel between those workers—white, black, and yellow—who want to venerate the capital and turn them into working cattle and living machines, and the workers, of all colors, who no longer want to recognize any master or rule of capital." In fact, Walker had been propelled to the gubernatorial seat by the Democratic Party, whose electorate rallied behind a disgruntled Republican to block the advancement of racial equality.[95]

Rather than attempting to correct Marx's shortcoming, emphasizing the centrality of the struggle for African American rights and its links with the labor question, the German American leadership took his analysis on the Irish question and applied it to the American case with no modification. In fact, Sorge was convinced that the Irish represented the bulk of the American working class and were the key to win the country. At the 1872 IWA congress in The Hague, Sorge explained that "the working class in America consists of 1) Irishmen 2) Germans 3) Negroes and 4) Americans" and that "to win over America we absolutely need the Irish."[96] As a result, between 1870 and 1873, Sorge and his followers sent several updates on the "progress" of the IWA among Irish workers—progress that the hostility between the German American and the Irish American communities made virtually impossible.[97] African Americans did not feature as a priority of the IWA. This move revealed the inability of the Marxist leadership of the IWA to grasp the significance of Black labor in the making and working of American capitalism.

The approach toward Black members was one of the aspects of discussion in the internecine struggle that led to the end of the IWA in the United States. The International had developed along ethnic lines since its inception. Section 1 was the first to receive credentials from London, but soon after, English-speaking sections had started mushrooming around the northeast of the country. Until 1871 at least, English-speaking and non-English-speaking sections had coexisted harmoniously. In those years, the IWA had met important successes: It proudly remained faithful to its internationalist outlook through the difficult times of the Franco-German war (a hard test for the German American and French American communities, shaken by strong nationalist afflatuses). It responded firmly to the end of the Paris Commune, a bloody and frightful episode whose blame the European elites entirely placed on the IWA's shoulders.[98]

But soon, intellectual and political differences came to the fore. The Yankee International was a composite group of political activists whose approaches were solidly rooted in the republican radical tradition of the country. Its membership spanned from the Woodhull sisters, flamboyant and talented women's rights defenders and visionary activists who challenged the personal and political actions gender norms of the time, to seasoned trade unionist William West, a disciplined follower of labor internationalism seeking to radicalize American trade unions.[99] The Yankee International was ecumenical and eclectic in its approach. It was a broad tent where the various strands of American radicalism came together. By its own approach, the group did not seek theoretical coherence. Rather, these American radicals brought "tactics, values, and conception of revolutionary change" apprehended during their antebellum militancy to a new problem: "the labor question."[100]

Abolitionism, argued Messer-Kruse, "was the sun under which all these diverse planets of reform orbited," and racial equality was well within the orbit of the objectives this coalition sought to achieve.[101] In the few demonstrations that the Yankee International organized independently, this predisposition came clearly to the fore. The American branches of the IWA were the main organizers of a demonstration in commemoration of the martyrs of the Paris Commune held in New York in December 1871, a march led by the Black Skidmore Guards.[102] In 1872, the American sections of the International supported Victoria Woodhull's presidential bid—an attempt to unite the National Woman Suffrage Association, spiritualists, and the IWA under the same umbrella. The campaign would feature the first woman ever candidate for the presidency (Victoria Woodhull) and the first-ever African American candidate for the vice presidency (Frederick Douglass, who in the end decided to turn down Woodhull's offer). More broadly, as thoroughly documented by Messer-Kruse, on multiple occasions, Yankee Internationalists reaffirmed their commitment toward racial equality and their attempts to open the ranks of the IWA to Black members.[103]

Disagreements over strategy made it impossible to turn the pro-racial equality stances of both wings of the International into a solid and coordinated policy of labor interracialism. While Sorge and his followers sought to "purify" the organization of every demand that was not strictly relevant to wage workers, Yankee Internationalists pursued a confused and uncoordinated policy, in which the request for an eight-hour work day went along with a strong pro-women's suffrage campaign, the establishment of a "universal government," and flirtations with monetary reformism. Ethnic frictions piled up on strategic differences. The two wings of the International had different cultural backgrounds and spoke different languages of radicalism, the Americans rooted in religion, spirituality, and republicanism, the Germans in the dry language of historical materialism. As David Herreshoff remarks, "Where the Germans said 'materialism,' the Americans said 'spiritualism'; where the Germans said 'gold,' the Americans said 'greenbacks'; . . . when the Germans spoke of 'class struggle,' the Americans spoke of the 'scientific reconciliation of labor and capital'; when the Germans urged 'the emancipation of the working class,' the Americans gave priority to 'the sexual emancipation of women.'"[104]

Sorge oversaw the ruthless political machinations that led to the expulsion of the Yankee International from the IWA. In the United States, he staged a coup that tightened the control of his faction on the North American federal organs. In Europe, when the contrasts between the American branches were brought to the attention of the 1872 IWA congress in The Hague, he gathered enough consensus to obtain the expulsion of Section 12 with no opposition in the general assembly. The American Internationalist and leader of Section 12 William West had attended the IWA congress hoping to get a chance to talk to Marx and explain the actions of his section. His hopes were vain. He was denied a meeting in London, and his speech in the IWA general assembly did not convince anyone to vote in favor of his group.[105]

Sorge had won the battle for the control of the association, but his victory came at a huge cost. In an unexpected twist of the events, the Hague Congress had turned conflict-ridden New York City into the designated seat of the IWA General Council. Karl Marx and Friedrich Engels had arrived at The Hague with the conviction that the First International in Europe had run its course. Surprising their allies as well, in The Hague, the pair successfully passed an amendment that required the General Council of the federation to move from London to New York City. Sorge traveled back to the States having secured control of the IWA North American Federation and on course to become the General Secretary of the association. But at that point, what he controlled was a mound of rubble. The Yankee International had collapsed on its own contradictions. Woodhull's presidential bid had ended in failure, after the Section 12 organ *Woodhull and Claflin's Weekly* was denounced for indecency for publishing an article on the extramarital affair of Henry Ward Beecher. Several American sections had seceded and continued political activism independently. Had the Yankee International really represented a unique and successful synthesis of a purely American radical and socialist ideology, as Messer Kruse suggests, it would have cruised toward triumph away from their oppressive German comrades. Instead, its attempts to continue as an independent organization rapidly evaporated. Even German American members slowly trickled out of the association, regathering in local parties such as the Workingmen's Party of Illinois and the Social Democratic Party of North America (based in New York City).[106] By 1874, the IWA was nothing more than a paper association.

Outside the IWA, German American socialist analyses on race and Reconstruction started to flourish again. In 1874, members of the Workingmen's Party of Illinois started the German-language weekly *Vorbote* (soon to be followed by the daily *Chicagoer Arbeiter Zeitung* and the weekly *Die Fäckel)* and hosted correspondence from German Americans in the South.[107] A series of articles, written by an anonymous German laborer who had moved to the South in the summer of 1874, gave a fresh perspective on southern racial relations. In an introductory piece titled "Capital against Labor, or the White-Baiting against Negroes," the German workingman had a hard time understanding the contradictions of southern racial relations. On the one hand, he accused former white slaveholders of still keeping African Americans under their control and maneuvering the economy of the state; on the other hand, he denounced the excesses of Black-controlled public authorities, who, in his opinion, favored too-openly Black litigants. Yet the German socialist already clearly identified the Black working class as the primary target of his socialist propaganda. Debating politics, he reported what he heard during his lunch-breaks—that Black workers were sick of their support for the Republican Party because they did not trust white politicians.[108]

The more he remained in the South, the more his understanding of southern racial and class politics improved. Soon after his opening article, the socialist reported two lynchings of African Americans, which occurred "simply because [they] have the misfortune of being colored."[109] It took him one more month to declare that "there are many socialist features among the coloreds, and they can easily become our best Party's comrades." The author, in fact, contended that, from several points of view, African Americans were actually better than northern whites because their minds were less "poisoned" and more receptive than those of the allegedly free white workers. "I meet here among the Negroes more sincerity and less sense of subjection than what I found in the industrial cities of the North, for example New York, where I worked for several years." And if in this article he was already convinced that "here English-speaking socialists would have a good field for agitation,"[110] in the last article sent to the *Vorbote* in December 1874, the German socialist openly spoke of a "race war" that was tearing the South apart. The activist was now aware that the "race question" completely influenced the way in which politics was organized. "Skin color made the party color," and, as a consequence, "the party struggle has become a race struggle." However, since most African Americans were wage workers, the race struggle was essentially a "class struggle, a struggle between the exploiters and the exploited." Blacks needed to use their voting rights carefully, otherwise the ruling class would not hesitate to "intern them into a reservation," as they were doing with Native Americans. Politicians, contended the socialist, were nothing more than "practical Darwinists" who were trying to enforce the idea that natural laws threatened the survival of anyone but the Caucasian race.

The German American correspondent of the *Vorbote* pushed his understanding of the relationship between race and class much further than many of his Northern comrades writing at the time. He clearly understood how dynamics connected to race discrimination still influenced and organized southern society. Race discrimination pervaded politics and economics, was reflected in the enforcement of civil rights, and created pervasive forms of social ghettoization. By declaring that "the white worker sees now in the colored workers a fellow sufferer, who sighs with him under the same yoke of wage slavery," the German American correspondent reiterated his adhesion to the socialist approach based on class solidarity.[111] However, he coupled it with the awareness that in the U.S. South, class meant race, namely, that racial discrimination was but a veiled way to perpetrate the dynamic of economic oppression experienced by freed Black workers.

Conclusions

In 1913, German American socialist leader and historian Hermann Schlüter wrote the first historical materialist history of the American Civil War. In the intention of the author, *Lincoln, Labor, and Slavery* was a book with a specific aim: to tell the history of the war from the point of view of the American working class. Schlüter argued that white workers in the United States had been lukewarm on abolitionism and slow to understand the implications of the Civil War because they lacked class consciousness. Due to the limited spread of industrial capitalism in the United States, American workers, unlike the English, failed to appreciate that the abolition of slavery was a necessary step for the "proletarianization" of the rest of the country that was indispensable to achieve socialism.[112]

Written with an emphasis on organized manufacturing labor and a teleological approach that was typical of Second International socialists, Schlüter's book left small room for a detailed reconstruction of socialist racial thought before and after the Civil War. By actively joining the chorus of voices that advocated an end to chattel slavery, antebellum socialists not only wished to participate in the political life of their new country but they were also enthusiastic about a radical fight that seemed to lead the way toward unexplored horizons. To oppose slavery meant to campaign against the conservative powers of the country, to subvert its fundamental economic structures, and to put the interests of working people center stage. The achievement of this objective provoked an enthusiasm that was perfectly captured in the message that Karl Marx sent to Abraham Lincoln at the end of the war.

For antebellum socialists, the struggle to abolish slavery had been the main way through which they dealt with issues connected to race. But after 1865, the nature of the problem radically changed. With emancipation, four million formerly enslaved men and women entered the ranks of the American waged working class. Understanding the best way to defend the newly acquired rights of African Americans and supporting their effort to improve their living conditions was now the burning issue. After 1865, the objective had become the achievement of real racial equality between Black and white workers. But for German American socialists, the goal soon started to be seen as a moving target. Socialist attempts to fit within the growing organized American labor movement pushed them in a direction that was incompatible with making racial equality a priority of their political action. If Weydemeyer had captured the gist of socialists' problems surprisingly early, during Reconstruction, none seemed to be able to move into his footsteps. Socialists remained firm in their commitment to racial equality, yet at the same time, they spent endless efforts cultivating the growth of an organized labor movement and almost no energy trying to understand why in these years African American workers remained so viscerally connected to the Republican Party rather than joining the ranks of the organized labor movement.

CHAPTER 2

"Geographies of Peoples"

Ethnicity and Racial Thinking in the Early SLP

In his eulogy at the grave of Karl Marx, Friedrich Engels famously compared the importance of Marx's theories to those of Charles Darwin. Opening his oration, Engels emphatically stated that "just as Darwin discovered the law of development of organic nature, so Marx discovered the law of development of human history."[1] Marx and Engels had a lifelong fascination with Darwin's theories. When *On the Origins of Species* was published in 1859, Engels was quick to define it as "splendid" for the contribution it made to secularizing the study of the human sciences.[2] In 1873, Marx had a copy of the second edition of *Das Kapital* delivered to Darwin at Down House, with a penned dedication.[3] But as much as Marx and Engels appreciated Darwinism, they saw it as a radically separate project from historical materialism. As Engels stated in his eulogy, the two theories had similar ambitions, but they discussed two completely distinct subjects. Darwin had brilliantly explained the mechanisms of evolution in the organic world, but his work was of no help in understanding human history. For that, the laws of historical materialism were needed.

Marx's and Engels's immediate followers seemed to think otherwise. Historians have proven the deep fascination socialists across the world felt for Darwinism and other theories of human evolution.[4] From Karl Kautsky to Eduard Bernstein, from Henry Hyndman to Paul Lafargue to Emile Vandervelde, hardly anyone in Second International socialism managed to escape the allure of grand theories linking the mechanics of social conflict to the problem of the evolution of the humankind. This fascination stemmed from the high intellectual reputation that social evolutionist theories commanded. Theories of evolution were embraced by scientists across various disciplines, made popular by media outlets, used by mainstream politicians to frame their policies, and as such, were seen as an encompassing framework that socialists had to acknowledge and integrate in their worldview.[5]

This chapter investigates the multiple ways in which American socialists discussed race and ethnicity through the key concepts of scientific racialism, Darwinism, and historical materialism in the first phase of the history of the Socialist Labor Party (SLP). At its foundation, the SLP had a strong ethnic-specific base, and the origins of its members had an enormous impact on socialist ideas of race in this period. Specifically, the German background of the vast majority of the SLP leaders of the time meant that the interpretation of racial conflicts in the United States was conducted with approaches, ideas, and standards that derived from a German cultural context. Due to intersecting immigration waves in the German American diaspora, intellectual backgrounds, and political positions, three main positions emerged in the early SLP.[6]

Adolph Douai epitomizes the first one. With his analyses of modern scientific theories of race, disseminated in the three most important SLP papers (the *Labor Standard*, the *Vorbote*, and the *Arbeiter Stimme*), Douai was a leading voice in the debate on race in the party. Douai's opinions were those of a generation of German immigrants born in the 1810s and 1820s, who mixed pre-Darwinian theories such as geographical determinism, naturalism, and Romanticism with their personal interpretations of Darwin's natural selection. Douai's writings illustrate the malleability of scientific racialism, a theory that, in those decades, went hand in hand with all manner of political stances, from the socialist egalitarianism that Douai himself expressed, to the libertarian laissez-faire outlook of Charles Spencer.

Douai was by no means the only German American discussing Darwinism in the SLP press of the time. The articles of August Otto-Walster and Paul Grottkau are evidence of a later generation of radical German immigrants who had no interests in pre-Darwinian scientific racialism. Both Otto-Walster and Grottkau had been prominent leaders in the socialist movement in Germany and had arrived in the United States when Otto von Bismarck's anti-socialist law was passed. Thanks to their reputation in Europe, they rapidly became leaders of the SLP. Otto-Walster was editor of the *Arbeiter Stimme* from 1876 to 1878 and of the St. Louis daily *Volksstimme des Westens* from 1878 to 1881, and Paul Grottkau edited the *Vorbote* from 1878 to 1882. When discussing racial relations in the country, both understood Darwinism as a pervasive and unassailable social theory that organized social interaction in a wider sense and was best married with socialist principles. Darwinism, for them, was an inevitable part of the social context of the time.

Alongside socialists debating race through scientific racialism and Darwinism, like Douai, Otto-Walster, and Grottkau, who represented the first broad approach on the matter, a third group of socialists, writing in the *Labor Standard*, presented a radically different point of view based on a strict adherence to historical materialism. This group was made of former members of the International Workingmen's Association (IWA) and had a multiethnic composition, and their approach was consistent with the internationalist point of view ascribed to post-1865 German Americans in the previous chapter. In their opinion, interethnic and interracial conflicts were not something biology could explain. For them, these conflicts needed to be interpreted as consequences of the capitalist dynamic of economic production. This group was made up either of Forty-Eighters, like Friedrich A. Sorge, or veteran European radicals, like the Irish leader Joseph P. McDonnell. The expansive and universalist breadth of the 1848 ideals made them deaf to the mounting appeal of exclusivist nationalism. Furthermore, the years spent in the United States made them disillusioned with party politics. They advocated for trade unionism as the key strategy to improve the conditions of American workers. With a focus on incremental improvements, workers' economic organization, and a fully inclusive attitude without regard to color or nationality, this group anticipated many of the attitudes embraced by the Knights of Labor in the 1880s. Taken together, scientific racialism—views held by Douai, Otto-Walster, and Grottkau—and the internationalist socialism of the *Labor Standard* group constitute the two broad points of view characterizing the socialist debate on race at the time of the founding of the SLP.

In 1876, the SLP was divided between a pro-electoral politics bloc and a trade unionist faction, which roughly overlapped with the scientific racialists being pro-electoral and the internationalists forming the trade unionist wing. Members of the party temporarily made peace in their dispute on political strategy, but quarrels rapidly reemerged, forcing the strongest trade unionist group led by Sorge to abandon the organization. As a result, by 1879, internationalism was a minority position in the SLP, and the party was ultimately led by those who were at ease with scientific racialist and Darwinist approaches. This circumstance fundamentally shaped the SLP's positions on race throughout the 1880s, as chapters three, four, and five will detail.

Adolph Douai: A Progressive Scientific Racialist

On July 19, 1876, Germania Hall in Philadelphia hosted a meeting with participants representing the past, present, and future of American socialism. With the city packed by visitors of the Centennial International Exposition, socialists found it appropriate to meet in Pennsylvania to kickstart

FIGURE 3. Portrait of Adolph Douai. Undated. Harry Ransom Center, Austin.

the first labor party inspired by socialist doctrines with ambition to become a national force. Friedrich A. Sorge and Otto Weydemeyer, the son of the pioneering Marxist Joseph Weydemeyer, brought with them the memory of struggles led by Marxists in the previous decades. The German-speaking immigrant Conrad Conzett carried the credentials of the Workingmen's Party of Illinois, by far the most proactive socialist group in the country at the time. Adolph Strasser and Peter J. McGuire, a couple of carpenters who would make history by founding the American Federation of Labor (AFL) in 1882, spoke for the newly created Social Democratic Party of North America based in New York. At the gathering, some 3,000 workers from across the country were represented. After a phase of factional conflicts between the different regional parties, the delegates decided to follow the example of their German counterparts who, in 1875, had come together in the *Sozialistische Arbeiter Partei Deutschlands*. The founding committee formed in Philadelphia in 1876 turned four organizations into a single national association: the Workingmen's Party of the United States (WPUS).[7]

Adolph Douai was not at the founding convention of the party, but his abolitionist credentials and long militancy in the labor movement helped him land the prestigious, if controversial, position of assistant editor of the three official newspapers of the new party: the *Labor Standard*, the *Arbeiter Stimme*, and the *Vorbote*.[8] The presence of several newspapers, located in different areas of the country, reflected the political divisions that still characterized the movement. Socialists were fundamentally divided on political strategy: Some believed that party politics was the road to improve the conditions of American workers; others were disenchanted with bourgeois politics and supported trade unionism instead. As it turned out, the trade unionists came together around the *Labor Standard* and the *Vorbote*, whereas political actionists took control of the *Arbeiter Stimme*. Douai was a veteran of the socialist movement, with experience as a journalist. He was also highly esteemed for his cultural achievements. His social prestige and staunch support for the socialist cause put him in the ideal position to operate as a link between the different factions that animated the party.

In this commanding and influential position, Douai contributed to shaping the party line on a set of issues. One of them was its racial ideology. Douai's centrality on race stemmed from his interest for a topic that had fascinated him for his entire life: scientific theories of human evolution.[9] In his autobiography, Douai claimed that in 1848, he had already begun describing himself as "a professor of the theory of evolution in natural science."[10] He went even further, writing that in the late 1850s, he would have included himself among the Germans who were "Darwinians before Darwin." He claimed that, without any training in natural history, he could trace humankind's origin from animals and reconstruct the link between geographical conditions and evolution. And he could do this well before Darwin published *On the Origin of Species*.[11] Douai called his area of enquiry the "geography of peoples." He published several articles under this title throughout his career, the first one in 1854 in the *San Antonio Zeitung*, the German language newspaper he founded while living in that Texas city. He also wrote a book on the topic, called *Land und Leute in der Union* ("Land and People in the Union"), which was published in 1864. In it, he discussed the history of the United States looked at through the prism of his theories of human development.[12] After 1876, Douai used his position as assistant editor of the three SLP papers to put forward his ideas on evolutionism and theories of race and to propose that scientific evolutionism should shape socialist policies on immigration and racial minorities.

The few remarks that Douai made on Darwinism in his autobiography demonstrate his full endorsement of Darwin's research. They also provoke questions regarding the way in which the socialist Douai interpreted and understood Darwin's revolutionary theories. In 1878, Douai opened an article in the *Vorbote* by arguing that "the great theory of Darwin brilliantly discovered that in nature there were two ways in which the great wealth of different types of creatures comes off, descent and adaptation." But in his next sentence, he developed an opinion with which Darwin would not readily agree:

> Living creatures will remain similar to parents as long as no other effect of nature changes that similarity (. . .). External events in nature include food, housing, the air we breathe, the shape and colors of the objects around us, and all the sensory stimuli they produce, the surface morphology of the soil, the climate of the locality, the enemies and the friends among the other living creatures; we prefer to group all these effects under the common name of "soil," or soil and climate.[13]

The point of view expounded by Douai shows the clear influences of pre-Darwinian approaches, especially geographic determinism. According to Douai, every change in geography causes a parallel change in the physical structure of the human being. If people remained in the same place, no modification intervened. But once, for whatever reasons, they moved, their bodies progressively adapted to the new environment. Douai thought that this process created a vast variety of living beings, out of which, through a Darwinian process of selection, only the fittest survived. In this way, while appropriating some elements of Darwin's theories, Douai put forward an original point of view whose origins need to be located in the debates on racial differences and evolutionism developed in Europe from the eighteenth century onward.

The fixation with geography was by no means confined to Douai; in fact, it dated to intellectual traditions started decades earlier. In the eighteenth century, as geographical discoveries gave rise to stories of exotic populations from different areas of the world, intellectuals began to theorize reasons for human physical and cultural differences.[14] For example, in his magnum opus, *The Spirit of Laws*, the French intellectual Charles Louis de Secondat de Montesquieu elaborated on a model according to which environmental circumstances decided not only human attitudes but also political and social features of the different human groups. For Montesquieu, climate and geography explained why despotism and slavery were common in Asia, whereas monarchies, republics, and more liberal customs proliferated in temperate areas like Europe.[15]

In the nineteenth century, naturalists and geographers started to ground their theses with firsthand data acquired from exploration and fieldwork. Geological observation led to the widely held belief that the earth was constantly evolving. Many extended this idea to the organic world, suggesting that both animals and humans were the product of centuries-long processes of evolution. But then the question became: How was evolution possible? In what way had living beings changed over time?[16] One of the more credited replies came from Jean-Baptiste Lamarck, who wrote a more sophisticated and scientifically grounded version of the geographic determinism theorized by Montesquieu. Lamarck expounded a theory that suggested that living beings developed physical features according to the surrounding geographical environment. According to Lamarck, humans and animals could pass on to their offspring characteristics developed during their lifetime. For example, the necks of giraffes had elongated because of the animals' repeated attempts to reach leaves at the very top of trees.[17]

In *On the Origins of Species*, Darwin corrected the ideas of the geographic determinists in a significant way, adding the fundamental point: random selection. Whereas Lamarck had argued that the animals managed to stretch their necks, Darwin maintained that out of a group of animals whose different features developed in a completely random way, only giraffes had survived because of their special ability to reach sources of food inaccessible to animals with shorter necks. This point on random selection had enormous implications and was one of the reasons why Darwin's theory had such an impact. With his idea of random selection, Darwin was suggesting that humans were not the perfect product of a superior divinity but rather the casual outcome of millions of years of random processes of evolution. This argument struck a significant blow to divine teleology. Darwin was made unacceptable to religious authority because of his idea that humans were essentially hyperdeveloped animals; his discoveries demolished the distinction between the human and the animal realms. Consequently, the idea that God had established the superiority of humans over animals and separated them from beasts by providing mankind with features such as a soul was now in question. These two arguments lay at the heart of the controversy Darwinism provoked in the realm of religion.[18]

Douai acknowledged the importance of Darwin's theory of random selection; however, he also contended that, while "Darwin and his school" had studied the impact of the "soil and climate" on multiple species, this study "had not happened with the same zeal . . . for the human race." Douai found this puzzling because the study of human differences through Darwinian methodology was "the easiest and most gratifying" task.[19] In a series of eight articles published in the *Vorbote* between December 1878 and January 1879, Douai embarked on a sweeping analysis of human differences according to Darwinian principles.[20] In this series, he offered one of the most comprehensive analyses of scientific racialism ever published in a socialist paper. While Darwinism was his starting point, Douai offered an original theory of human transmutation that significantly revised the theories of the English scientist. To do this, he utilized multiple approaches, spanning the early nineteenth-century naturalism of Alexander von Humboldt to the linguistics of Wilhelm von Humboldt and August Schleicher. Although at times incoherent and controversial, Douai's theory cast a significant light on the racial thinking of an early generation of German American immigrants who interpreted racial policies through the lens of scientific evolutionism.

Douai set out to discuss "the main characters of the soil and climate individually" and to provide a coherent explanation about how human beings have evolved across millennia. He reviewed every geographical area, starting from the tropics and the poles and moving toward the temperate zones. For each human group, Douai offered explanations of their physical, cultural, and social traits. Douai's methodology was revealing of the many influences that characterized his approach. He combined historical information, considerations on nutrition, data on the availability of food and domestic animals, geographic circumstances, technological developments, and linguistics. Therefore, even though he apparently based his theory of transmutation on geography alone, in reality, he formulated an analysis that was holistic in its methodology and scope. Douai placed African Americans, "[N]egritos," Malaysians, Native Americans, and "half-breeds of the white, yellow and black races" on the lowest scale of human development, whereas "in the temperate climates," he maintained, "We find both the largest variety of bodily and mental development and the only progressed culture."[21] Douai connected human development to the technological, cultural, and social status, or sophistication (defined by him) of the respective cultures and societies: Peoples living in the tropics, Malaysia, or Africa were the least developed, and Europe and the United States were at the top of the scale. In Douai's analysis, the biological and cultural levels were inextricably intertwined. The "white race" not only had a higher level of technological development, it was also "mentally and physically superior."[22]

From a scientific point of view, at times Douai's points were rather naïve in describing the effects of geographic circumstances on the human body. For example, he argued that people living in the tropics have dark skin because the heat prevented their lungs from breathing out all the carbon dioxide in their blood. As a result, according to him, some dioxide ends up under the skin and darkens its color. Douai provided a further detail to prove his theory, writing that at birth, "Negro children are fairly white because they only begin to breathe at birth, and only later progressively darken."[23] Yet elsewhere, his arguments were grounded on carefully considered scientific theories, while informed by progressive and open-minded beliefs.

Consider Douai's discussion on monogenism and polygenism. The clash between monogenists and polygenists had characterized a large part of the theorizing on race during the nineteenth century in the United States. Its implications went way beyond the interests of scientists and naturalists and were directly involved in debates on slavery in the country. Grounding their arguments on controversial interpretations of the Bible, polygenists openly argued that African Americans and people of other non-white races were strikingly different because they were not created at the same time as the white race. Historian Reginald Horsman argued that these scientists were moved by a deeply engrained need to situate the white race higher on the scale of human development. "At the heart of the polygenetic position," contended Horsman, "was a refusal to believe that other people who appeared in every way 'savage' and physically different could have sprung from the same ancestors." In some cases, polygenetic positions combined with anti-evolutionism: Not only were all the other races inferior to whites but also this inferiority was cast in stone and biologically fixed.[24]

According to historians Adrian Desmond and James Moore, the ultimate reason that motivated Charles Darwin to formulate his revolutionary theory of evolution was precisely the will to refute the polygenetic race theory.[25] Darwin's was an attempt, essentially, to defend universal brotherhood and undermine the strongest argument in the hands of polygenism, namely, the idea that God created men differently.[26] Adolph Douai placed himself within the realm of Darwinian monogenism, even though he offered his own version of the theory of human evolution. Douai openly rejected polygenism, writing that "no naturalist today would regard the different human races as originally different."[27] Unlike Darwin, however, he believed that different human races existed. Darwin had not been against the idea of hierarchy in human groups. As historian Robert J. Richards stressed, Darwin "aligned the human groups on a developmental path, from 'savage' races to the 'civilized.'" But he refrained from using the term "race," which he considered indistinguishable from that of species.[28] Yet crucially, Darwin restricted the different levels of human advancement to *non*-biological fields: From a biological point of view, men and women were all equal. For Darwin, differences may occur in the realm of political, cultural, or social advancement but not in the realm of biology. Moreover, even the different levels of development of human groups were modifiable over time. The classification was not cast in stone but was flexible and changeable.

Unlike Darwin, Douai believed that physical, as well as cultural and social differences, divided human beings. For Douai, humans were divided into three races (the white, the yellow, and the Black) that had originated from the same species. Each of these groups had different innate features. Some were weaker than others, and some were more advanced than others. Douai suggested that evidence coming from geological investigation and linguistic evaluation proved that the different human races were born at different times. But, despite their differences, none of the races were going to disappear. Quite the contrary, he continued; evidence showed that the different races would continue to mingle and evolve. "If all three races—the black, the yellow, and the white, with their half-breeds—were the same age old, the yellow, being tougher and more warlike, would have extirpated or plundered the weaker black race long ago, and the white, which is mentally and physically superior to both, would have destroyed or subjugated both of them."[29]

According to Douai, historical linguistics explained why the logic of replacement and extermination was not applicable to relationships between human races. Linguistics had significantly grown in importance and prestige during the nineteenth century in Germany. Throughout the century, various scholars, from Wilhelm von Humboldt to Friedrich Schlegel to August Schleicher, had contributed to its dissemination. Through the study of commonalities and differences in ancient and modern languages, linguists had imparted valuable information on the pattern of movement of humans across the millennia. The discovery and study of Sanskrit in the late eighteenth century had enabled scientists to postulate the existence of a group of Proto-Indo-European languages with common grammatical, morphological, and phonic traits. This crucial demonstration showed that most of the humans that now inhabited India, the Middle East, and Europe had come from one common group.[30]

In the mid-nineteenth century, linguistics was rarely analyzed in conjunction with Darwinism. Only after 1869, with the publication in English of Schleicher's short pamphlet *Darwinism Tested by the Science of Language* did the conversation begin.[31] Douai, writing a decade after the publication of Schleicher's pamphlet, showed great familiarity with Schleicher's work and demonstrated his own ability to correlate the theory to modern scientific evolutionism. Linguistics gave Douai solid scientific arguments to prove that humans continuously mixed and changed, and while Douai did not refrain from the idea of superior and inferior races, he did contend that among the human races, hierarchy itself was in constant evolution.

Together with linguistics, the Romantic naturalism of Alexander von Humboldt had an even more significant impact on Douai's thinking. Douai adopted a methodological approach, taken in every respect, from the vast literature published by Alexander von Humboldt, the founder of modern historical geography. Alexander, the oldest of the Humboldt brothers, grew up reading Immanuel Kant's books and discussing his theories with Johann Wolfgang von Goethe, Friedrich Schiller, and his brother Wilhelm.[32] His travels in South America between 1799 and 1804 and his published accounts of them inaugurated a new method of study encompassing the interaction of man and his geographic environment.[33] Historian Laura Dassow Walls argued that Humboldt's scientific method was based on four mandates: explore, collect, measure, and connect. This methodology required the naturalist to physically experience the place, rigorously classify and analyze the evidence collected, and studiously connect all the elements acquired, with the ultimate goal of producing a holistic view of the natural world. His main work, *Cosmos*, was a five-volume attempt to synthesize his grand theory of nature into a unified system. This work went from emotional responses to natural landscapes to the explanation of theories connected to geographical phenomena. His work was a powerful expression of early-nineteenth-century Romanticism. With its commingling of different disciplines, it became enormously influential, not only for scientists like Charles Darwin but also for the artists among the transcendentalists and for painters of the Hudson River school in the United States.[34]

Humboldt died in 1859. At that period, Douai was a schoolteacher in Boston. His love for Humboldt was so renowned that the local German association asked him to organize an event of commemoration for the deceased Prussian naturalist.[35] On reading Douai's work, it is not difficult to see how much Douai relied on Humboldt's theories; he imitated the same all-embracing analytical style and used a wide-ranging multidisciplinary approach to reconstruct the development of the different races by putting together different elements in a logically consistent structure. Douai's use of the "soil and climate" methodology to investigate the "geography of peoples" was an attempt to update Humboldt's comprehensive scheme in light of the recent discoveries in human evolution, geographic determinism, and linguistics.

Douai followed in the footsteps of his intellectual mentor when it came time to discuss the subject of racial differences. In *Cosmos*, Humboldt had argued that mankind was distributed in varieties, "designed by the somewhat indefinite term *races*." However, the differences between human groups were so numerous that to give a sharp, clear, *scientific* definition of the idea of race was essentially impossible. Humboldt embraced the notion of "the unity of the human species" and wholeheartedly rejected "the depressing assumption of superior and inferior races of men."[36] He further contended that while there were "nations more susceptible of cultivation, more highly civilized, more ennobled by mental cultivation than other," divisions based on inherent racial features simply did not exist. All men and women were "in like degree designed for freedom; a freedom which, in the ruder conditions of society, belongs only to the individual, but which, in social states enjoying political institutions, appertains as a right to the whole body of the community."[37]

While replacing Humboldt's culture-based humanism with his bricolage theory of human biological transmutation, Douai ultimately agreed with Humboldt's egalitarianism. Douai was a staunch supporter of the free movement of people, and he thought that migrations benefitted the human species from a racial point of view. As a result of the continuous movement of people, he reasoned, it was extremely rare to find "pure" races. But the more the races mixed, the better. Humans naturally tended to concentrate in hospitable places in the temperate areas of the world. These areas, with their "colorful mixtures," gave rise to "the most progressive breeds" and "the most advanced races."[38] With his progressive Lamarckism, based on the belief that human physical, social, and cultural traits continuously changed, Douai furnished a version of scientific racialism that held to Humboldt's core tenets. Human races were in constant flux. Even the groups at the lower levels of the human scale of development could improve for the better and rapidly achieve the top of the scale, and moreover, Douai supported policies designed to achieve this. When, at the end of his series of articles, he got around to discussing the American continent, Douai asserted that climate conditions made the Americas an inhospitable place for humans to live. "Humanity is in constant danger of degenerating here," he claimed. Only by being constantly "refreshed by new immigration and imported culture" could the human population continue to thrive.[39]

Douai translated into practice his staunch pro-immigration policy. He supported an open-border policy in all cases, including for Chinese immigrants who, from 1882, were being stopped from entering the United States by the Chinese Exclusion Act. Not surprisingly, Douai's support for open borders was highly controversial. Moreover, there were elements of his theory that led him to progressive political positions. For example, given the comprehensiveness of his theory, Douai produced analyses that paid attention to the impact that social and economic conditions had on the development of human groups, thus increasing the pointedness of his political commentaries. Douai was one of the few socialists to openly campaign for the political organization of the African American community, a position which relied as much on his relatively sophisticated understanding of the socioeconomic condition of Black Southern communities as it did on his egalitarian racial thought.[40]

Douai's case attests to the fact that the adoption of scientific racialism did not necessarily tie with the defense of white supremacy. With his theories, Douai confronted regressive interpretations of Darwinism that justified social and economic inequality on the basis of the alleged natural inferiority of certain racial groups. Instead, he offered a version of scientific racialism that fit with principles of working-class solidarity and internationalism. His was a unique voice in the Gilded Age socialist context. With his articles, Douai drew on German naturalism, linguistics, Lamarckism, and Darwinism, and he brought to the debate a highly informed, if at times contradictory, understanding of scientific racialist theories. While failing to produce a fully coherent point of view, Douai's articles demonstrate an attempt to interpret the socialist doctrine in light of modern scientific theories of race, using the science to harness the credibility and effectiveness of the socialist doctrine.

The Inevitability of Darwinism: Paul Grottkau and August Otto-Walster

Douai was arguably the only socialist intellectual to employ such detailed theories of race in his work, but many others also used Darwinism as an interpretative lens to discuss the contrasts between different racial and ethnic groups. For the generation that followed Douai's—born in pre-unification Germany of the 1830s and 1840s—it was no longer a question of needing a holistic explanation of the differences between human groups. They had grown up in the intellectual milieu where the "theory of evolution" expressed in scientific terms was no longer a novelty. For them, on the contrary, the problem was to determine to what extent the theory of evolution could be used to interpret human facts. The *Socialist* reported an opinion on Darwinism that perfectly contextualized this issue:

> It seems blind absurdity to attempt an explanation of human nature on the theory of evolution. The theory utterly fails to even hint at the facts with which we are confronted, when we begin to study the moral side of human

> life. The law of the survival of the fittest might have produced excellent teeth and claws, but it could never have evolved the human heart . . . This theory of man's origin is becoming popular on account of the materialistic tendency of modern thought, and is fast supplanting the old ideas derived from traditional superstition; but it must forever be rejected by those who discern the spiritual mysteries of human life.[41]

This article struck at the heart of a debate between opposing systems of thought raging in imperial Germany in the last decades of the nineteenth century. Germany, with its prestigious universities and world-renewed intellectuals, was the global leading hub of humanist knowledge. A historicist approach, nurtured by the philosophies of theorists such as Wilhelm von Humboldt, Johann Gottlieb Fichte, and Johann Gustav Droysen, had organized much of Germany's self-perception in the leading up to German unification in 1871. The colonial encounter and the concurrent renewed interest in natural sciences created the conditions for this hegemonic system of thought to be challenged. Although Germany did not start its own colonial endeavor until 1884, the debate on human differences provoked by the spread of imperialism revealed the shortcomings of a theoretical framework that was only centered on Western culture. In the German context, the assault on the powerful humanist canon was led both by anthropologists and Darwinian thinkers, although the two schools of thought took divergent paths. German members of the socialist movement tended to embrace Darwinism and evolutionism, seeing it as a means through which the rigid stronghold of the humanist academic canon could be broken.[42]

The material published in the German-language socialist press in the United States confirms socialist support for Darwinism. German American socialists of the 1870s not only embraced it, they saw it as fully compatible with the socialist doctrine and applicable to American contexts. In May 1878, the *Vorbote* published an article by Paul Grottkau titled "Darwinism in the Economic and Political World." Born in Berlin in 1846, Grottkau had been a member of the Lassallean Allgemeiner Deutscher Arbeiter-Verein (General German Workers' Association) and editor of the *Berliner Freie Presse*. He was warmly welcomed by the German American socialist community in Chicago when he first arrived there at the beginning of 1878. His fame in Germany certainly facilitated his career in the local socialist movement, and within six months of his arrival, he was nominated editor of the *Arbeiter Zeitung* and the *Vorbote*, the daily and weekly papers of the Chicago section of the SLP.[43]

In his article, Grottkau explained why Darwinism was so popular among employers and the ruling class: "The bourgeoisie cheers Darwinism, because it thinks that with this hard, inhuman doctrine of naked and brutal struggle it can justify the legitimacy of the capitalist mode of production. Because, so these gentlemen say, each person fights for his existence, and only the better, the more appropriate survives, whereas those who go down have no right to exist."[44] Grottkau did not contest the interpretation of Darwinism furnished by the capitalists. In his opinion, the fact that the "struggle for existence" ruled political and economic relations was based on scientific evidence. But he did show the way in which Darwinism and socialism could coexist just as easily. Grottkau argued that in this phase of history, according to the Darwinian process, it was legitimate for big businesses to destroy and incorporate small businesses, just as in the future, it would be legitimate for the socialist Cooperative Commonwealth (the largest possible form of economic production) to destroy and incorporate capitalist businesses.[45]

Grottkau was not the only one to hold this position in the SLP. August Otto-Walster expressed similar opinions in his writings. Otto-Walster was born in Dresden in 1834. In 1869, he worked at the *Dresdner Volkszeitung* and cooperated with August Bebel and Wilhelm Liebknecht to found the Marxist *Sozialdemokratischen Arbeiterpartei* (Social-Democratic Labor Party). Otto-Walster was a refined and much-appreciated intellectual. He was a prolific writer who published several novels exploring working class life in pre-unification Germany. In 1876, he relocated to New York after accepting the offer of the SLP to work as editor of the official paper, *Arbeiter Stimme*. In 1878, he moved to St. Louis to become the editor of the *Volksstimme des Westens*, a step forward in his career, considering that St. Louis had one of the biggest sections in the party and the *Volksstimme* was one of the few socialist dailies in America.[46]

In October 1878, Otto-Walster commented in the press on a talk given by Oscar Schmidt, an early supporter of Darwinism. In his talk, Schmidt had rejected the idea that Darwin's theory and socialism were compatible. A debate on this topic had exploded in 1877 in Germany after Rudolf Virchow, perhaps the country's most prestigious anthropologist, had argued that Darwinism should not be taught in schools because it was dangerous, a view confirmed by the fact that even socialists embraced it. As reconstructed by historian Angela Zimmerman, Virchow led a school of anthropologists that was highly skeptical of biological evolutionism and Darwinism, an approach that they dubbed as "monkey doctrine."[47] Virchow's association of Darwinism with socialism had provoked an immediate hostile reaction from Darwinian scientists. Zoologist Ernst Haeckel, the most celebrated and popular advocate of Darwinism in Germany, vehemently attacked Virchow. Haeckel argued that Darwin had scientifically proven the inequality

FIGURE 4. Portrait of August Otto-Walster. Undated. SPD Collection, International Institute of Social History, Amsterdam.

of men and was at odds with the egalitarianism of socialism. The Virchow-Haeckel debate had a long echo in Germany, because in it, academic polemics on an explosive new doctrine like Darwinism intersected with political debates on socialism in a moment when Chancellor Otto von Bismarck was gearing up to approve his anti-socialist legislation.[48]

Otto-Walster was keenly aware of the crucial importance of this debate. In his commentary, he took the occasion to expound a carefully phrased position: "Socialism does not state that all men have the same predispositions, but rather demands that in the struggle for existence the individual be granted the most complete use of all his inborn qualities, so as, for example, not to throw up as an unhappy winner an ignorant yet devoted millionaire like Vanderbilt."[49]

Eventually, Otto-Walster sought a way to make Darwinism and socialism harmonious. He argued that socialism did not contest the Darwinian principle that men were unequal and that the struggle for existence regulated social intercourse. But he insisted that it did demand fair and equal rules of engagement so that everyone could have the chance to use their qualities and succeed in the struggle. Otto-Walster, for his part, aimed to attack pro-bourgeois biases, but ultimately was at ease with a social model that implied structural inequality.

The opinions of Adolph Douai, on the one hand, and of Paul Grottkau and August Otto-Walster, on the other, exemplify the way in which German American socialists approached differences of race in the 1870s and early 1880s. In this period, the SLP was a site where scientific theories of evolution were used to conceptualize and explain racial differences. Still, socialists did not produce a single and coherent position on the topic. By taking into account the intellectual debate in pre-unified Germany and by describing the generational differences within the German American socialist community, one can, nevertheless, identify two general approaches to the issue. The first is characterized by the early nineteenth century eclectic mix of Darwinism and pre-Darwinian geographical determinism represented by Douai, and the second is Grottkau's and Otto-Walster's attempts to amalgamate Darwinism and socialism. While not being anti-egalitarian or racist in themselves, these approaches conceded the possibility that structural inequality, based on biological, social, and economic conditions, was a reality inscribed in the natural laws that governed human interaction. This concession severely weakened the emancipatory power of the political message socialist activists were trying to spread.

Against Darwin: Internationalist Trade Unionism

Marx and Engels welcomed the publication of Darwin's *On the Origins of Species* with enthusiasm. In 1859, Engels wrote to his friend: "Darwin, by the way, whom I'm reading just now, is absolutely splendid. There was one aspect of teleology that had yet to be demolished, and that has now been done. Never before has so grandiose an attempt been made to demonstrate historical evolution in Nature, and certainly never to such good effect."[50]

As the quotation aptly shows, the aspect of Darwin's theory that both Marx and Engels enjoyed most was its capacity to explain evolution without religion. Marx confirmed this idea two years later. In presenting Darwin's book to Ferdinand Lassalle, he wrote that here for the first time teleology in the natural sciences is not only dealt a mortal blow, but its rational sense is also empirically explained."[51]

Marx's and Engels's enthusiasm was an expression of the anti-religious sentiment generated in Germany by the liberating theories of Darwin. The two were looking for confirmation of their materialism. Darwin's theory provided a powerful argument against Hegelian idealism, the model in contrast to which Marx and Engels had framed dialectical materialism. As stressed by historian Richard Weikart, however, Marx and Engels did not incorporate any other aspects of Darwin's point of view into their theoretical plan. By the time Marx had read Darwin's work, contended Weikart, the key tenets of his materialistic methodology were already in place. Marx's understanding of the world was based on the distinction between human and animal. His theory was devoted to explaining the dynamics that regulated human interaction. Biology and natural sciences were peripheral areas in Marx's system of thought. Therefore, continued Weikart, "Marx's evolutionary view of society did not in any way derive from or depend on biological evolution."[52]

It is not surprising, then, that the German American socialists who most closely followed Marx and Engels were less proactive when it came to embracing Darwinist approaches. This is evident in the opinions expressed in the *Labor Standard*, the newspaper controlled by the SLP group that considered trade unionism to be the primary work of the party. This group was composed of former members of the North American section of the IWA, most of them recent immigrants to the northeast of the United States who spoke English. Among its more prominent leaders were Friedrich A. Sorge and Joseph P. McDonnell, the editor of the *Labor Standard* from 1876 to 1882.

McDonnell had a radical background surpassing Sorge's. He was born in Dublin in 1847. During his youth, which was spent between Dublin and London, McDonnell had been a vocal advocate of Irish nationalism, a supporter of the Paris Commune, and a member of the IWA, serving as the organization's Ireland secretary in the early 1870s. McDonnell had been jailed several times for his political activities, and Herbert G. Gutman noted that on his arrival in New York in 1872, "Few other immigrants carried to industrializing America so full and so complete a set of radical credentials."[53]

This group brought to the SLP the internationalist inspiration that had animated the IWA, as explained in the *Labor Standard* in 1877: "If capital does not care to import French Canadians, Italians, Poles and heathen Chinese by the ten thousand, to abate the wages of labor and increase its own profits, what more necessary thing have we to do than to organize ourselves with the laborers of all nations to keep the wolf from the door first, and to break down private capital next?"[54]

In the newspaper, the problem of national and racial differences was rarely analyzed by itself. The issue was more often mentioned in connection with the dynamics of the job market and immigration. But here, the interests of the American workers were never given first place. Labor internationalism was applied in a consistent, almost rigid way.

On July 7, 1877, the *Labor Standard* published an article written by its correspondent "Middleton" (a pseudonym). McDonnell so warmly embraced the content of this piece that he decided to forgo his own weekly column in order to make space for Middleton's. Using simple language and an easy-to-follow logical progression, Middleton explained why American wages were falling so rapidly. He explained that, as a consequence of global interconnection, high American wages had fallen to the level of low European wages. At this point, "having exhausted the civilized world in the hunt for cheap labor," capitalists had turned to China.[55] But Middleton did not indulge in any protectionist temptation. Instead, he argued, "It is useless to prevent the importation of the products of cheap labor, so long as we import the cheap laborer." Middleton adamantly concluded his case by declaring that "the best protection for labor at home, is the improvement of the *Laborer* abroad."[56] He refused to place any blame on the workers who had immigrated to the United States:

> The French, German, English, Irish, Italian, or even Chinaman are not less fond of high wages than the American. No better evidence of this is needed, than the fact that they will leave their homes, their friends, and all the social conditions under which they have lived from childhood, and come to a country whose whole manners and customs, and even the very language, are all entirely strange, if not repulsive, to them. All this they will do in order to obtain high wages. It is therefore clear that their object is to improve their own condition, rather than impair ours.[57]

Placing himself in the position of immigrants, Middleton demonstrated a profound empathy for their circumstances, and put forward a political strategy that sought to satisfy both American and immigrant workers.

The trade unionists of the SLP did not only focus on immigration and national differences; they also concentrated on racial inequality. In a speech McDonnell gave to a crowd in New York during the Great Strike of 1877, the *Labor Standard* editor celebrated the interracial unity of workers by declaring that "it was a grand sight to see in West Virginia, white and colored men standing together, men of all nationalities in one supreme contest for the common rights of workingmen. The barriers of ignorance and prejudice were fast falling before the growing intelligence of the masses. Hereafter there shall be no north, no south, no east, no west, only one land of labor and the workingmen must own and possess it."[58] Class solidarity, according to McDonnell, should make no exceptions. He thought that the worsening of the workers' situation opened new spaces for them to unite despite their proclivity to balk at ethnic and racial differences.

The contrast between scientific racialism and internationalism helps put the changes in the labor scenario that took place between the late 1860s and the late 1870s in the right perspective. During Reconstruction, IWA leaders failed to forge interracial alliances because they focused too narrowly on wage workers and Irish immigrants. But the situation had changed by the end of the decade. In the context of the late 1870s and early 1880s, with its intellectual landscape made up of exclusivist nationalism, Darwinism, and scientific racialism, the position of the internationalists once again represented a progressive voice in the American radical movement. At a historical moment when the failure of Reconstruction and competition in the job market favored the spread of racial and ethnic discrimination, internationalists kept a global perspective and managed to shun the calls for protectionism and white supremacy. Their decision to leave aside political action and focus on trade unionism had two positive effects: First, it gave them a chance to work for small, incremental improvements that could win the favor of the workers; and second, by abandoning electoral politics, they did not have to back political campaigns antithetical to socialist ideals, like, for example, the closure of the Pacific borders.

However, the epoch of the internationalists in the SLP was short lived. The Sorgean group joined the WPUS-SLP in 1876 on the condition that the party would not take part in elections until it was strong enough to achieve some solid result. This clause, approved in a last-minute deal during the Foundation Congress, was violated just three months later by the Newark section of the party led by a proponent of political action, Peter J. McGuire. The Newark section's activity opened a year-long debate, where the two opposing factions faced one another with no intention of surrendering their respective positions. Paradoxically, the matter was settled to the advantage of political actionists by a series of protests led by trade unionists—the Great Strike of 1877. This caused a momentary increase in the socialist vote and allowed the supporters of electoral politics to overtake and exclude the defenders of trade unionism. Sorgeans formally remained in the SLP until the end of 1877 but did not take part in the Second Congress of the party in December 1877, and by 1878 had founded their own organization, the International Labor Union (ILU).[59]

With the ILU split from the SLP, the Sorgean-Marxist strand of thought secured a firm place in the American radical world. The ILU enlisted among its members some activists from the eight-hour movement, such as Ira Steward and George E. McNeill.[60] And in the end, Sorge managed to achieve what had been his goal since 1869: to fuse Marxist trade-unionism with U.S.-bred republicanism in the manner of the National Labor Union. However, in the ten years it took Sorge to accomplish this result, the American labor world had completely changed, and former NLU members no longer had prominent positions of leadership. According to Sorge himself, the ILU managed to organize a few successful events in New England, but after a couple of years, the organization could not sustain itself and was dismantled. In a series of articles that Sorge wrote for the theoretical journal of the Social Democratic Party of Germany *Neue Zeit* in the 1890s, Sorge blamed repressive anti-trade union regulations for the quick demise of his organization. Even if a meeting called by the ILU attracted a large turnout, he argued, the organizers could not find workers who would agree to accept positions in their assemblies, let alone enroll in the organization. They feared having their names published in the *Labor Standard* because it most certainly would have guaranteed a swift dismissal from their jobs. Despite an initial flurry of interest, then, the union was forced to close in 1880.[61]

The principles of the ILU did not disappear from the world of organized labor. But rather than having been revived by Gompers's AFL, as Messer-Kruse has suggested in *The Yankee International*, they were upheld by the largest trade union federation of the 1880s, the Knights of Labor.[62] The promotion of measures to improve the lot of workingmen and women without considerations of race or ethnicity showed up again as a key aspect of the Knights' organizing principles in the 1880s. Not only that but the Knights put into practice the intuition of Middleton. Animated by the conviction that organizing workers *in loco* was the best strategy against cheap labor in the United States, the Knights opened sections of the trade union federation in Europe and attempted to tackle the problem of immigration by improving the conditions of potential immigrants while they were still in their place of origin. This was similar to what had been attempted by the IWA in the 1860s. The ideals of ethnic and racial equality sketched by ILU members were translated into deeds by the Knights of Labor.[63] Sorge and his group had pointed to a possible alternative for socialists. When in the early 1880s the failure of the SLP convinced numerous socialists to abandon political action, many joined the Knights of Labor and continued their political activism in that organization. The ILU opened a path that was later followed by many other socialists.

Conclusions

Scientific racialism and internationalist trade unionism were the two main approaches used by the American socialist movement in the late 1870s and early 1880s to discuss and address racial diversity. Because of the large German American component in the SLP and the specific features of the German American community in the United States, it is possible to identify the intellectual origins that animated debates in the party. The writings of Adolph Douai, for example, combined pre-Darwinian approaches, such as the holistic methodology of Alexander von Humboldt and the linguistic methods of Schleicher, with Lamarckian and Darwinist elements. A second group, exemplified by Paul Grottkau and August Otto-Walster, saw Darwinism as an eminently positive theory and sought ways to connect it with socialism. Finally, a third group, epitomized by Friedrich A. Sorge and Joseph P. McDonnell, rejected approaches based on scientific theories and relied on race-blind internationalism in their approach to national and racial differences.

These divisions intersected with political factions within the party; the Sorge/McDonnell group corresponded with a defense of trade unionism in opposition to political action and participation in elections. The Sorge/McDonnell faction had a short life in the SLP, remaining in the organization only between 1876 and 1878. As this group moved on to found a new movement (the International Labor Union), socialists within the SLP who supported scientific racialist and Darwinist points of view took the lead in the party. It is important to stress that the dividing lines between the different groups were more blurred than they might appear. Several elements were at work here. Firstly, those who used race-based approaches were not necessarily racist or white supremacist. Secondly, a minority of internationalist trade unionists were present in the large Chicago section of the SLP, and they remained in the party after the bloc around Sorge split in 1878. So, while internationalist positions continued to be represented within the SLP, from 1877 onward, the SLP was a party where socialists embracing scientific racialist and Darwinist points of view found a comfortable home. The next chapter details the specific concerns that arose out of these ideological positions as they pertained to the "Chinese question."

CHAPTER 3

Must They Go?

American Socialism and the Racialization of Chinese Immigrants, 1876–1890

The size of the crowd in the square facing the new San Francisco City Hall was beyond the wildest expectations of the rally's organizers. On the morning of July 23, 1877, the Workingmen's Party of the United States (WPUS) issued an appeal for a meeting in support of the Great Railroad Strike in the eastern states. By the end of the day, the party's leadership stood in front of a crowd of ten thousand people. The rally was a success and a glorious showcase of working-class activism. With several speakers alternating at the podium, the crowd unanimously approved resolutions for the eight-hour workday and against the violent repression of the labor demonstrations in the East, condemning the "two great parties" as "the slaves of the money ring" and "the tools of monopolists."[1]

The agitation did not end when the workers' meeting adjourned in the late afternoon. The "hoodlum element," as the *San Francisco Examiner* labeled it, gathered at "the outskirts of the crowd" and, not finding in the words of the speakers something "congenial with their own desires," "started off for a little diversion on their own book." The WPUS-called rally turned into a violent and uncontrolled mob that rampaged for three days. During the afternoon rally, the WPUS chair James D'Arcy had defined the violent repression in the East as "a disgrace to our civilization" and had described the socialists as "a law-making and law-abiding people." A couple of hours later, the noise of smashed windows and the blaze of fires made his words sound hollow and meaningless. The violence rapidly took on racial overtones. For three long nights, a mass of unemployed white workers vented their rage and frustration against Chinese-owned shops and businesses across the city. By the end of the week, when the calm was restored by an ad-hoc "Committee of Safety," few remembered the immense and peaceful meeting called by the socialists. The end of July went down in public memory—quite accurately—as the moment when the largest anti-coolie-labor movement in United States history got its start.[2]

The mixture of working-class activism and white supremacy characterizing the history of California in the 1870s and 1880s has been a source of fascination for U.S. labor historians.[3] It interests historians perhaps because, with the small number of Chinese immigrants in the population, it is not obvious what the mob was fighting about. When President Arthur signed the Chinese Exclusion Act on May 6, 1882, the Chinese population in the United States totaled one hundred and three thousand. Chinese immigrants were only around 1.6 percent of the six million foreign-born individuals recorded in the 1880 U.S. census. Compared to the total of the U.S. population, which in that year amounted to 59 million people, they were 0.17 percent of the total. Surely Californians had a different perception of the problem: The western state hosted around seventy percent of the entire Chinese immigrant population of the country (75,218 people), making its population ten percent Chinese.[4] What is more, Chinese immigrants, who were overwhelmingly male and in a working age, were overrepresented in the ranks of the California working class. Yet the localized nature of the issue hardly justified the level of attention that Chinese immigration received across the country in the 1870s and in the 1880s. Nor did it explain the necessity to discuss and sign an ad-hoc bill to shut the western border—"the first federal law ever passed banning a group of immigrants solely on the basis of race or nationality."[5]

When it organized the July 1877 rally, the WPUS was less than one year old and could only count two small sections in San Francisco and a handful of members in California. Within two months of the rally, the party was replaced in the news by the sudden and unexpected growth of the Workingmen's Party of California (WPC), which would dominate the Californian political scene until the early 1880s. Historians tend to conflate the opinions of the socialists of the SLP with those of the members of the WPC, but in the 1876–1890 period, the two parties marched in parallel yet had differing opinions on Chinese immigration.[6] Exploring the SLP's position on Chinese immigration opens a window on the ways in which the "Chinese question" influenced the discussion on race in the American Left. Alexander Saxton captured the contradictions among Gilded Age socialists, writing that members of the SLP "circled uneasily at the fringes, torn, as radicals have been so often, between the conflicting desires to be ideologically correct and to be 'where the masses are.'"[7] Looking at the contradictions faced by socialists helps us to understand the ways in which a movement constitutively bound to working-class internationalism reacted to a strongly exclusivist political project like the one supported by the WPC.

The SLP's position on Chinese immigration mirrored the internal contrast between internationalist trade unionists and scientific racialists. Initially, the former decided the official position of the party, and in 1877, a resolution based on the distinction between *importation* of labor and *immigration* was passed. Aligning themselves with a section of the Republican and progressive political class, internationalists maintained that free Chinese immigrants were welcomed to come and stay in the United States, while the importation of indentured or "coolie" workers ought to be immediately stopped.[8] But this plank was dropped at the 1879 convention and was not replaced by any new official position. Evidence suggests that at this point, the majority of the SLP rank and file was against Chinese immigration. Many socialists (in both the English- and the German-language press) used pseudoscientific arguments to conflate the image of the Chinese immigrant with that of the coolie and indentured worker and concluded that China as a whole was an "enslaved" country whose inhabitants ought to be kept away from the free United States.[9] By 1882, a small group of socialists was still campaigning for the free immigration of Chinese, but the rest of the SLP was committed to an anti-Chinese immigration position. In the aftermath of the Exclusion Act, the anti-Chinese position became more entrenched and consistently held within the SLP. By the end of the 1880s, not a single article in the socialist press defended the rights of those Chinese immigrants who remained in the United States.

The socialist shift from a moderate pro-Chinese position to exclusivist white supremacism was the result of many interlocking dynamics. To an extent, socialists went with the flow: As the national debate on Chinese immigration evolved in the late 1870s and early 1880s, it became evident that the overwhelming majority of the white working class, especially in California, supported exclusion. SLP leaders were uncomfortable with the open racism of the WPC. But they admired its political success, describing it as a triumph of labor over capital. These were the years when the SLP was stepping up its involvement in party politics. Scientific racialism provided the ideal framework to pursue electoral success among a white supremacist electorate. But the more this happened, the more the position of internationalists in the party became untenable. In this regard, the causal chain worked both ways: The SLP's flirtation with the WPC pushed more internationalists outside of the party. Concurrently, as more internationalists abandoned the party, the party moved more speedily toward Chinese exclusion.

The weakness of the internationalists' position on Chinese immigration had origins that socialist debates on the subject help clarify. Internationalists articulated their open-border position on the distinction between "importation" and "immigration" of Chinese workers, but was this distinction sound? Were Chinese immigrants really "coolie workers"? The process that brought thousands of Chinese to the United States had unique features. It involved a specific sort of transpacific human traffic organized by Chinese-led mediators (the Six Companies). Often, Chinese workers willingly entered abusive forms of employment, accepted for their temporary and remunerative nature. Yet white commentators in the socialist press systematically failed to fully comprehend the features of these interactions. Socialist commentary on Chinese immigration conflated different levels of analysis, showing lack of empathy and understanding toward the difficult circumstances of Chinese workers. Socialists were prone to generalizations and assumptions, which explained the Chinese through racialized and Orientalist stereotyping rather than circumstantiated and evidence-based analysis of the reality that brought Chinese workers to the United States. The socialist conversation on the "Chinese question" shows how pervasive Orientalist stereotypes were and how they were influential in shaping left-wing politics.[10] It encapsulates the slippery slope into which internationalism occurred. The most progressive wing of the SLP genuinely sought to defend an open border—an extraordinary move in a context in which the condemnation of Chinese immigrants was almost total. But by arguing that "importation" existed, and by turning a blind eye on the specific conditions of Chinese workers, it facilitated the process that turned exclusivism into the most common position in the American Left.

"Without Regard to Nationality": The Socialist Labor Party and the Search for a Pro-Chinese Immigration Position

In September 1878, the abolitionist Wendell Phillips sent a letter to the citizens of San Francisco. The topic was "Kearneyism," a reference to the philosophy of Denis Kearney, the most important leader of the Workingmen's Party of California and inventor of the organization's slogan, "The Chinese must go!"[11] In the letter, Phillips revived his long-term commitment to the rights of Chinese immigrants. At the apex of his influence as leader of the Radical Republicans, in 1870, Phillips had successfully led a campaign for the rights of Chinese immigrants to freely migrate to the United States.[12] Almost a decade later, this message was revived against the white supremacist sentiments unleashed by the victory of the WPC. "Indeed," he argued, "I detest the shallow, heartless, and narrow views taken there [on the Pacific coast] on the subject [Chinese immigration]." The Chinese, like "all the millions from any race that will or can come here," were "sorely needed to fill up the vast wastes in our possessions between Omaha and the Pacific . . . The Chinese are a painstaking, industrious, and marvelously capable people. Statesmanship and political economy, as well as Christianity, bid us welcome such help in subduing the continent—not violently to trust them out." The letter concluded with a direct attack on Irish immigrants, like Kearney himself, who had arrived in America no more than thirty or forty years ago, and now wanted to close the door to Chinese: "Shame on the Irishman who, after his country's four centuries of protest and rebellion, borrows from England the self-same infamous and hateful weapons, to use them against Chinese!"[13]

Kearney's political career had started on the doorstep of the socialist WPUS. In the immediate aftermath of the July 1877 protest organized by the socialists, Kearney started seeking a political group where he could carry forward his anti-Chinese crusade. Kearney knocked at the doors of the WPUS to become a member of the organization. As recalled later by labor leader Frank Roney, the party did not trust Kearney's labor credentials and sent him away. When his application was rejected, Kearney swore that "he would form a party and beat those fellows."[14] His revenge started immediately in the choice of name for his new organization—Workingmen's Party of California—which recalled almost word by word that of the party who had dared to reject him.[15]

Socialists had good reason to doubt Kearney's labor credentials. He did not have the pedigree of a labor leader. In fact, Kearney was hardly a workingman at all. Saxton describes him as "a producer in the Jacksonian sense," with a burning ambition and a fascination for "the familiar syndrome of the self-made men."[16] After the foundation of the WPC, Kearney became its most prominent leader by acclamation of the crowd. He outmaneuvered his political enemies, sensing in the anti-Chinese crusade the opportunity to advance in stature and rise to national fame.

Kearney had found himself in the right place at the right moment. For a short period after the start of the gold rush in 1848, California's authorities and the American ruling class as a whole welcomed immigrants from China. American entrepreneurs saw the growth of trade and exchanges with China as a way to establish the country as a "Pacific nation."[17] The U.S.'s plan for geopolitical hegemony in the Pacific, however, soon had to deal with a sudden change in the public perception of Chinese immigration. When the gold rush boom of 1848–1849 came to an end, California passed a Chinese-targeted "foreign miners' license tax" that imposed a payment of three dollars on every foreign miner who did not wish to become a citizen. As well, other governmental bodies imposed special fees on boats carrying Chinese immigrants and promulgated discriminatory statutes, such as one requiring each Chinese person to provide proof of his or her "good character." Workers' anti-Chinese sentiments were institutionalized in the 1860s, when white western laborers founded "anti-coolie" clubs to defend their interests. Originating in the 1860s, a decade of relative economic expansion, the clubs grew in numbers amid the worsening economic crisis of 1873–1877.[18] By the end of the 1870s, California formed the perfect environment for a demagogue like Kearney to thrive.

The birth of the WPC put American socialists in a difficult position. Inevitably, socialists and the WPC found themselves tapping into the same pool of potential voters. But while the WPC had a clear position on Chinese immigration, socialists had to decide which side they would take. Was Chinese exclusion a worthwhile price to pay for the triumph of a labor-led party? At the 1877 New Haven congress, socialists took what seemed a clear position on this issue. The assembly passed a simple but straightforward resolution to the effect that "the importation of Coolies under contract must be immediately prohibited, and the Coolies already in America released from similar obligations."[19] In a few words, this resolution marked a neat distinction between the WPC and the Socialist Labor Party (as the party renamed itself at the New Haven convention). While Kearney's organization openly endorsed the expulsion of all Chinese immigrants in the United States, the SLP's plank operated a conceptual separation between contracted workers, who presumably were forced to migrate to the United States and were employed in unfavorable and exploitative working conditions, and free Chinese workers. The resolution asked for an end to the exploitation of Chinese immigrants and, at least implicitly, favored the idea that free Chinese workers be given the opportunity to remain in the United States and to work alongside laborers of other nationalities.

Even though the SLP convention's proceedings are silent on the debate leading to the approval of the resolution, a broader look at the socialist party press gives a clear picture of which groups in the party were behind the resolution. Labor internationalists writing in the *Labor Standard* had, since 1876, focused on distinguishing between importation and immigration. This distinction, clearly acknowledged in the resolution, was an attempt to disentangle class solidarity from considerations based on race and "nationality." In June 1876, the *Labor Standard* wrote that socialists "do not object to the Chinaman as a Chinaman, but we object to him as a coolie, the same as we would object to a French, English, or German, if he comes to this country under the same economic conditions. We object to the system, and not to the man; as we objected to slavery, and not to the negro."[20] Making a difference between importation and immigration, and emphasizing the ways in which Chinese workers were hired, made race and culture insignificant in the evaluation of workers' relations. The *Labor Standard* article further elaborated that "we [socialists] do not object to the Chinese on account of their being 'heathen' and calling their god by a different name than ourselves, for we hold that while any man strictly follows the dictates of his own conscience, he is entitled to the respect of all good men."[21] In this way, the socialists mentioned cultural and religious differences as a way to stress their own respect for diversity and to distance themselves from those who attacked Chinese immigrants because of their race and culture.

Internationalists frontally attacked the WPC's anti-Chinese slogan in an article published in the *Labor Standard* in 1878 and reissued in the *Socialist* in 1879: "The cry that the 'Chinese must go' is both narrow and unjust. It represents no broad *or* universal principle. . . . We have certainly a right to protest, and use every available means against the capitalistic combinations through which thousands of poor and ill-fed beings are imported to this country from China, Italy, and elsewhere, but we have no right to raise a cry against any class of human beings because of their nationality."[22]

Socialists used the nineteenth-century terminology of "nationality," but what they meant to stress was that ethnic or racial identity should *not* be used to decide whether someone was entitled to certain basic rights, including the right to travel to the United States in search of better working conditions.[23]

The content of the resolution approved by the SLP in late 1877 firmly placed the party amongst the supporters of the Chinese immigrants' right to migrate and settle in the United States. SLP leader and co-editor of the three official newspapers of the organization Adolph Douai made it clear that an open border to free Chinese workers was the official position of the party during a congressional commission set up in 1878 to investigate the causes of the economic depression in the country. Abram Hewitt, Democratic member of the House of Representatives from New York, chaired the hearing in which Douai was called to testify. Asked by a congressman if he favored restricting Chinese immigration, Douai answered that "we would not restrict anyone . . . We demand that Chinese emigration under contract ought to be stopped immediately." "Not otherwise?" urged the congressman. "Not otherwise," replied Douai.[24]

With their anti-coolie work and pro-immigration position, the SLP put itself in a position that was at odds with the WPC. At the same time, the position defended by the socialists sheds light on some limits and shortcomings of their alleged racial egalitarianism. Socialists articulated their position from within the conceptual arsenal of working-class internationalism, and they offered a labor-based point of view whose goal was keeping the border open to Chinese immigrants. Yet internationalists were not immune from the public conversation on Chinese immigration that was actively distorted by racial prejudice and stereotypes. The distinction between importation and immigration—upon which the socialist point of view rested—took for granted some circumstances, namely, that indentured work was widespread among Chinese immigrants and that a clear distinction between "imported" and "free" Chinese workers was easy to track. But was that really the case? The answer to this requires investigating how the debate within the SLP evolved and how working conditions for Chinese laborers as well as Orientalist stereotyping shaped it.

Socialism and "Anti-Coolieism"

With its short and generic formulation, the SLP resolution on Chinese immigration was designed as a compromise to accommodate conflicting interests and points of view in the SLP. By distinguishing between importation and immigration, the resolution safeguarded the key values of free movement and internationalism favored by militants who supported trade unionism. At the same time, its attack on "coolies under contract" gave some ammunition to socialists interested in electoral politics. Acknowledging the allegedly illegal ways through which Chinese workers arrived in the United States, the resolution allowed the socialists to tap into the anti-Chinese sentiment that was becoming popular in white working-class circles.

Despite the general assembly's attempt to solve internal tensions in the party, the anti-coolie resolution failed to quell the debate on the issue. The German-language San Francisco section of the SLP did not take part in the convention. But two months later, it sent an official letter of protest to the party leadership. German American San Franciscans did not mince their words. "A resolution like this could only make us ridiculous here and harm the interests of our party on the Pacific Ocean."[25] To succeed, a radical change of direction was needed. The San Francisco section suggested to replace the second part of the resolution, which currently stated, "And the Coolies already in America released from similar obligations," with the phrase, "and the Coolies already in America returned to their home."[26]

Even though the California socialists came from the same cultural milieu as their comrades in the East, it is evident that specific labor circumstances of the West Coast had had a significant impact on them. The number of words being replaced in the resolution were few, but the conceptual gulf between the two proposals could not have been wider. While the original proposal safeguarded the rights of free Chinese immigrants to settle in the United States, the revised proposal promoted deportation as the only viable solution. German American San Franciscans expanded on their motivations to defend such a position. They said that the pro-Chinese settlement resolution failed to acknowledge that Chinese workers "[were] not" and "[did] not want to be" free workers. "They do not accept our language, customs, and manners, they do not want to assimilate to the Caucasian race in any way."[27] With their stubborn insistence on accepting incredibly poor working conditions, the article contended, Chinese immigrants threatened to lower working standards across the board. Self-preservation obliged white workers to defend themselves, the socialists concluded, and the only possibility was that Chinese immigrants be returned to their homes across the ocean.

The crucial conceptual point that differentiated the two positions was a consideration of the "nature" of the Chinese immigrants themselves. Embedded in the distinction between importation and immigration defended by internationalists was the premise that the enslavement of the Chinese workforce was a temporary and practical circumstance; once Chinese workers had been "freed" from their status of enslavement, they would join the ranks of the working class and would be entitled to the same level of solidarity as any other workers. But for the San Francisco socialists, the "servile" condition of the Chinese workforces was something that did not depend on the mode of employment. It was innate and impossible to eradicate. It did not matter who employed them and how they were employed. Chinese workers were "naturally enslaved."

How such divergent positions could coexist in the party (and indeed in the country) can be understood by exploring the racial undertones of the socialist analyses of "coolieism." In 1879, a socialist activist writing under the pseudonym Rusticus responded to the letter that Wendell Phillips had sent to the population of San Francisco.[28] Rusticus wanted the readers to know the specific conditions of exploitation experienced by Chinese workers, and he centered his denunciation on a crucial theme: the abuse of the Six Companies against Chinese workers. The Six Companies were mutual-support associations that ran San Francisco's Chinatown. They replicated a model widespread in China: the *huiguan* or guilds organized on a regional, class, and clan basis. In China, if a person moved from a specific province to another area of the empire, they could rely for support on the local *huiguan* from their province that had been established in the new location. In the United States, these *huiguan* reproduced similar patterns of regional and class solidarity, functioning as the first point of contact for newly arrived immigrants.[29]

For Rusticus, the Six Companies were not welcoming societies for mutual assistance but rather a sophisticated system of transpacific labor exploitation. The Six Companies, Rusticus wrote, "own all the ships, and all the

Chinese stores on the Pacific Coast and many thousand slaves, whom they hire out in this free country." By charging large sums of money for a trip to the United States, where workers would come attracted by the possibility of future earnings, they tied free Chinese workers to exploitative relationships, forcing them into years-long debt peonage. Chinese immigrants were hired out and kept in an enslaved and degraded condition by having their wages distributed by Chinese "bosses," who could speak some English. Preventing Chinese immigrants from learning English was a way to keep them under the Six Companies' control.[30]

Indeed, Rusticus had captured the exploitative nature of the monopolistic hold exercised by this group of associations. The Six Companies had control of the Chinese workforce and did not hesitate to use it in an abusive way. The Six Companies gradually extended the profitability of labor importation by moving from simply organizing the journey to providing Chinese workers with lodging, jobs, and basic necessities in exchange for a percentage of the wages received. Historians Peter Kwong and Dušanka Miščević explain that membership in the *huiguan* was not voluntary. The Six Companies had a strict system according to which no Chinese immigrant was able to return to China without a certificate issued by their association which attested that all debts and dues had been paid. The *huiguan* did not hesitate to use violence against those who did not comply with their rules.[31]

What Rusticus failed to appreciate, however, perhaps because he *could not* appreciate it, was that the Six Companies' influence in America's Chinatowns was the result of the specific historical circumstances in which the Chinese presence in the United States had unfolded. Historically, the Chinese Empire had not allowed its inhabitants to migrate to other countries for work. Having its workforce move abroad to enrich other countries was perceived as unjustifiable economic damage and a source of embarrassment. But the Opium War, together with the repeated and insistent threats to Chinese territorial integrity from European powers and Japan, forced the Beijing Court to abandon this approach. In the mid-nineteenth century, the empire was no longer able to control its borders and prevent the migration of its workforce abroad.[32]

Entrepreneurs located in the ports of southern China sensed a business opportunity and began organizing Chinese migration to the United States. Shipping companies run by American, European, and Chinese businessmen launched transpacific trips to the United States. Over time, they expanded their ties in the United States and forged solid alliances with local *huiguan* until they controlled every aspect of life for Chinese immigrants on the West Coast, from running funeral services to providing electricity in Chinatown.[33] The Six Companies filled the void left by the weak Chinese authorities and even started behaving as a semi-official Chinese embassy, petitioning the White House for the protection of Chinese economic and social interests.[34] Only in the late 1870s did the Qing Empire try to reign in the situation by sending a "spokesperson" from the Beijing Court to Washington, DC. As historian Shih-Shan Henry Tsai has stressed, this change of approach came about because Chinese authorities understood that the revenues sent home by Chinese immigrant workers could help alleviate the financial crisis in the Empire. But the Beijing Court always maintained that the Chinese presence in the United States was to be temporary and exceptional—an approach sanctioned in the 1868 Burlingame Treaty, which forbade the naturalization of Chinese immigrants.[35]

To some extent, socialists like Rusticus captured the ambivalent circumstances in which Chinese immigrants found themselves. In his article series, Rusticus described the mechanisms used by the Companies to keep Chinese workers under their control. If a free Chinese immigrant was "no longer satisfied to work for wages; if he accepts something of the American spirit of enterprise and starts out in business for himself, and if his business should come into competition with an establishment of the Six Companies then he is ostracized from the Chinese population altogether."[36] Moreover, socialists writing in the press correctly identified the presence of a class tension within the Chinese American community, with a handful of businessmen united in the Six Companies maintaining control over the large majority of the Chinese workers. Rusticus demonstrated that he had an expert eye when it came to recognizing class differences within America's Chinatowns. He wrote that white workers on the West Coast could easily spot the difference between "the slave" and "the master who imports him . . . already by sight—by the cut and make-up of their clothes."[37]

Yet Rusticus seemed to have scarce appreciation for the implications of the class tensions in the Chinese American community and for the motivations that led Chinese workers to migrate. The nature of Chinese immigration to the United States was temporary and earning-focused. Chinese workers came to the United States for short periods of time to cumulate money and return to their homeland as quickly as their material conditions allowed. During their time in the United States, Chinese workers were knocked about by converging situations of conflict: under pressure at home as a result of their "unpatriotic" decision to leave the country for money, controlled by organizations in the United States that sought to gain a large profit from their labor, attacked by white workers who resented their competition.

A consistent adoption of an historical materialist framework of analysis would have put Rusticus and the SLP in the position of seeking a cross-racial alliance with this exploited Chinese workforce. Their migration was motivated by nothing more than the same global dynamics of exploitation of working peoples that hit American workers in the United States. Instead, introjected racial prejudice led the socialists to identify the Chinese presence in the United States as the ultimate cause of their problems. Rusticus used the alleged Chinese lack of patriotism and unwillingness to integrate as a motivation to call for the closure of the western borders. "Have you ever heard of a Chinaman helping to fight the war of Rebellion [the Civil War], although Chinamen immigrated here twelve years before?" And further: "Can you tell me how many Chinese American citizens—children born of Chinese parents and brought up in our country and in our schools—are registered in proportion to the number of Chinese immigrants from 1849 to 1879?" It did not matter that Chinese people *did* fight the Civil War—if only within very small numbers that reflected their minuscule presence in the country in the 1860s. Nor that Chinese workers were *legally prevented* from laying roots in the country as a result of the Burlingame Treaty.[38]

Rusticus's solution consistently followed up from his prejudiced idea that the Chinese presence in the United States was an irredeemable problem. While frontally attacking the Six Companies and suggesting that the people of California enter a legal suit against them, Rusticus applauded Kearney's Workingmen's Party of California for its role in reducing the number of Chinese immigrants. It was "to the credit of [Kearney's] movement that the immigration of the Chinese has decreased so much during the last two years," he wrote in the *Socialist*.[39] Rusticus did not entertain the idea that the socialists could cooperate with Chinese workers to fight the oppression of the Six Companies nor did he think class solidarity could cut across racial lines. Ultimately, the political solution that he offered to Chinese immigration was in line with the position expressed by the German American section of the SLP in San Francisco: Forced deportation was the only viable alternative to solve the "Chinese question" once and for all.[40] Rusticus did not make explicit the premise that subtly but clearly underpinned his argument: A belief that Chinese immigrants, whether they were enslaved by the Six Companies or not, were a servile workforce that was unwelcome in a free America.

Rusticus's position is exemplar of how considerations of class and race intertwined to structure socialist support for the closure of the western borders. Comparing the position of internationalist socialists with the stance of anti-immigration supporters like Rusticus and the German American San Francisco SLP section outlines the differences within American socialism on Chinese immigration. On the one hand, the resolution that the SLP congress approved in 1877 rested on a simplistic concept of importation.

Quite naively, it seemed to suggest that it was possible to draw neat lines between "imported" and "free" Chinese workers. It further seemed to imply that Chinese immigrants had full control of their status—namely, that they were free to interrupt their relationship with the Six Companies at their will. Both assumptions showed the inability of the socialists to fully understand the specific conditions of exploitation in which Chinese immigrants found themselves—a circumstance that made it impossible for the socialists to articulate a full-fledged and functional approach toward Chinese immigration.

On the other hand, in no respect should this position be equated with those of anti-Chinese socialists. Rusticus and the German American San Francisco SLP socialists either implicitly or explicitly premised their opposition to Chinese immigration on a conceptually racist assumption about the "nature" of Chinese immigrants and on the flawed idea about their capacity for integration in the American society. Even with its limits, the internationalist point of view was successful in avoiding the dead end of white supremacy and exclusivist nationalism.

Chinese Immigration and the Conceptualization of White Labor Internationalism

Between 1877 and 1882, the SLP quietly but surely moved away from internationalism and toward a full-fledged defense of anti-Chinese exclusion. To understand this, we must investigate the impact that scientific racialism had on the American socialist movement. Many supporters of Chinese exclusion, both within and outside the socialist movement, sought to deflect accusations of racism by cloaking their arguments in class-based arguments. But a sizeable group of American socialists did not feel any need to conceal their ideas. Rather, they openly embraced pseudoscientific racialist theories and sought ways to make them compatible with the tenets of historical materialism. The result was a proudly defended version of white supremacist working-class internationalism, one in which the stadial evolution toward socialism intersected with the allegedly immutable laws of racial science.

To a certain degree, socialist racialists built on the set of exotic and Orientalist stereotypes that were widespread in the American society of the time. As documented by Stuart Creighton Miller, Americans relied on the imagery brought by early nineteenth century missionaries, traders, and diplomats that presented the view of Chinese people as naturally slavish, immoral, and uncivilized.[41] Concurrently, post-Emancipation attempts by former-Confederate plantation owners to replace freed Black workers with Chinese workforce in the South and the extended use of Chinese labor in low-paid mass projects like the Central Pacific Railroad contributed to strengthening and perpetrating the image of the Chinese worker as a "coolie."[42] It did not matter that Congress had formally banned the coolie trade in 1862 and that the immigration of Chinese workers, despite having the exploitative features described above, was in no way the same as the forms of indentured work occurring for decades in the Pacific, South America, and the Caribbean during this period.[43] For the vast majority of white workers, the process of identification of Chinese immigrants with the category of "coolie worker" was an exercise in racial imagination rather than a careful consideration of the real working and living conditions of Chinese Americans themselves.[44]

In the hands of the socialists, the generic set of anti-coolie stereotypes widespread among white workers was defined in a specific historical materialist sense. Socialists took the coolie imagery, refined it using racial theory, and tied it to their own critiques of American capitalism. In line with postbellum American labor movements, socialists articulated their attacks in the language of slavery and emancipation. The popular German American socialist daily *New Yorker Volkszeitung* openly labeled Chinese immigration "gelbe Sklaverei" (yellow slavery) and compared it to antebellum chattel slavery.[45] From the point of view of the capitalist, socialists contended in the *Volkszeitung*, Chinese immigration was more advantageous and efficient than antebellum slavery. Chinese workers "do not even cost capital to buy, like the negro slaves." The Six Companies ("the yellow slave traders") delivered them "free of charge to the hireling at the door." Chinese workers "cannot become citizens and dispute landowners' political rule in the country."[46] What is more, capitalists could rely on the fact that Chinese immigrants were exemplary workers. Evidently unaware of the multiple examples where Chinese people had resisted employers' exploitation, the *Volkszeitung* stated that Chinese workers "obey and are willing to learn."[47]

Socialists writing in the *Volkszeitung* constructed their concepts of "capitalism" and "communism" through the racialized understanding of Chinese immigration. China was a country where "capitalism is so ancient that whites could go at school there and learn about it." The alleged capitalist nature of the Chinese society and economy in this model had nothing to do with the degree of industrial development of the country. Instead, what made China a capitalist country was the ability of its elites to enslave Chinese workers. "This yellow race has been bred for tens of thousands of years by the forces of nature and their history to live, flourish, and play the obedient slave, or the devastating robber, in every climate and soil." In the telling of this socialist newspaper, the specific breeding received by Chinese workers had a crucial impact on their interpersonal and human features; the prolonged period of "enslavement" had turned them into a subhuman entity with no independent will. In another article, the *Volkszeitung* intoned that "slavery in China is a four-thousand-year-old institution, which lives on as a dogma in the slaves themselves and is voluntarily observed by them with a religious sense." Chinese workers "bring Chinese slavery with them," continued the article, and "establish here a life according to Chinese laws, and continue to pay obedience to the Chinese emperor."[48] Servitude and obedience were part of Chinese history and were inscribed as an essential part of Chinese workers' background, a feature existing in itself and not dependent on their mode of employment. The article claimed that Chinese workers were coolie workers and, as such, were naturally slaves. Ultimately, then, the *Volkszeitung* concluded, the "Chinese question" became "the question of whether the capitalist or communist culture should prevail," with capitalism meaning labor exploitation and communism standing as a symbol of free, humane, and emancipatory culture, a feature of the much younger and "advanced" white culture.[49]

In some cases, socialists realized the contradictions between socialism and contemporary racialism and tried to establish some sort of consistent correlation between the two theories. A case in point is Leo, an unidentified socialist militant from St. Louis. Leo contended that Chinese workers should be given the chance to enter the United States, but only if they undertook "cheap labor" and "especially if, as is the case with the Chinese today, they do not seek to stay and mingle with us." Questioned on his racism by another militant, Leo replied: "I believe in race, and in this point I am supported by many of the most prominent Socialists and enlightened thinkers of the day. To mingle the blood of four hundred millions of Chinese . . . with that of forty millions of whites and four millions of Africans, would deteriorate the whole mass, and yield a human product as bad, or worse, than the mongrel mixture of red, white and black races of Mexico and South America."[50]

Leo was correct to suggest that many "prominent socialists" believed in some sort of evolutionism and scientific racialism—even though hardly anyone would have embraced miscegenation theories with the same eagerness as him.[51] But eventually, he also felt troubled by the anti-egalitarianism embedded in the racial theories he defended. Leo specified that he did not, "in this letter, wish to inculcate that the Chinese, because they are heathens, are also barbarians. I merely assert that their civilization is different from ours, and that at present we cannot assimilate."[52] The imperatives of modern racialism became the means through which Leo explained socialists' inability to deal with the problems of Chinese workers. "I think a great deal of the question of justice to the poor Chinaman," wrote Leo, "but at present I am too deeply interested in dragging from starvation and degradation our own dear wives and children, and saving them from the death-grip of our accursed monopolies . . . to pay too much attention to the inhumanely persecuted Mongolian just now."[53] In Leo's mind, racial solidarity overtook class solidarity as the organizing principle that should guide the political choices of the American socialist movement. Leo's choice did not come as an afterthought, but was a thoroughly argued decision based on a combination of socialist and scientific racialist arguments.

But what if Chinese workers could bridge the racial difference that divided them from white workers? Articles published in the *Volkszeitung* discussed precisely this possibility, showing yet another nuance of the process through which socialists normalized white supremacism via an adhesion to alleged scientific racialist theories. In the logic embraced by socialist scientific racialists, the point was to "force" Chinese workers to move beyond the enslaved nature inculcated in them by their Chinese education. The *Volkszeitung* proposed one simple solution for achieving this: grant Chinese immigrants American citizenship. "It is clear that those Chinese who sign up for civil rights cannot be coolies any longer, but must have finished their service to the Six Companies, or having immigrated freely, because by becoming citizens here they expose themselves and their families to the heaviest penalties in China."[54]

The antithetical thinking adopted by this socialist commentator—a measure sought by Chinese immigrants but denied them by American legislation—was seen as the way to solve the basic problem between white and Chinese workers in the United States. The socialist proposal revealed how racialist principles organized socialist thinking. Given that "Chinese-ness" was equated with "servitude," if there were a way for Chinese workers to divest themselves of this feature, then clearly, this path should be taken. By becoming citizens, suggested another *Volkszeitung* article in early 1882, Chinese workers would become "less dangerous than if we wanted to make a despised and degraded caste out of them." The article claimed that they would also lose those cultural and racial features that made them incompatible with white workers. "You then learn to speak the language and you know how to be with them. They gradually adopt our ways and ways of life and lose what is disgusting for us."[55] For the *Volkszeitung*, forced assimilation was fully compatible—in fact, it was necessary—for the full respect of the civil rights of Chinese immigrants. "We workers must not forget that here civil rights and human rights are guaranteed," explained the article, "and that we must not deny this, if we do not want to cut the ground away and delegitimize all our aspirations towards true democracy, towards the destruction of classes and towards justice."[56] As the article spelled out, for Chinese workers "citizenship [was] a true liberation from slavery," thus Americans should not prevent it but rather should favor it. But only by embracing the stereotype that China was irremediably tied and corrupted by slavery could this argument function.

In the crucial years between the approval of the SLP resolution on coolie work in 1877 and the passage of the Chinese Exclusion Act in 1882, the socialist press offered a disparate range of positions on Chinese immigration. The party debate developed along unique lines, involving a significant degree of attention to the peculiar living and working conditions of the Chinese workforce in the United States. Socialists showed familiarity with the working and living conditions of Chinese immigrants, but this knowledge was rarely used to cultivate class solidarity between white and Chinese workers. Instead, scientific racialism organized socialist approaches toward the Chinese. At times, the alleged imperatives of racial laws gave socialists the justification to neglect the issue of Chinese exploitation. In other occasions, following scientific racialism led to counterintuitive proposals, such as the request to offer them naturalization. Yet for a clear majority of socialists, race remained a more important lens than class in approaching the issue of Chinese immigration to the United States.

The SLP and the Workingmen's Party of California

From the point of view of a white worker interested in the labor cause, deciding between the WPC and the WPUS was a matter involving personal political convictions but also strategic considerations about potential political success. The example of Frank Roney is a case in point. A veteran leader of the Irish republican movement, Roney left Ireland to escape imprisonment and arrived in San Francisco in 1875.[57] Roney's first involvement in the organized labor movement coincided with the beginning of the anti-Chinese agitation of 1877. In his autobiography, the Irish leader explained that after the San Francisco City Hall demonstration of July 1877, he pondered which movement to join to contribute to the cause of organized labor in California. "I had previously read the platform of the Workingmen's Party of the United States," wrote Roney, "and, feeling that it advocated the adoption of measures that were essential to the comfort and happiness of the whole people, I was seriously considering the advisability of applying for membership in that organization."[58]

After the San Francisco public authorities attempted to stop anti-Chinese and labor protests by arresting dozens of workers gathered on the sand-covered space in front of City Hall, including many leaders of the

Workingmen's Party of California, Roney decided to join the WPC instead.[59] Roney's anger had been provoked by "the actions of the city authorities in attempting to suppress free speech and free assembly," but it is plausible to assume that an unspoken element in Roney's joining the WPC was probably the greater potential of that organization to achieve political success.[60] Indeed, Roney might have had more theoretical affinity for the socialists, but he surely saw that the WPC was creating a network of supporters across the city unmatched by the WPUS. For an ambitious agitator like himself, the Californian labor party was the place to be.

Roney's stance on the "Chinese question" illustrates how political expediency was a factor for many white activists on the West Coast. In his autobiography, Roney voiced his concerns for the anti-Chinese sentiments he had seen in San Francisco. He considered such sentiments "unreasonable and antagonistic to the principles of American liberty." Restrictions on Chinese immigration were "brutal and such as no self-respecting civilized people would dream of imposing upon the members of any race within their midst."[61] If Roney could write these words in his autobiography, how could he join a party whose war cry was "the Chinese must go"? Roney recognized this contradiction and offered a justification that revealed his sacrificing principle on the altar of practical circumstances: "I never warmed for that feature of the agitation [anti-Chinese activism]. I realized that the cry was superficial, but agreed to sail under the flag so emblazoned in order that I might have other and real subjects considered by the people, which I deemed to be of far greater importance to their permanent well-being."[62]

Roney's path was followed by many. Some members of the German American San Francisco section of the WPUS—the same group that sent the letter complaining about the 1877 resolution—had taken part in a meeting to write the platform of the WPC in December 1877. Subsequent reports from the West Coast socialists show that the ties between the SLP German-language section and the WPC had become so close that the SLP National Executive Committee decided to disband the section altogether. In May 1878, Charles Beerstecher, another former member of the SLP who joined the WPC for personal gain, successfully submitted a resolution to the assembly of the WPC that recognized "the Socialistic Labor Party of the United States as a kindred organization, having for its purpose and end the emancipation of the workingmen."[63] Many California socialists were stunned by the political success of the WPC, and they struggled to stay away from its alluring orbit. The WPC, for its part, had so little to fear of the socialists that they eagerly listed them as their allies.

Saxton describes the WPC's political trajectory as a frustrating list of missed opportunities. In the hands of leaders like Kearney and Isaac Kalloch, flamboyant orators with no real interest in working-class issues, the WPC squandered its political chance to introduce legislation that would provide concrete benefits to the working people, like the eight-hour working day or increased wages and protections.[64] Details about this internal strife filtered through the eastern socialist press, illuminating the relationship between the socialists and the WPC. The *Labor Standard* made its position clear by hosting a letter from an anonymous "trade unionist," who labeled Kearney as a "would be Caesar" and a "presumptuous highbinder."[65] A few weeks later, the socialist paper doubled down by publishing a long chronicle of events by Roney's associate Edward Henckler, a party leader. The article explained why, following the results of the elections of the party nominees to the California Constitutional Assembly, a group had decided to abandon the party. It reconstructed how Kearney had bulldozed and ignored the party leadership, using his popularity with the party base to pack the lists with his supporters and keep the organization under his control.[66] "As a Socialist it is impossible for me to follow Kearney with his 'The Chinese Must Go' any longer," concluded Henckler, "and there are thousands of good, thinking workingmen in the same fix."[67] Frank Roney was one of them. During this time, he had been on the front line in the attempts to counter Kearney. Discredited when his faction lost the elections, Roney left San Francisco to accept a job in a mining camp in Nevada.[68]

The attempt of Roney and his supporters to "sail under the flag" of anti-coolieism to advance labor issues lasted just a few months. Roney never openly challenged Kearney on his anti-immigration stance—yet with his departure, the (already quite minimal) possibility that the WPC would tone down its anti-Chinese message were lost for good. As the anonymous letter to the *Labor Standard* put it, anti-Kearney and pro-labor members "want not an anti-Chinese movement but a labor movement." With the expulsion of Roney, the WPC's anti-Chinese platform became the sole alternative.

Yet this did not stop eastern socialists from looking at California with some hope. Kearney's bullying of his internal opponents had no impact whatsoever on the expected political triumph of the WPC at the State Constitutional Convention. The labor party took thirty seats out of ninety, an incredible performance when compared to those of other labor parties across the country. From the pages of the *Labor Standard*, Adolph Douai saluted this result with enthusiasm. The WPC's victory was "a highly encouraging sign of the times. It is a sign that, all over the world, our ideas are spreading and beginning to bear fruit, and that many other such agreeable surprises are in store for us."[69] Douai was sorry that the platform of the Workingmen's Party did not advocate an eight-hour working day, but he "hoped that such a plank may find its way into the new constitution of the State to be framed and be adopted by the ratifying popular vote."[70]

On the "Chinese question," Douai expressed his disenchantment. Apparently ignoring his own open-border stance, he saw the WPC's victory as positive news that would avert a more violent confrontation between the highly distressed white working class and big business over the closure of the western border. Not one word, however, was spent on the fact that the WPC had a position that was at odds with that of the SLP. Nevertheless, Douai's position seemed to reflect the broader approach that existed in the socialist movement at large. Time and time again, the socialist press discussed California as a land of political conquest and possibility for labor's cause, a pioneering social experiment that prefigured a future of success for the movement across the nation.

Denis Kearney, allegedly the architect of the WPC's success, was perhaps the most frequently discussed subject in the socialist press. Socialists did not know what to make of him, and the opinions varied significantly over time. Writing in the aftermath of the Constitutional Assembly election, August Otto-Walster expressed a moderate skepticism. As a consummate analyst of radical and socialist matters, Otto-Walster was suspicious of the fact that Kearney had become so wildly popular in the span of a couple of months. "How could Kearney gain such a reputation outside of California so quickly?" Otto-Walster pointed to the "bourgeois newspapers," who "treated him ten times better than they ever treated a worker agitator." That this was happening could be a sign, Otto-Walster pointed out, that "Kearney's Platform is so far removed from a socialist platform that even the worst socialist-minded organs have found themselves compelled to portray it as either anti-socialist or at least harmless."[71]

Commentary in the socialist press persisted for months, invigorated by the stunning victory of the WPC candidate, Isaac Kalloch, as San Francisco's mayor in November 1879 and by Kearney's visit to the East, where he tried to forge a coalition with the Greenback Party and the socialists so as to present a joint ticket at the 1880 presidential elections.[72] Proceedings of party conventions in these years attest to the fact that the SLP continued to live in the shadow of the WPC, too weak to impose any of its own political goals. In the report of the SLP's 1879 convention, for example, the San Francisco sections of the party reported that they were "doing their best to educate the rank and file of the W.P.C. in [SLP] principles," although for the moment, they decided not to nominate an SLP ticket, "deeming it unwise and imprudent at present to divide the forces of the labor movement."[73] One year later, the San Francisco section attempted to return to the resolution approved at the 1877 general congress by proposing for consideration the following plank: "The importation or immigration of Chinese or other servile races to be strictly prohibited, and those now here returned as fast as practicable, at the expenses of the U.S. government."[74]

Even though the resolution was not carried by the assembly, the SLP slowly but surely moved in the direction encouraged by the San Francisco socialists. In socialist circles, the conversation was firmly entrenched within the "coolie work" framework. Scientific racialist voices grew in strength, pushed by opinions coming from California and by the reluctance of the party leadership to confront the racism of the WPC. Overall, it is clear that the party was more interested in exploiting a potential alliance with the powerful WPC than it was in engaging it in a principled battle for the defense of Chinese immigrants.

The national debate on Chinese immigration played a role in the gradual movement of the SLP toward anti-Chinese positions. In February 1879, President Rutherford Hayes vetoed the so-called Fifteen Passenger bill, a law approved by Congress limiting American vessels to no more than fifteen Chinese passengers per trip. Hayes's veto was issued on matters of form, not content. It maintained that the new law was in conflict with the terms established by the 1869 Burlingame Treaty and therefore could not be upheld. But President Hayes did not oppose the underlying objective of Congress. He appointed a commission, led by University of Michigan President James Burrill Angell, to travel to China and negotiate a new treaty. Saxton commented that 1879 "marked the turning point of the campaign for federal intervention." The national debate and its outcome had made clear that the supporters of free Chinese immigration had lost the argument. "Principled opposition to Chinese exclusion had ceased to have any political substance. It was now a matter of time, of face saving, of certain peripheral readjustments."[75] Chinese exclusion was on its way. Three years later, Arthur signed into law the Chinese Exclusion Act.[76]

The socialist response to the closure of the western borders attests to how far to the right the party had moved. After the approval of the bill, the powerful Chicago section of the SLP sent a report in which it declared that two of its leaders had attacked as "un-American and un-Socialistic" the anti-Chinese measure. The corresponding secretary of the party, Philip Van Patten, reluctantly published the report in the monthly party paper, the *Bulletin of the Social Reform Movement*, adding in parentheses his response to it: "Abstractly perhaps they are right, but as 'self-preservation is the first law of nature' and there are many Socialists who deny that it is our duty to permit the lowering of our standard of living, or further degradation of our working people, it is at least unwise in our friends to go out of their way to create dissension over this subject."[77] A couple of lines below Van Patten's response, the SLP's San Francisco section celebrated the approval of the Chinese Exclusion Act and the fact that "all political divisions over these questions have ceased and white people are nearly unanimous in demanding that John 'must go.'"[78]

By 1882, pro-Chinese-immigration socialists were now a minority who did not enjoy the support of the SLP leadership. That leadership, meanwhile, was keen to make the most of the consensus achieved in white workers' circles in California. Analysis of the socialist press confirms that the approval of the Chinese Exclusion Act suppressed even the few voices that in 1882 were still arguing against the closure of the American borders to Chinese immigration. Immediately after the bill's approval, the *Volkszeitung* published a short article that borrowed its title from the WPC motto, "The Chinese must go!" The article demanded that Chinese be prevented from entering the United States and also that the "yellow mass" already living in California be sent back to China. Other comments followed along the same line, suggesting that Chinese workers should pay compensation for any damages incurred during the period of free immigration and asking that Chinese people in America be ordered to close their businesses in order not to interfere with businesses run by white people.[79]

The Chinese Exclusion Act did not suffice to stop racist violence against Chinese immigrants and, in actual fact, led to a worsening of the situation. Kwong and Miščević suggested that "it was as though the Senate vote [which passed the bill] had sent a signal to the vigilantes for an 'open season' on the Chinese."[80] Between 1882 and 1890, a sustained series of episodes of racial violence hit Chinese communities across the country. In the words of Chan Kiu Sing, a Los Angeles social commentator and police court interpreter, "They call it exclusion; but it is not exclusion, it is extermination."[81] This heightened anti-Chinese sentiment was reflected in the socialist newspapers as well. In 1885, the *Volkszeitung* published an article from Eureka, California, which chronicled a town meeting to discuss the forced expulsion of all the Chinese from the city. The article denounced the fact that these Chinese would end up in San Francisco.[82] Ten months later, in an article titled "Chinesen gegen Weißen" ("Chinese against whites"), published originally in the *San Francisco Abend Post*, there were complaints about hidden agreements between the Six Companies and capitalists to exclude white workers from factories.[83] In another piece, the socialist newspaper reacted vehemently to an article in the *New York Times* that suggested Chinese repatriation was not viable because whites were no longer capable of doing certain kinds of physical jobs performed by Chinese immigrants. On the contrary, the *San Francisco Abend Post* asserted, whites would happily replace Chinese and, like white Southerners, who they absurdly claimed began working in the fields after the abolition of chattel slavery, would begin to occupy jobs previously held by Chinese immigrants.[84] Arguably the most overtly anti-Chinese piece in the socialist press in this period was published in 1886 in the *Volkszeitung*. It discussed whether the Anti-Chinese League was "un-American" or not. The journalist listed all the typical anti-Chinese tropes, from the fact that they were only interested in exploiting and monopolizing lands, mines, and industries, to the accusation that they were completely unwilling to integrate, made no contribution to American culture, and chose instead to remain isolated in their ghettoes. Lamenting that there were already six million African Americans and many millions of white immigrants in the United States, the article concluded that the aversion toward the Chinese was completely justified.[85]

In 1886, the SLP started a new official newspaper in English, the *Workmen's Advocate*.[86] Its first mention of the "Chinese question" confirms the trend seen in the *Volkszeitung*. With the headline "The Chinese Pest," the article attacked "the so-called moralists, religionists, or mere commercialists" who would like to reintroduce Chinese immigration to the United States. In conclusion, the article summarized and endorsed a pamphlet written by Washington D. Ryan, which argued, "Our present civilization cannot stand against an unrestricted influx of syphilitic, leprous, cunning and vicious barbarians. And as it is to the working people that our civilization must look for maintenance and progress, to them also must we appeal to defend our people from the Chinese scourge, the direct result of private capitalism, the degrading monster which Labor must in self-defense destroy."[87]

If at the end of the 1870s such overtly racialized attacks on Chinese immigrants formed only one part of the socialist press's coverage of the "Chinese question," eight years later, they had become the norm. From the *Workmen's Advocate*'s 1886 article onward, not a word was written in favor of Chinese immigrants. In the *Workmen's Advocate* and in the *Volkszeitung*, Chinese people were accused of a wide variety of crimes, from vice and prostitution in San Francisco's Chinatown to monopolizing the American cigar market using illegal practices, from enslaving women at work to raping and killing children.[88] The 1880s were arguably the worst years for Chinese immigrants. Abandoned by local and federal authorities, they became scapegoats for social and economic tensions and suffered racial and cultural segregation and victimization. While rare voices opposed these trends, the socialists were not among them.

Conclusions

The debate on the "Chinese question" deeply divided the SLP. At first, the leadership of the party reacted by approving a platform founded on a conceptual distinction: Free Chinese immigrants should be allowed to stay in the country; indentured and "coolie" workers should be freed from their bonds and then allowed to remain in the United States. While this position was progressive in embracing free Chinese workers as immigrants to the United States, as well as seeking to undermine the exploitative dynamics linked to much Chinese immigration, it also used and perpetuated the derogatory "coolie" concept in which not only class identities but also ascribed racial identities were intermingled. The concept of the Chinese "coolie" laborer, which took root in socialist thought and among labor leaders and the white working class more widely, was reductive and misleading. While Chinese immigrants were subjected to specific forms of exploitation and oppression, they were *not* indentured workers. Socialists projected an image of Chinese immigrants that was shaped by underlying racial prejudices and led them to prioritize affiliations of race over affiliations of class in their political analysis of the "Chinese question."

Categories of race and class were interwoven in socialist discourse, and the SLP and associated socialist groups and newspapers could never disentangle them. The fact that the SLP did, at one early point, incorporate a pro-Chinese element into its platform suggests that there was, at that time, a chance that the intermingling of race and class might be addressed on a political level. But to have done so would have required a deeper understanding of the experience of racial prejudice toward (in this case) Chinese immigrants. The socialist commentaries in their press barely scratched the surface on that score. Furthermore, socialists were driven by political expediency and prioritized support for (and from) white workers over commitment to a race-blind internationalist position. And both federal law and specific workers' political organizations, such as the WPC, turned decisively against Chinese immigration—in deeply prejudicial, racialized terms. The approval of the Chinese Exclusion Act in 1882 pushed socialists toward an anti-Chinese position, a tendency that was definitively espoused in the SLP by the end of the 1880s.

CHAPTER 4

"Regardless of Color"

The SLP and African Americans, 1876–1890

In 1879, the Socialist Labor Party (SLP) adopted an official position on labor organizing across racial lines. Convened in Allegheny, Pennsylvania, for the 2nd General Congress of the party, socialists approved a resolution stating that:

> Whereas, The so-called Democrats (landlords) of the South joined hands with the so-called Republicans (capitalists) of the North; and
> Whereas, This combination of the wealthy men, both North and South, is made for the sole purpose of destroying the liberties of the common people of both sections of our country; therefore, be it
> Resolved, That we urge the working people of the South, regardless of color, to unite with their brothers of the North against the attempts of the ruling class to further impoverish and enslave them by depriving them of the possession and enjoyment of the fruits of their labor.[1]

For the first time in the history of American socialism, a socialist-inspired organization had included in its declaration of principles a plank that clearly referred to the problem of race and committed the party to political action on the issue. The resolution's invitation toward "working people of the South, regardless of color" to cooperate against capitalism clearly positioned the party in favor of organization beyond racial lines and across all sections of the country (even though the reference to the northern "brothers" betrayed the male-centric conception of this plan).

The Workingmen's Party of the United States (WPUS) was founded only four months before the presidential election that led to the end of Reconstruction. While socialists were organizing their sections and starting their political activity, Americans headed to the polls to cast their votes for Rutherford B. Hayes and Samuel J. Tilden. When a bipartisan electoral commission settled the election in favor of Hayes in January 1877, the WPUS had its three official newspapers hitting the streets of American cities. Hayes's victory set in motion the process leading to the creation of the Jim Crow South. But the instauration of this new racial order was far from sudden, uniform, or coherent. The relentless efforts of African American women and men to defend their civil rights and achieve economic independence, supported by the attempts of white allies in the North and in the South, made the triumph of Jim Crow a process that took decades to be completed. In the immediate aftermath of Reconstruction, the South was a land of social and political conflict. A "New South" was in the making, but what it would look like was still too early to tell.[2]

Telling this history from the point of view of Gilded Age organized socialism is no easy feat. The WPUS, with its mostly northern, white, and immigrant membership, had close to no presence or impact in the complicated work of reconstruction of the South. On the role of socialists with regard to the creation of interracial labor alliances and the defense of African Americans, Philip S. Foner is trenchant, writing that the SLP was "oblivious to the increasing attacks on [Black] political rights . . . the deteriorating economic position of the black sharecroppers and craftsmen, and the exclusion of blacks from Northern industry."[3] Expanding the analysis to non-English language sources complicates Foner's assessment, as local German-language papers prove socialists' commitment to racial equality and allow a closer look at the interaction between socialists and African American communities in places like St. Louis, New Orleans, and Cincinnati. As evidenced in the previous chapter, racial prejudice heavily influenced the socialist analysis of Chinese immigration. Even the most progressive wing of the party failed to come to terms with and understand the specific socioeconomic conditions experienced by Chinese immigrants. The same is not true for African Americans. Socialists had a better familiarity, understanding, and comprehension of the situation and problems of Black workers. Yet Foner's overall assessment stands. The "Negro question" was not a priority of socialists in the 1876–1890 period.

But why? Through the prism of Gilded Age organized socialism, this dilemma serves as a stark reminder of the fractured and volatile composition of the Gilded Age radical political landscape, in which the sources of division vastly outnumbered the potential sources of solidarity. The broader picture is one of an organized socialist movement that was firmly enmeshed in large ethnic communities (the German, the Scandinavian, the Jewish) located in the North and the Midwest and whose members seemed to be unaware or unable to understand the features of the "racial pact" that made it impossible for African Americans to escape the harsh realities of the post-Civil War South, move north, and enter the ranks of the northern industrial working class.[4]

But a closer analysis shows further trends. Supporters of labor internationalism were the most proactive in their attempts to reach out at African Americans. They understood the fact that Black laborers—whether they were industrial workers, farmers, or sharecroppers—were a crucial component of the American working class whose inclusion in the socialist movement was a key precondition for political success. Yet, as a result of their scarce knowledge of southern politics, internationalists offered analyses and tactics that barely managed to cut through the intricacies of southern politics and local social and economic dynamics. Conversely, the political wing of the socialist movement, gathered in the SLP, found itself better positioned to seek to create a Black socialist membership. The SLP had a presence in cities like Cincinnati and St. Louis, where a sizable and growing Black population existed. But precisely in these realities the key limitation of socialist policy towards African Americans came to the fore. Socialists kept insisting that African American workers joined their fight for improved working and living conditions through party politics and trade union activism. In doing this, they did not realize that African Americans had problems that confrontational opposition towards employers and local politicians could not solve. In this period, African American protests took various forms, from "traditional" labor uprisings in urban settings to physical and spontaneous acts of resistance against racist violence, such as the "Kansas Exodus," a mass migration of the Black workforce from several areas of the Mississippi valley toward Kansas. The limit of socialists was to expect African Americans to conform to socialist strategy rather than supporting African American dissent in whatever form it came.

These limitations piled onto problems created by the fragmentation of the United States's labor political world. Especially in the South, the SLP was outperformed by political competitors that were more able at responding to the needs of Black Americans. The Greenback Labor Party (GLP), a movement solidly rooted in the South and with some capacity to organize workers across the racial line, for example, had a short period of relevance that coincided with the SLP's most important electoral successes at the end of the 1870s. The SLP and the Greenback Labor Party competed for the same electoral pools, and in the South, the GLP limited the growth of socialists. In an attempt to stretch its presence further south, the SLP tried to join a coalition led by the GLP at the presidential elections of 1880. Mismatching class politics made the coalition unstable and unsuccessful at the polls. The final part of this chapter details the devastating impact that the 1880 failure had on the American socialist movement at large.

"Merely from a Social-Democratic Point of View": The SLP and a Strategy for African Americans

The 1877 New Haven convention ushered in a new epoch for the American socialist movement. Firstly, it ratified the internal division that had already splintered its membership. Of the trade unionist faction, neither Friedrich A. Sorge nor Joseph P. McDonnell took part in the assembly. The delegates convened acknowledged that the *Labor Standard* was no longer under the control of the party, dropped the charges that some members had levied against McDonnell, and embraced political action, while at the same time recognizing the importance of union activism. In a last straw against Sorge, they added the label "socialist" to the name of the party, a move that the old Marxist leader had explicitly forbidden just a year before.[5]

Away from New Haven, Sorge, McDonnell, and the other internationalists established their new trade union federation, the International Labor Union (ILU), in earnest.[6] The *Labor Standard* was the common forum where members listed the features the future organization should have. One such feature was its interracial composition. A correspondent from North Carolina began his message by informing northern comrades that "the condition of our colored fellow workmen in the Southern States is very deplorable."[7] The socialist reported that he had traveled around the state and seen with his own eyes the oppression of freed Blacks, who "[had] been taken from a kind of serfdom to another." Commenting on the perverse effect of the sharecropping system that had replaced slavery in vast areas of the rural South, the correspondent wrote that "many of them are in a more wretched condition than they were in during the worst days of chattel slavery." At the same time, African Americans "are not willing slaves. There is a wonderful amount of intelligence amongst them and it only needs the introduction of the labor movement to rouse them from their prostate state." The socialist found Black workers "deep in their hatred of oppression and ready to embrace any chance by which they can emancipate themselves." He closed his piece arguing that "the interests of white and black workmen are alike and they must stand by each other" and expressing the hope that "steps will be taken to bring our colored fellow workmen into the proposed Labor Union."[8]

Marie Andreef-Edger, the wife of the English positivist thinker Henry Edger, was a reader of the *Labor Standard.* In early 1878, she sent a letter to the paper including an appeal for the integration of Black workers. In the message, she stated that a Russian friend, a worker on an Ohio farm, had managed to get in touch with some Black workers and intended to distribute some copies of the socialist newspaper amongst them. Andreef-Edger added that African Americans were eager to join the movement.[9] P. E. Collie from Philadelphia further expanded on the ILU's perspectives in the South. Drawing upon their experience as wage worker in Florida, Collie argued that the Southern society was essentially divided into three classes: "1st. Whites who had possession before the war—patricians; 2nd. Whites who had no possession before the war—crackers-plebians [*sic*]; 3rd. Negroes who do all the labor and are considered only when needed—outcasts."[10] The Democratic Party gathered the support from the first two classes of citizens, the Republican Party among the third. However, "During election times the negroes are flattered and deceived by both parties . . . White workingmen in the Southern States should do their utmost to create splits in the political parties and to bring our colored brothers into the labor ranks."[11]

In the political fray dividing socialists in the 1878, Adolph Douai remained one of the few if not only leaders in communication with all factions. At New Haven, SLP delegates offered him the editorship of the new English-language national paper of the party that would replace the *Labor Standard.* Douai rejected the proposition after it was established that the paper would be published in Cincinnati.[12] Yet after the convention, he continued to address his correspondence both to the *Labor Standard* and to the papers of the SLP, especially the *Vorbote.* In his letters and articles, Douai proved to be the socialist leader that more than any other sought to elaborate a comprehensive strategy to reach out to African Americans.[13]

Douai was adamant on the need of the socialist movement to address its propaganda to Black workers. In the *Labor Standard,* he contributed on the planning of the strategy of the newly founded ILU by assessing its perspectives among American farmers. In this context, Douai wrote that the Black population of the South deserved "our kindest and most careful attention. They are the almost only laboring people there; few of them are anything but wage slaves. Without their gathering into our fold, one half of the country must remain adverse or indifferent to our movement."[14] Douai added that the "enlightenment" of African Americans should begin in places where socialist trade unions had some presence, such as Baltimore, Washington, DC, Louisville, and St. Louis. By organizing African

Americans, argued Douai, "we might achieve what otherwise cannot be done—we might loosen the hold of their white employers on them, and weaken the unnatural fellowship of those egoistic ex-rebels with the farmers and mechanics within the National Party of the North."[15]

Douai returned to the subject six months later, this time for the SLP audience. If in the *Labor Standard* article he had already hinted toward a slightly more structured political analysis of the role of socialists in southern politics, in the columns of the *Vorbote,* Douai put forward an even more robust political plan. He analyzed the subject "merely from a social-democratic point of view" in order to understand what "we can expect from the Negroes for the purpose of supporting our propaganda."[16]

Douai articulated a comprehensive and quite consistent investigation of southern social and political dynamics that considered class and race relationships. He divided the southern society into four groups—former planters and "their comrades in the exploitation of working Negroes" (upper-level bourgeoisie such as merchants, the clergy, lawyers, and politicians); Black "wage workers and wage slaves"; the "indigenous poor whites of the South"; and the "immigrant white working population"—giving accurate information on their size and features.[17] Then he proceeded to denounce the "racial pact" that kept the South together, the white alliance between former masters and the local poor population. "Of course, there is no spiritual bond between the slaveholders and the poor native whites beyond the hatred for Negroes; they hate each other quite cordially." But it was the help of poor whites that kept Southern elites in power.[18]

Douai recognized that it would be a struggle for socialists to enter this political and social scenario. Yet he contended that the example of the Greenback Labor Party, which had received around a million vote in the 1878 local elections, gave socialists hope. Douai's expectations were cautiously pinned to a reorganization of southern politics along class lines. Betting on the fact that sooner or later, the interests of land owners would align with those of northern capitalists, Douai envisioned a future in which the political power would be in the hands of a broad coalition of employers with no significant party distinctions. This circumstance would create the ideal situation for socialists to gain ground. In this scenario, a virtuous dynamic of class cooperation would tear down racial rivalries. "The poor whites of the south would be compelled to compete with the big employers for the negro votes in order to obtain a decisive majority in every southern state." As a result, the white worker would have incentive to help Black workers and protect their rights. "The negroes would receive support and legal protection from the poor whites and the immigrant workers." Socialists and northern immigrants would ease the transition by promoting "a tremendous effort" to "spread education and political understanding among these poor whites."[19] Douai's plan was more the result of his own hopes for the South than a realistic assessment of the perspectives of southern politics. At the same time, his proposal attested to the attempts of socialists to envision interracial forms of class cooperation in a reformed South. The southern white working class, traditionally considered beyond the reach of political progressives, was given an unusual central place in Douai's scheme.[20]

A surprising and problematic omission in Douai's article was the lack of emphasis on African American resistance. Douai wrote his piece just one month before the African American exodus toward Kansas made it to the first pages of Northern dailies.[21] Migration to Kansas was just the most notable of the myriad of ways in which Black sharecroppers and urban workers had been regularly challenging racial discrimination in the South since 1865. African Americans used legal methods to defend their recently acquired civil rights, their opportunity to receive an education, and their chances to become economically independent from white landowners and businessmen. They signed petitions, used the franchise, and entered lawsuits and appeals. Yet this enormous work of civic and political resistance was not duly acknowledged in the socialist press of the time. At least theoretically, socialists understood that Black farmers and urban workers had a key role to play in the spread of the socialist message in the South, yet they did not seem to realize that the spontaneous acts of rebellion of African American sharecroppers and workers were precisely what socialists were looking for to provoke a destabilization of the American capitalist system, that the South was reorganizing itself on the basis of a very rigid white supremacist order.[22]

Socialist absence from the South surely had a role to play in creating this blind spot in socialist literature. Southern socialist voices were the exception rather than the norm, and a brief analysis of the geographical spread of the party is highly instructive to understand why. In 1877, the SLP had eighty-nine sections, seventy-seven of which were located either in the Northeast (forty-seven) or in the Midwest of the country (thirty). Of the remaining, nine were in the South (four in Kentucky, one in New Orleans, and four in St. Louis) and three were in the West (two in San Francisco and one in Sacramento).[23] With the exception of New Orleans, the SLP did not have any organized presence in the Deep South. The party was hundreds of miles away from the political centers of southern politics, which had a clear impact on the perceived priorities of the party.

The SLP was also poorly positioned to develop a sustained interaction with African Americans, who, in this moment, were still predominantly living in the South. Apart from the handful of militants in New Orleans, the SLP did not even have a single section in any of the states where the Black population was over thirty percent, such as Alabama, Virginia, Florida, Georgia, Mississippi, and the Carolinas. Where the SLP was more powerful and had some say in local politics, the African American presence was almost negligible. In New York City, Chicago, and Detroit, where the largest SLP sections were, the percentage of African Americans in 1900 was still below two percent. The situation was the same in SLP-rich areas like Massachusetts, Pennsylvania, and New Jersey, whose Black population fluctuated between 1.1 and 3.7 percent. These figures are even more telling when compared with those of the foreign-born population, namely those communities where the SLP had its stronghold. To focus just on the three cities mentioned above, in 1900, in the greater New York City area, the Black population was 1.8 percent (60,666), versus the thirty-seven percent of foreign-born people (1,270,080). The figures were similar in Chicago (1.3 percent versus 34.6 percent) and Detroit (1.4 percent versus 33.8 percent).[24]

This circumstance did not mean that there was no interaction between organized socialism and the African American community. For a start, the SLP attracted a small African American membership. Firm numbers are hard to reconstruct, but in the pages of the socialist press, it is possible to find mentions of a Black presence in the socialist movement. In August 1878, the Baltimore section of the party wrote in its regular report to the *National Socialist* that "the colored men are now taking an interest in the movement and an attempt will be made to organize there."[25] Some months later, in the Chicago-based *Socialist*, "Elmo" informed the SLP membership that in St. Louis, "a well-attended meeting of colored men was held . . . at the call of the colored men's section of the Socialistic Labor Party. These people are taking great interest in our cause."[26] Also, the Chicago section welcomed its first two Black members in 1878 and the Black agitator George Mack joined the New York City section in January 1879.[27]

There were also circumstances in which the pattern identified above broke down more explicitly. The first case is the already mentioned New Orleans. The largest Southern port city, New Orleans had a strong African American labor contingent and a small socialist presence, at least in parts of the period under scrutiny. The second case is Cincinnati. Although not technically in the South, Cincinnati had a growing African American population, given its proximity with the Mason-Dixon line, fluctuating between the three percent in 1870 and the five percent in 1900.[28] The Ohio case is made even more crucial by the presence in the SLP ranks of Peter H. Clark, a prominent Black political leader. The last case is St. Louis, the fourth largest American city in 1880 and home of a large African American community that grew significantly when the SLP had one of its biggest sections there, in the aftermath of the 1877 Great Strike. By focusing on these three cases in some details, a clearer picture of the racial politics of Gilded Age socialists emerges.

New Orleans

Ludwig A. Geissler was a steadfast and regular source of information about the deeds of the New Orleans SLP section in the first years after the end of Reconstruction. Between 1878 and 1880, Geissler sent several letters to the St. Louis-based *Volksstimme des Westens*, the *Vorbote*, and the *Labor Standard* informing northern socialists on the progress of socialism in the southern city. Socialists started on the right foot in 1878. By the end of the year, the SLP could count on an English section, a German section, and a French section. As soon as Spanish-language material reached the city, wrote Geissler, New Orleans socialists were planning to open a Spanish section, and they were also considering to start an independent women's section.[29] New Orleans socialists thanked their northern comrades for the financial support received to contrast the epidemic of yellow fever that hit the city in the last months of the year, and the list of people that received financial support confirmed that socialists were organizing across racial lines. Geissler listed "two Octoroons and one Negro" amongst the people helped by the financial fund set up by the SLP.[30]

Yet it soon turned out that New Orleans's socialist outpost was built on shaky ground. After a silence of six months, a long report informed *Volksstimme* readers that the activity in Louisiana had dramatically slowed down. Two problems had dragged the SLP down. First, the Greenback Labor Party had entered the city's political scene. The party was a direct competitor of the SLP and it had created no small problems in the recruitment of new members. Second, an outbreak of yellow fever had taken its toll, killing some of the most talented socialist organizers including "Cordes," his wife Methua Szumanowski, and the "brilliant" Irishman Lawrence Murphy. The strenuous work of the German-speaking and the French-speaking contingents of the section stopped an attempt to outmaneuver the party leadership, but as a consequence of this failed coup, the party's Central Executive Committee and the ward clubs had disbanded. The group was nothing more than a small committee for events organization. "We held several meetings in the gymnasium . . . we bought a red flag, feasted our beautiful community, and have been working for some time now to get the non-socialist workers into a grand demonstration in favor of the eight-hour movement."[31]

Geissler sent one last letter in April 1880, and news on the party was reduced to a minimum. The German activist was more interested in the labor turmoil that agitated the city. The Black workers on the plantations of the St. John and St. Charles parishes went on strike for better wages, although their protest was suppressed by military force. In town, the longshoremen had responded to the contractors' attempts to break the power of the unions. They had succeeded. Geissler could not help but notice that the Black working class was the backbone of labor activism in Louisiana: "The blacks are showing a sense of independence and superiority to many white workers."[32] Geissler was right. In the 1880s, the unique successes obtained by New Orleans longshoremen rested on the solid foundations laid by Black organized labor.[33] The New Orleans working class was on the move, but socialists could only nod from the sidelines as this progress unfolded. Adverse circumstances and political competition from the Greenback Party made their presence irrelevant in the Louisiana city.

Either Black or Red: Peter H. Clark in Cincinnati

The 1877 congress of the SLP had moved the seat of the National Executive Committee (NEC), the leading body of the party, from Chicago to Cincinnati. The Ohio city was chosen because it housed one of the strongest sections of the SLP, which in November 1877 achieved a stunning twenty percent in the municipal elections.[34] The strike of July 1877 had stirred Cincinnati's labor movement, and the party leadership genuinely believed that the Ohio industrial city, with its strong community of German American radicals and its expanding working class, could be the ideal location from which to lead the party toward a better future.

The success was helped by the inclusion on the socialist ticket of Peter H. Clark, a Black teacher who had joined the organization in the first months of 1877. Clark, defined by his biographer Nikki M. Taylor as "America's first black socialist," had a distinctive background. He was born as a free person in Cincinnati in 1829. His father, owner of a barbershop, gave his son a full education. Though public schools were not open to African Americans in Cincinnati, Clark attended private colleges both for primary and secondary school. He completed his studies in 1848 with a diploma from the Cincinnati High School, a private institution founded by the Methodist church minister Hiram S. Gilmore.[35]

During his long political career, Clark cooperated with several key African American leaders, including the Republican leader John Mercer Langston, Frederick Douglass, and Booker T. Washington, changing his political

FIGURE 5. Portrait of Peter H. Clark. *Cleveland Gazette*, June 3, 1886.

affiliation several times across his life. An early supporter of Black nationalism and emigration to Africa, he joined the Radical Abolitionist Party in 1856 and had close relations with the freethinkers and the German American socialist groups led by August Willich in the late 1850s. After the Civil War, he became a leader of the Cincinnati Black community for the Republicans, a position he retained until the early 1880s with two interruptions, the first in order to join the liberal Republican faction in the early 1870s and the second to support the SLP between 1877 and 1879, although there are doubts that he actually left the Republican Party in this period. With his move to the Democratic Party and his support for segregated schools in his native Ohio in the mid-1880s, he lost all credibility in the local Black community and was forced to move to St. Louis for the remainder of his life, where he continued his job as a teacher without any further involvement in politics.[36]

Historians have debated the significance of Clark's experience in the SLP. For Philip S. Foner, Clark's short-term membership in the party demonstrated the inability of socialists to address the "race question." The presence of the Cincinnati leader in the SLP was a solid chance to promote the adhesion of African Americans to the socialist party. However, Foner maintained that socialists' obliviousness toward race forced Clark to abandon the party. Clark's biographer, Nikki M. Taylor, further elaborated on this. She suggested that, during his time in the SLP, the Black leader did not connect socialism and race discrimination: "[Clark] never developed a racial critique of socialism: he never criticized either the Workingmen's or the Socialistic Labor Parties for being conspicuously silent on the issue of race or for failing to make any substantive efforts to recruit or organize African American workers. . . . For him, socialism offered a solution to *economic* inequalities—not racial ones."[37]

There are few doubts that Clark's early resignation from the party represented a blow for the socialist movement in Cincinnati. However, Foner's position that his abandonment was motivated by the SLP's lack of understanding of the problems of African Americans should be questioned. Similarly, whilst Taylor was correct in arguing that Clark did not develop a "racial critique of socialism" for the period in which he remained in the socialist organization, Clark had a slightly different understanding of the relations between race and socialism than the one Taylor ascribed to him. As I detail below, between 1877 and 1879, Clark described socialism as a solution for economic inequalities *and* racial ones. The Black activist understood the situation of African Americans in the South as a matter of class and racial exploitation, and he believed that the triumph of socialism could put an end both to economic exploitation and to racial discrimination. This is the reason why Clark did not develop a racial critique of socialism and why he did not leave the party because of its lack of policies on African Americans. Clark understood socialism as a race-blind political project, though one which could ultimately deliver racial equality too. He left the party when its strength faded, and he acknowledged that there was no hope of achieving any of the political objectives socialists had in mind.

There are few doubts about the quality of Clark as a pioneering leader of the rights of African Americans. His profound commitment to the cause of racial equality emerged early in his life, when he rejected the possibility of replacing his father in the family-owned barbershop because he did not want to work in a state of subjection to whites. With his anti-slavery political activities in the 1850s, he established himself as a clear-headed and talented leader. His sophisticated understanding of racial prejudice is documented by the words he proclaimed in a speech of 1873:

> I do not forget the prejudice of the American people; I could not if I would . . . It stood by the bedside of my mother and intensified her pains as she bore me. It darkens with its shadow the grave of my father and my mother.

> It has hindered every step I have taken in life. It poisons the food I eat, the water I drink and the air I breathe . . . Hercules could have as easily forgotten the poisoned shirt which scorched his flesh, as I can forget the prejudices of the American people.[38]

There was no aspect of the life of an African American individual which was not determined by racial prejudice. In this passage, Clark eloquently explained the personal and intimate nature of the problem, a reality that affected African Americans and left them no possibility of escape.

Clark gave this speech three years before joining the SLP. Already in 1875, he was addressing a meeting of the Sovereigns of Industry, a workers' society that later took part in the founding of the Cincinnati section of the party. In his speech, he praised the virtues of cooperation, as opposed to the avarice and inhumanity of capitalism.[39] Clark delivered his first speech as a socialist in March 1877, during a rally organized by the WPUS. He started the talk with a comment on his sudden switch, saying that he "had been a socialist in heart long before the Republican Party had an existence." It is likely that here Clark was referring to specific biographical circumstances. Clark encountered socialism early in his youth, thanks to the Owenite and Fourierist ideas of the director of his high school, Hiram S. Gilmore. The close connection with Gilmore provided Clark with his first job as a stereotyping apprentice at the studio of Thomas Varney and his wife, Maria. The couple was famous for their radical activities, which spanned from communitarian socialism to land reform and anarchism. During these experiences, the young Clark became acquainted with radical and anti-capitalist literature.[40]

For some time, Clark had been divided between a pragmatic and reflexive approach focused on the defense of African Americans' rights and a more global and radical outlook devoted to the fight against economic inequalities. In the mid-1870s, as a politician extremely sensitive toward the mood of the electorate, Clark sensed that the latter attitude could boost his chances to earn political success. In the speech he gave at the socialist rally of March 1877, Clark boldly declared that "the ideal of a workingmen's democracy which is now attracting the attention of the civilized world will before long triumph over the dominancy of the present party." He moved on to expound an interpretation of international economic dynamics that would have had Karl Marx nodding with approval. He attacked international capitalism, arguing that Otto von Bismarck and the English employers shared their interests with the American ruling class. Then, he went on tightly connecting class and race exploitation together. "Then come into our country. Go into the South and see the capitalists banded together over the poor whites. They carefully calculate how much, and no more, it will require to feed and clothe the black laborer and keep him alive from one year to another." Clark continued, intoning that "not a foot of land will they sell to the oppressed race who are trying to crowd out the degradation into which capital has plunged him."[41]

Clark was talking to an audience of white American and immigrant workers, to whom he articulated the dynamics of race discrimination as a manifestation of class exploitation. Like Douai, Clark argued that the alliance between white capitalists and poor whites, rooted in a shared antagonism to Blacks, was creating African Americans' condition of inescapable segregation.

Six months later, Clark delivered a speech in Augusta, Ohio, where he made the connection between race discrimination and the class question even clearer. Against the inhuman tyranny of economy and industrial organization, he maintained, workers should hold high the torch of morality. The "progress of the race," made possible by the abolition of chattel slavery, served to demonstrate that "there is an underlying and undying moral law governing the relations of men with their fellowmen . . . The Social Democracy came before the American professing a faith in this underlying moral law." After a detailed investigation into European and American salaries, Clark wrapped up his speech by contending that "if he [the American laborer] does not resist at the ballot box, we shall have a Nation of industrial slaves or paupers, governed by an aristocracy of capital." Class and race once again traveled together in Clark's analysis. "Already in the South this condition of affairs is realized. The unfortunate freedman lies hopelessly in the power of the capitalist, nor does any hope save that held out by migration present itself. There is no remedy for this tendency, save that offered by socialism."[42]

Clark used socialist theory to address what he considered the most burning aspect of African Americans' segregation: economic exploitation. In this phase of his political career, Clark did not have a focus on civil rights, but he genuinely believed that with the success of socialism, a twofold result would be achieved: not only the improvement of workers' economic conditions but also the creation of a more equal system of racial relations. With his adhesion to the SLP, Clark did not abandon his commitment toward race equality; on the contrary, he attempted to find a different path to achieve it.

There is a good deal of truth in Foner's claim that the departure of Clark was a lost opportunity for the SLP. The political weight of Clark in Cincinnati's local scene is excellently described in an alarmed article of the Republican *Cincinnati Enquirer* about the "colored vote" in 1877, where a supporter of the GOP denounced the lack of political rewards for the Black electorate. "The consequence," argued the writer, "will be that, in the ensuing election that takes place this fall, a great many colored men will vote for the Democratic ticket, a large number will follow Peter Clark and vote for the Workingmen, and others not vote at all."[43] Clark was an important political leader who was able to influence the Black vote in Cincinnati. Therefore, the SLP's inability to prevent Clark's departure was a significant problem. However, it is doubtful that Clark abandoned the SLP because of socialists' blindness on the "race question." Unlike Foner's account, the evidence discussed in this chapter suggest that his decision was provoked by several causes, amongst which are the dynamics within the Cincinnati section, the inability of the SLP to provide the Cincinnati Black community with political protection, and, finally, personal interest, namely, Clark's growing disappointment with the inability of the SLP to secure any political position for him.

The radical activist William Haller had a key role in bringing Clark into the SLP. A sergeant in the Union army during the Civil War, Haller was elected to the City Council of Cincinnati in 1865 but lost his seat almost immediately, after he revealed his "red" commitment to workers' rights. Later, he was part of the Labor Reform Party (the political spinoff of the National Labor Union) and of the People's Party, the same short-lived organization August Willich had joined in 1873. In the WPUS, he arguably achieved the apex of his political career. Not only did he immediately join the party but he also launched a weekly newspaper, the *Emancipator*, which helped to establish the local reputation of the WPUS during the 1877 strike.[44] Clark and Haller had known each other since a national convention of the Labor Reform Party in 1871. It was Haller who invited Clark to the meeting of the Sovereigns of Industry in 1875 and later convinced him to join the WPUS.[45] Haller clearly understood the importance of having a Black member in the Workingmen's Party. When Clark joined the WPUS ticket as school commissioner in 1877, Haller saluted the event by writing that he "of all the candidates on the ticket, most thoroughly represents the contest between laborers and capitalists, of the proscribed race, whose sorrows made the name of the United States the synonym of robbery and murder throughout the world; his nomination is therefore above all others the finest vindication of the claim, that the 'Workingmen's Party' is a purely cosmopolitan organization."[46]

Clark himself acknowledged the importance of racial inclusion and cosmopolitanism in his friend's thinking, when, at the time of Haller's death in 1881, he was called on to deliver his eulogy. Arguing against Haller's opponents, Clark made the point that "this assemblage, composed of men of various races, various religious views, various conditions of society, shows that all men did not believe the slanderous charges . . . That all races should be represented here is eminently proper, for the cry of the oppressed in any land found a ready response in his heart."[47] There can be little doubt about the strength of Haller's commitment on interracialism within the WPUS. But the point is that Clark did not abandon the WPUS/SLP because of conflicts about this position. There are other, more relevant elements to consider.

Clark mentioned some critics of Haller during his funeral speech; in fact, Haller had many. Since his early steps in the labor movement, Haller had been a stubborn and intransigent defender of electoral politics. In his opinion, the ballot box was the "Archimedes's lever" given by the American political system to rapidly overthrow exploiters and achieve control of government.[48] He did not believe in trade unions, compromises, or piecemeal improvements. Even when Sorge and his followers left the party in 1877, he was still complaining about the excessive attention the SLP gave to trade unions. In 1878, he was hired by the St. Louis section as an English-language agitator, but his experience lasted only a few months because the leaders of the section did not agree with his anti-trade union stance. Returning to Cincinnati, he escalated the conflict between the National Executive Committee of the party led by Philip Van Patten and the German section and was eventually expelled from the party in 1879.[49] Clark seemed to share Haller's antipathy toward trade unions. In a speech during the July 1877 strike, he declared that "trades unions, Grangers, Sovereigns of Industry, cooperative stores and factories are alike futile. They are simply combinations of laborers who seek to assume toward their own unfortunate fellows who are not members the attitude that the capitalist assumes toward them."[50]

One may wonder, then, whether the progressive unpopularity of Haller's and Clark's position had a role in provoking the Black teacher's abandonment of the party. The resignation letter Clark sent to the NEC of the SLP gives further elements to consider. Clark referred to an attempt to remove him as principal of the Gaines High School, the Black institution he had led since 1866. He reported that he could stop it only because the Black community "came as one man" to rescue him. Clark continued, saying, "I really belong to that people; I really belonged to them from my childhood."[51]

This episode encapsulates the mix of motivations behind Clark's resignation, which arose out of several intertwined interests. As he clarified in his letter, the separation was not intellectual. In the letter, Clark specified that he still considered himself a socialist, and that he still believed that "there is not, under the sun, any method except through the party, by which the difficulties that surround the Labor platform can be solved."[52] Therefore, the real reasons for his resignation lay elsewhere. First, it must be noted that with the expulsion of Haller from the party, Clark lost the connection who had brought him into the organization and was left as one of the few members of the party still defending an anti-trade unionist stance. Secondly, the complete fiasco of the SLP at the 1878 elections, in which Clark was on the socialist ticket for Congress, made evident that the SLP was not destined to have the central role in the local and national political scenario that Clark had envisaged in 1877. Third, and crucially, the local Black community was not interested in following him into the socialist ranks. By remaining a member of the SLP, Clark was at a dead end: Not only did his affiliation threaten his job but more importantly, as a politician, the Black leader was not able to provide any sort of protection to the Black constituency that had supported his political career until now. Ultimately, Clark had no alternative but to reenter the Republican ranks; to keep his job and to keep defending the interests of the political constituency that gave him his political position, he had to abandon the socialists.

Clark expressed some of the most advanced and fully developed analyses of the relation between class and race to be found in the socialist press of the time. He believed that racial discrimination was intimately connected to economic inequality, and from this point of view, he saw socialism as a theory that could address both issues. Albeit in an unstructured form, Clark articulated opinions that anticipated those of Black socialists writing decades later, like Hubert Harrison and W. E. B. Du Bois.[53] But his attempts to combine the fight for racial equality and the struggle to achieve socialism failed in the face of the SLP's political weakness.

St. Louis and the "Negro Exodus"

Clark's resignation was the last nail in the coffin for the SLP in Cincinnati. Prostrated by internal infighting on political strategy, at the end of 1878, the socialist party had lost any significant influence in the local political scene.[54] However, elsewhere in the country, socialists had more success translating the vast public interests in labor politics sparked by the 1877 Great Strike into a more stable political presence. In St. Louis, the size and duration of strike were unprecedented, to the point that historian David T. Burbank described the event as "the first general strike in U.S. history."[55] Despite the scare generated by this unexpected workers' revolt, socialists managed to establish an infrastructure that would lend them continuous influence in St. Louis local politics for the following years.

Starting as a resolute but peaceful attempt by the railroad workers of East St. Louis to negotiate better wages, the 1877 St. Louis strike had turned into a week-long general revolt that united workers across all levels of craftmanship, race, and nationality, forcing the city to a complete halt. In a precarious leadership position of this unforeseen outburst of protest were the socialists of the WPUS. On Sunday, July 22, 1877, WPUS members moved to East St. Louis to show their support for the railroad workers on strike. In the space of twenty-four hours, and without much political planning, the spontaneous gathering had turned into a nonstop series of demonstrations and rallies. A committee of five was created to coordinate the protest and agree on a list of demands to present to the city authorities. All of them were members of the WPUS. But soon, the strike leaders realized that they were losing control over the crowd. By Wednesday, July 25, three days after the first demonstration, the committee called off further marches to avoid the risk of violence. The Democratic newspapers of the city repeatedly boasted that the "Internationalists" were amassing weapons in their deposits and were ready to turn the city into a new Paris Commune. Despite these insisted denunciations, the strike ended peacefully on Friday, July 27, without a single shot fired. The allegedly incendiary revolutionaries were caught while attempting to jump from the windows of the party headquarters to avoid arrest. They were jailed in disgrace. In two days, the federal troops stopped the last remnants of the strike, and by the next Monday, calm had been restored to the city.[56]

The events in St. Louis are not only a powerful symbol of the impressive level of social conflict in the United States in 1877 and of the weaknesses of the political parties that were supposed to represent workers. They are also a crossroad in the relationship between Black and white workers and about the role that organized socialism had or could have had in leading forms of protest across racial lines. The protest was interracial from its very beginning. An unidentified "Negro speaker," who was later included in the first provisional committee of the strike, addressed the first general rally at Lucas Market.[57] The *St. Louis Daily Tribune* reported that on Tuesday morning, W. H. M. Knight, a Black steamboatman, asked the crowd: "Will you stand to us regardless of color?" He received resounding answers of, "We will, we will." Newspapers continued to record the presence of Black workers in the following days too.[58]

However, in the words of the WPUS leader and member of the strike committee Albert Currlin, who was interviewed by the *St. Louis Daily Tribune* two weeks after the strike, the moment when the strike leadership started to realize that it was no longer able to control the "mob" was precisely when a vast group of African Americans joined the protest. "On Wednesday," Currlin told the reporter, "there was a large crowd gathered about that we didn't want to have anything with. They were loafers and niggers and made up nothing but a mob."[59] The German socialist went on to detail how, having failed to keep the demonstration limited to "only workers," the socialists decided to abandon the rally. "Before the hour for starting a gang of niggers, it looked like about 500, came to Turner Hall and sent word that they wanted to join our party. We replied that we wanted nothing to do with them, and it was this gang that started and led the processions that did the mischief."[60]

The appeal for solidarity made by the steamboatman Knight on Tuesday was falling on deaf ears. White socialists did not want to mingle with Black workers, and some quickly came to blame them for the failure of the strike.

Historian Alison Clark Efford suggested that Currlin's response needs to be contextualized within a wider analysis of the midwestern German American community. The appeals for economic citizenship launched during the strike of 1877 came at the end of a period in which the German American community had explored the possibility of joining forces with African Americans to fight a common struggle for social and economic rights. According to Efford, opinions such as Currlin's demonstrated that by 1877, that project had failed. German Americans had abandoned progressive and egalitarian principles during the early 1870s in order to pursue their own nationalist agenda and to obtain social prestige in the American society. By analyzing the coverage of the strike in German language papers, Efford concludes the German American bourgeoisie saw German American socialists as a threat to their recently acquired social status, and the interracial nature of the strike acted as a further confirmation of the potential danger to the established order created by socialists. "Black protestors," contends Efford, "symbolized the anarchy that socialists had unleashed on the city."[61]

Efford provided a solid rationale to contextualize the socialist approach in the complex ethnic dynamics of the German community in the United States. Currlin represented the paradigmatic example of a worker prioritizing his own personal gain over the principled defense of racial equality, a pattern that closely matched those of many other immigrant workers cashing in on their acquired whiteness. However, if Currlin's opinion is reframed within the parallel history of the development of a racial politics in the American socialist movement, his voice loses part of its exemplar power and becomes one opinion in a cacophony of many discording sounds.

Currlin was a low-rank leader of the St. Louis section of the WPUS, which in the aftermath of the strike became one of the leading lights of the American socialist movement, together with Chicago, Detroit, and New York City. The St. Louis section boasted around one thousand activists divided between its German-speaking branches (six hundred), English-language branches (three hundred), and French and Bohemian groups (the remaining one hundred).[62] Right after the strike, the section made a move that proved its growing strength by starting a new German-language daily, the *Volksstimme des Westens*, the second existing in the country after Chicago's *Arbeiter Zeitung*. St. Louis German socialists invited to edit the paper one of the most prestigious German-speaking socialist intellectuals in the country, August Otto-Walster. Otto-Walster had arrived in the United States in 1876 invited by the WPUS, yet the position he had been invited to hold had disappeared in a year, when the *Arbeiter Stimme* had closed for lack of funding. The editorship of the *Volksstimme* was his occasion to shine.[63] The *Volksstimme* regularly published for over three years (from 1877 to 1880), a time span that can easily be identified as the peak of socialists' influence in St. Louis.

The *Volksstimme* joined one of the most packed and high-quality journalistic scenarios of the country, reflecting the importance of St. Louis on a national scale and the strength and significance of the local German American community. The city had two German-language dailies: the Democratic *Anzeiger des Westens* and the Republican *Westliche Post*. The *Anzeiger* was one of the oldest German-language papers of the country. Since 1835, it provided St. Louis German Americans with a conservative and ethnic integrationist point of view. The *Westliche Post* had been purchased by Carl Schurz and Emil Preetorious in the late 1860s. Under their leadership, it became a leading Republican voice not only in St. Louis but across the entire Midwest. St. Louis could also count on several English-language dailies with a national reputation. In 1877, the *St. Louis Globe-Democrat* and the *St. Louis Daily Times* were the two highest-circulation papers. The scene further expanded in 1878, when the U.S.-naturalized journalist Joseph Pulitzer bought the defunct *St. Louis Post* and *St. Louis Dispatch* and merged them into the *St. Louis Post-Dispatch*, the paper that launched his career across the country.[64]

In this period, St. Louis was in the midst of a ruthless competition with Chicago to become the most important industrial and transport center of the region. Authorities campaigned through any means available to attract new businesses by making their cities better connected and more efficient in the production, packing, and shipping of goods across the country. St. Louis could count on a peculiarly good position: It was the "Gateway of the West," with goods traveling by train from the Northeast and the Midwest to the West, but also a historic crossroads on the Mississippi for people and material going from south to north. From 1877, St. Louis could also count on another powerful ally in Washington, DC, former-Missouri senator Carl Schurz, who was appointed as secretary of the interior by President Hayes in 1877.[65]

St. Louis was organically part of the South, and for this reason, the attention of public opinion toward the socioeconomic conditions of the southern states was prominent. This was reflected in the *Volksstimme*'s coverage. More than any other socialist weekly or daily of the time, the *Volksstimme* featured a wealth of information on the living conditions and issues of African Americans in the South. But Otto-Walster edited a paper whose position on African American rights was hard to discern. In the pages of the *Volksstimme,* one could find opinion pieces that could easily have been included in a pro-slavery publication written by southern white supremacists during the first half of the nineteenth century. In an article published in November 1877, for example, R. Mills deemed as inevitable the extinction of Native Americans, rejected the idea that African Americans were "culture capable," and invoked a race war against Chinese immigrants.[66] The paper also featured openly anti-Black reports on Southern matters from conservative German-language papers like the *New Yorker Staats Zeitung.* These articles described the "mass of colored citizens" as "still incredibly ignorant," adding that "the only thing it knows is the value of money." According to the *Staats Zeitung*, the Southern Black male population was divided between an old generation unable to work as a result of the marks left by the physical exploitation they had suffered before Emancipation and a younger generation characterized by "work-shy, hedonistic and confrontational" behavior.[67] Such descriptions spread negative stereotypes of the African American population among the socialist readership and were consistent with the opinions of its leader, Currlin.

However, the socialist daily also published material defending the opposite side of the argument. A week after the *Staats Zeitung* article, the *Volksstimme* reprinted a letter signed by a group of New Orleans women to former Union army general Benjamin Butler, invoking his help against racial violence in the South.[68] Another public appeal, a desperate "cry for help" addressed to the president, to congressmen, and to the Republican and the Democratic Parties, appeared in the *Volksstimme* in April 1879. The appeal, written by an assembly of African American citizens of New Orleans, detailed the situation of despair of Blacks in Louisiana, commenting on how they were beaten and persecuted for their support for Republicans and how they were denied the opportunity to improve their present state of ignorance and poverty: "If you call us uneducated, so this is not the fault of us, but of whites, because they call it a crime to teach us to read the Bible."[69] The *Volksstimme* attached a short note to the appeal, in which it mocked with irony "the 'noble race' that is born here" (i.e., white Americans) and its alleged "Great Republic" for failing to respect the rights of its citizens. Finally, another article, this time reprinted from the *Milwaukee Herald*, attacked the anti-emigration laws approved by Mississippi and other states, arguing that the Southern aristocracy was still violating African Americans' basic civil rights by disposing at will over their freedom to move.[70]

This variation of political positions was not uncommon in nineteenth-century dailies. In many of them, especially of the low-budget type like the *Volksstimme*, original reporting intermixed with "fillers" taken from other newspapers, creating eclectic mixes with no discernible political coherence. However, quite often the editors of the paper reserved for themselves the top-left spot on page two, right under the newspaper header and info, for articles that, at best, represented the line of the paper. In this section, in May 1878, Otto-Walster published an editorial in which he sought to provide a comprehensive analysis on the possibilities the socialists had within Black communities in the South.

Otto-Walster offered a balanced summary of socialist perspectives. He remarked that the SLP had friends in the South who could spread its credo. However, he quipped, the tasks of these agitators were made difficult by numerous circumstances. First, influential leaders of the African American community, such as Frederick Douglass, had turned their back on workers and were now supporters of "the harmony between capital and labor," in line with the new course of the Republican Party. Second, Blacks had scarce opportunities to receive free education and to step outside the influence of conservative Black churches. And lastly, Social Democrat agitators were caught between the two fires of the Democratic and Republican Parties, powerful party machines that they could not rival. Party authorities should focus on urban contexts like St. Louis, Louisville, Baltimore, and New Orleans, suggested Otto-Walster, where circumstances for socialists were more favorable.[71]

While this strategy was more realistic and concrete than any of the others produced by SLP leaders of the time, at its heart was a fundamental misunderstanding of African American electoral behavior and priorities. A goal of Otto-Walster's article was to explain "why blacks voted Democratic" in 1876. Identifying the Republican Party as the party of big business, Otto-Walster attacked the South's occupation through the Union Army and "carpetbeggers" as corrupt and inefficient. Discussing the 1876 presidential elections, he contended that Black voters saw that Republican occupation was on the verge of ending and they preempted it by throwing their support behind the only group who could defend their interest: white Southern landowners. "They chose the smaller of two evils, determined to fight it at a later stage." Otto-Walster was eager to attack the Republicans, and Schurz in particular, a key adversary of the socialists in St. Louis. Yet in doing so, he ended up fundamentally mischaracterizing the behavior of the Black electorate. Otto-Walster seemed to not recognize the real reason why Blacks had apparently voted Democratic in 1876: voter suppression. African Americans had no faith in southern whites, as Otto-Walster alleged. Instead, violence and intimidation had kept Blacks away from the polls or forced them to vote Democratic.[72]

Otto-Walster's poor analysis of the 1876 presidential election is perhaps indicative of a wider lack of understanding by the socialists of the circumstances experienced by African Americans in the South. Further evidence of this is given by their failure to lend a hand to Blacks when an occasion was presented at their doorstep. Frustrated by poverty and white violence, in 1879, thousands of Blacks from Louisiana, Texas, and other southern states traveled along the Mississippi River and through St. Louis in order to settle in Kansas. As detailed by historian Nell Irvin Painter, the "Kansas Exodus" began in the first months of 1879, even though its organization had been underway well before, thanks to the work of Henry Adams and Benjamin "Pap" Singleton.[73] Socialist reactions to African American "Exodusters" were cold, to say the least. On the day of the arrival of the first boats on the levee, the *Volksstimme* reported on the event, wondering who told African American southerners "that a trip North would be as the arrival in the Promised Land for Jews" and further questioning what would happen once Black workers had spent the little money they carried along with them.[74] In a series of other articles published in 1879, the *Volksstimme* gave further details about the presence of African Americans in town. It reported some initiatives undertaken by the city authorities to control the flow of immigration and detailed the opinions of Republican politicians on the origin of the phenomenon. The socialist paper blamed the Republican authorities for failing to find credible solutions for the groups of African Americans forced in St. Louis by their lack of funds to continue the journey to Kansas. However, despite reporting on the event, nowhere in these articles did the *Volksstimme* express the idea that the SLP should offer relief to the Black Exodusters in their attempt to reach Kansas.[75]

Taken together, the three examples of New Orleans, Cincinnati, and St. Louis convey the image of a party that maintained a theoretical commitment to interracial organizing but regularly failed to turn this intention into practice. In the first fifteen years after its foundation, the SLP oversaw only brief moments of influence on local labor politics. The end of the 1870s was one of them. In its official documents, the SLP singled out the situation of African American labor as exceptional and incomparable to those of other groups. As the resolution approved in 1880 attests, socialists understood that a racial divide existed and that unity between white and Black workers must be proactively sought. Cincinnati and St. Louis represented perhaps the only two circumstances in which socialists had favorable political conditions to attempt to conduct a systematic effort to do so (in New Orleans, the SLP was always too weak to attempt anything). Yet in neither of these cities did the local party move in that direction. The motivations of these failures are similar. Neither in Cincinnati nor in St. Louis were socialists able to find a way to coherently link together the priorities of the Black electorate with the goals of their white and immigrant membership. African Americans' spontaneous attempts to subvert racial oppression, like the Kansas Exodus, were dismissed as problems of the Republican Party and never understood as part of a broader attack against racist institutions. Currlin's response to the 1877 strike was not representative of the overall behavior of the SLP. In the late 1870s, socialists were open to interracial organizing, as the presence of Peter H. Clark in the party's National Executive Committee attests. But even when Clark campaigned from the socialist camp, the gap between the Black and the white ethnic electorates was not bridged. Socialism remained a political project not suited to address the specific problems of Black Americans.

The SLP in the 1880s

On a broader political scale, a key difficulty socialists struggled to overcome in their attempt to spread south was the presence of a party that insisted on a similar section of the electorate and had a much stronger presence in southern states: the Greenback Labor Party.[76] The GLP was born in 1878 from the Greenback movement, an organization founded by western and southern farmers to demand the institution of a non-gold-backed currency of exchange. Over time, the movement had included in its program labor issues such as shorter working hours and the increase of wages, and by 1878, it had managed to elect fifteen congressmen and poll around one million votes. The GLP had sections in many southern states, such as Arkansas, Georgia, Louisiana, South Carolina, Tennessee, Texas, and Virginia. Unlike the SLP, the GLP had the means, expertise, and social position to activate interracial forms of cooperation with Black farmers and workers whenever local conditions allowed it.[77]

By the late 1870s, the GLP started spreading north and entered in direct competition with the socialists. Sometimes, the encounters between the two parties created resentment; on other occasions, the two organizations found ways to cooperate and work together. As documented by historian Mark A. Lause, SLP branches in Detroit, St. Louis, Baltimore, Philadelphia, Boston, Newark, and Grand Rapids hosted GLP speakers, took part in GLP meetings and organized joint events. In St. Louis and New York, the GLP and the SLP filled joint candidacies for specific posts. The SLP and the GLP had features that seemed to suggest that cooperation could be mutually beneficial. In the North, the GLP and the SLP competed for support among industrial workers, but the ethnic makeup of the organizations was different. While the socialists had their stronghold in the German American community, the GLP proliferated among Irish immigrants. Geographically, the two parties complemented one another: The GLP had the bulk of its presence in the South, the SLP in the North.[78]

Perhaps some of these arguments crossed the minds of SLP leaders, as well, because from 1878, moderate and English-speaking members of the SLP started toying with the idea of creating a common front. The *Irish World* was a weekly paper founded by the Irish immigrant Patrick Ford in 1870 in New York City. Across the decade, the paper became one of the leading voices of the Irish American community. In 1879, Ford changed the name of the paper to *Irish World and American Industrial Liberator* and turned it into the quasi-official publication of the GLP. Ford was a supporter of Henry George's theories of land redistribution. But in this period, his paper hosted a wealth of material on socialism in the United States. SLP leaders, like the corresponding secretary Philip Van Patten, and regular SLP correspondents like W. G. H. Smart, John F. Bray, and Frank Roney published in the paper, quite often to defend the SLP or to introduce the core tenets of socialism to the *Irish World* readership.[79]

An occasion to turn intentions into practice came in 1880. In preparation for the presidential elections, the fifteen independent congressmen elected in 1878 under the banner of the GLP led an effort to federate several labor groups across the country and present a presidential ticket. The GLP leadership did not seem to have particular interest in the socialists of the SLP, who had a small electoral following and a controversial political reputation. Instead, their main goal was to forge an alliance with the Workingmen's Party of California of Denis Kearney, which, in 1879, had just won the mayoral elections of San Francisco, and with other independent southern groups. But socialists saw in this coalition an opportunity to strengthen their movement and extend their geographical reach across the country. Even though the proposed coalition did not meet the favor of the most radical wing of the SLP, the party leadership decided to go ahead, attend the June convention held in Chicago, and endorse the GLP ticket composed by James B. Weaver and Barzillai J. Chambers. Eventually, the party assembly decided to call for a general vote of all sections, at the end of which a delegation of socialist leaders was sent to the August 1880 general convention that would decide the coalition's presidential ticket and platform.[80]

The farmer-labor formation that was to be christened in Chicago had the potential to mount a serious challenge to the Democratic-Republican party system that was slowly becoming the main infrastructure of the national political scene. This was especially true in the South, where Black voters had been part of the Greenback political strategy since its inception. But unity between Greenbackers, Grangers, workers, and socialists proved hard to achieve. The SLP sought to carve for itself a space in a coalition that was already shaken by acute conflicts between moderate and radicals, southerners and northerners, laborers and farmers. Fully conscious of its precarious position, the SLP leadership set an extremely low bar to agree to enter the coalition. The party leaders confirmed their intention to skip the vote on the presidential candidates, determined to accept whomever the convention decided to nominate. Instead, the only request presented was that the meeting tabled a vote on a simple and straightforward resolution that attacked monopolized control over "land, air, and water."[81] The resolution received a warm reception from the floor, but the control of the conservative wing on the convention's procedure was so strong that the SLP resolution was not voted until after the presidential ticket had been decided (at 6 a.m. of the last day of the convention). Even then, moderates maneuvered to have the resolution removed from the platform that was printed in the most important papers following the convention.[82]

Despite the treatment received during the convention, the SLP delegation decided to go ahead and support the GLP presidential ticket. This provoked a furious reaction from the most radical wing of the party. Several sections decided to ignore the decision of the SLP leadership. Large swathes of the SLP membership in Chicago and St. Louis campaigned against the GLP ticket. Others simply stayed away from the polls. In peripheral areas, the confusion was complete. The New Orleans section sent a letter asking that the comrades up north simply stop fighting because they had no idea what was going on.[83]

Why were radical socialists protesting the coalition with the GLP? Did racial policy—and perhaps the possibility that the SLP adopted the same interracial approach of the GLP—have a role to play? Consider the perspective of one of the staunchest opponents of the coalition with the Greenbackers: Albert R. Parsons. Parsons would go down in history as one of the Haymarket martyrs sentenced to death in 1886 and as the husband of the famous leader Lucy Parsons. Before turning to anarchism, though, Parsons had been one of the most important leaders of the powerful Chicago section of the SLP. Despite his adhesion to allegedly "foreign" doctrines, Parsons was a full-fledged American radical. A native of Montgomery, Alabama, during the Civil War, a teenage Parsons had sought adventure and glory as a "powder monkey" (carrying powder to the guns) and scout in the Confederate army. In 1868, aged twenty-three, he founded a weekly in Waco, called the *Spectator*, in which he advocated "the acceptance, in good faith, of the terms of surrender, and [support for] the thirteenth, fourteenth, and fifteenth constitutional amendments and the reconstruction measures securing political rights of the colored people."[84] The paper was short-lived, and political enmities forced him to move to Austin, where he took up several paid positions through the Republican-dominated Texas legislature. Parsons had a brother in the senate's Republican ranks and was considered a rising star in the party. In the early 1870s, Parsons was tasked with restoring Republican control of parishes marred by racial violence against African Americans, in this way continuing his activism in favor of African American rights started in Waco. Yet Republican power in Texas was not destined to last. By August 1873, with Republicans on course to lose their control of the state legislature, Parsons resigned his positions. Life for him and his Black wife, Lucia, secretly married in September 1872, had become unbearable. The couple decided to leave Texas behind and seek better fortune north, in Chicago.[85]

The socialist leader wrote in his autobiography that, once settled in Chicago, he had rapidly become interested in the "labor question," investigating as a journalist at the *Inter-Ocean* the case of the "Relief and Aid society," an organization set up to distribute funds raised after the Great Fire of 1871. Parsons soon found out that workers had good reason to denounce the corruption of the society. Crucially, he further added that he "also discovered a great similarity between the abuse heaped upon these poor people by the organs of the rich and the actions of the late southern slave-holders in Texas toward the newly enfranchised slaves." Parsons connected his former commitment toward African American civil rights with the defense of wage workers in Chicago. He identified a common pattern of exploitation, based on what he termed "a great fundamental wrong at work in society and existing social and industrial arrangements."[86] Even if Parsons did not further elaborate in this section of his short autobiography, it is reasonable to assume that the "great wrong" he was referring to was economic inequality—the unbalanced allocation of resources which caused the state of poverty experienced by both white workers in Chicago and Blacks in the South.

On the basis of this background, it is highly unlikely that Parsons's argument against the GLP had anything to do with the will to keep African Americans outside the party. In fact, his fundamental reason to oppose the coalition was connected to the Greenbackers' class politics. Arriving in Chicago as a Republican activist, in the years spent in Illinois, Parsons's political ideas had undergone a deep process of radicalization. An expert typographer, tireless organizer, and brilliant orator, Parsons was one of the gravitational centers of the SLP's Chicago section. In Chicago, the party had its most numerous and influential cradle of activists. Solidly rooted in immigrant and native union federations, between 1876 and 1880, the SLP had been a constant thorn in the side of the city's leadership, with an electoral peak reached in 1879, when the socialist mayoral candidate, Dr. Ernst Schmidt, polled twenty percent of the vote. Yet in 1880, Parsons saw no reasons to rejoice in this result. Despite the socialists' popularity, the party was having no impact on the city's political system. Workers' conditions had constantly worsened in these years, but socialists had not reached any degree of political control. In this situation, the last thing the SLP needed was to dilute its identity in a coalition that clearly did not support the socialists' program. Parsons found allies for his battle for the soul of the party: Paul Grottkau, the *Vorbote*, and almost the entire German American community of Chicago opposed the coalition with his same vehemence. Controlling the city's party press, Grottkau and Parsons pushed this fight to its extreme consequences. In November 1880, Chicago SLP's section filled its own "purely socialist" candidates against the GLP ticket. The result was to split the already minuscule socialist vote into two. The disaster was complete.[87]

Parsons's trajectory shows how in the early 1880s, radical class politics stood in the way of a political opening that might have led to a more articulated socialist racial politics. SLP leader George Schilling reasoned that "a fusion with the Greenback party would give us a wider, and for that reason, a more useful field for the propagation of our ideas."[88] Parsons and his allies ignored this argument. The two factions had no real disagreement on the idea that the party should welcome Black members and that an expansion beyond the industrial North was desirable. Yet how to achieve these goals was the real issue. Radical members were not interested in compromising their political goals to make room for political movements that had found a way into southern politics. Moderate socialists failed to convince them. The national political circumstances did not help to quell divisions in the socialist movement: The GLP ticket was a complete fiasco, with 300,000 votes cast in total, less than a third than the vote GLP congress candidates had polled two years before.

The 1880 elections started a long phase of decline of American socialism. The SLP began immediately hemorrhaging members in two directions. Some abandoned electoral politics altogether. Peter J. McGuire, the arch-supporter of the ballot box who had angered Sorge by running at a local election in New Jersey months after the foundation of the WPUS in 1876, dusted off his past as a carpenter and founded the United Brotherhood of Carpenters and Joiners of America, a forerunner of the American Federation of Labor.[89] Entire sections of the SLP threw themselves into union organizing, in some cases furnishing the crucial social infrastructure upon which the 1886 agitation led by the Knights of Labor was built.[90] Parsons, growing disillusioned with party politics altogether, led a faction of radicals outside of the SLP to found a "socialist revolutionary" movement. By the end of 1882, he and the core of his group had replaced the SLP in Chicago. August Spies had succeeded Grottkau as the new editor of the German-language papers *Vorbote* and the *Arbeiter Zeitung*, whilst in 1883, Parsons had founded the *Alarm* to address the English-speaking section of the Chicago working class. That same year, the group federated with a faction of New York socialists, amongst which were former SLP members Justus Schwab and Wilhelm Hasselmann. In two years, this new political formation joined forces with the anarchist International Working People's Association (IWPA). While identified as "anarchist" from this moment onward, this group retained its strong links with local trade unions and continued to pursue the objective of a socialist revolution. By then, the English-section of the SLP in Chicago was reduced to "a corporal's guard," in the words of George Schilling. One of its most important leaders, Thomas Morgan, retired from politics, whereas Schilling temporarily stepped back from active engagement, only to join the anarchist faction in late 1882. In the same year, the SLP moved its National Executive Committee from Detroit to New York, the only place where it still retained some followers. In April 1883, Philip Van Patten, the steadfast corresponding secretary who had coordinated the party since 1877, disappeared, leaving behind a suicidal note. Only years later, he confessed to George Schilling that he had left exasperated by the party's infighting. In December 1883, a disheartened German American member advanced a proposal encapsulating the situation of deep crisis of the party. Perhaps now, "the Party should no longer engage in politics, but concentrate all its efforts upon the support of the movement in Germany and the 'scientific development' of Socialism."[91]

The trajectories of socialists outside the SLP confirmed the importance of political contingencies in shaping socialist policies toward African Americans. Socialist revolutionaries like Parsons, Spies, and the IWPA remained fundamentally uninterested in making their radical anti-electoral politics message more palatable for African Americans. In the rare occasions when the IWPA press debated the issue, the significance of race was downplayed. Lucy Parsons wrote on the subject in 1886 in the *Alarm*. Commenting on the lynchings of thirteen Blacks in the Carrollton, Mississippi, area, she denied that "outrages" were "heaped upon the Negro because he is black." "Not at all," she wrote. "It is because he is poor. It is because he is dependent."[92] The *Alarm* implicitly made it clear the mismatch between the goals of the group and the political priorities of many African Americans. In 1885, the paper commented on a petition by A. B. Lee, an African American man from Wisconsin, who said that it was "very wrong to withhold from the law-abiding negro" the elective franchise, "a right which many of the worst enemies of any government enjoy; communist and Anarchists, the dregs and scums of Europe and America." The *Alarm* caustically responded to this attack on anarchism by saying that anarchists had no use of the franchise, which they considered a futile exercise with no real political value.[93]

A distinct trajectory characterized those who dedicated themselves to trade unionism. In some areas of the country, the explosive growth of the Knights of Labor in the 1880s was favored by the presence of activists who had cut their teeth in socialist politics in the late 1870s, as Richard Oestreicher's study on Gilded Age Detroit so masterfully demonstrated.[94] Philip S. Foner listed in the SLP's ranks the protagonists of a flagship episode demonstrating the Knights of Labor's egalitarian approach to race. During the 1886, Knights of Labor's national convention in Richmond, Virginia, the Black delegate of New York's District Assembly 49 (DA49) and SLP member Frank J. Ferrell tested the limits of Southern racial infrastructure. When Ferrell was denied entry to the hotel that was supposed to host the NYC delegation, the entire group walked out in solidarity. They attended collectively a theater representation, to the scandal of Richmond's white-only audience. Ferrell spoke in front of Virginia's governor Fitzhugh Lee, introducing Knights of Labor's Grand Master Workman Terence V. Powderly with a speech celebrating racial equality. Foner stressed that Ferrell and many other DA49 members were also part of the SLP at the time of the Richmond convention.[95]

These examples proved that trade unionism was an ideal incubator for an egalitarian policy of race and class within the socialist movement. Yet this egalitarianism flourished outside and not within the SLP. Ferrell and his comrades may have been party members, but the SLP's official press did not report on their trip to Richmond (which was abundantly discussed and detailed elsewhere).[96] Possibly, this was the consequence of the fact that in the second half of the 1880s, the SLP went through a period of perpetual crisis. Plagued by political disagreements, decimated by splits, the party became a tiny organization active almost only in the New York City area.

Throughout the Gilded Age, political and party memberships were volatile. Very often, people belonged to several organizations at the same time, and they rarely could afford to pay their dues regularly. Lines between trade unions and anarchist and socialist organizations were blurred, to say the least. At the moment of his arrest in Chicago, Parsons was an IWPA member but also a Knight of Labor. One of the closest allies of Ferrell in Richmond was Victor Drury, a member of the International Workingmen's Association in the 1860s, then in the SLP until 1882, then close ally of Johannes Most in the American anarchist movement and leader of the Knights.[97] In this period, it is possible that many leaders of Central Labor Unions and the Knights of Labor across the country continued to carry the SLP's red card in their pockets, yet what is sure is that the SLP had no infrastructure in place to coordinate the actions of its members. In her report from the United States, Eleanor Marx optimistically wrote that the SLP was "beginning to reap their deserved reward." Yet she could not avoid dealing with a problem becoming more evident across the decade. "Whilst the Germans will in the future, as in the past, direct the thoughts of their fellow-workers . . . they will have to be content after a time to stand aside, and let the so-called leadership of the movement pass into the hands of the English-speaking peoples."[98] Emancipating from its ethnic insularism in the 1890s became the way through which the SLP entered a new phase of its history, opening up new chances to amend and improve its racial politics.

Conclusions

Between 1876 and 1890, socialists repeatedly discussed the place of African Americans in the American society. For some socialists, such as Douai and Clark, the problem of racial discrimination was connected with economic inequality. Racial prejudice was seen as a feature of society which caused the economic and social segregation of African Americans. Yet elsewhere, socialists either did not understand the specific problems of Blacks or openly embraced white supremacism and supported the idea of the biological inferiority of the Black race.

This diversity of opinion around race in the SLP demonstrates that, between 1876 and 1890, socialists did not have clear theoretical tools to systematize racial discrimination within their thinking. Socialists did make efforts to connect African Americans' struggles with those of workers in general, attempting to go beyond the color line, but appeals for interracial cooperation were scattered and formulated in abstract terms. The general political record of the party on African Americans was weak. Although some members of the party called for the inclusion of African Americans and sought the approval of a resolution invoking an interracial coalition between southern and northern workers, sections in Cincinnati and St. Louis did not undertake any significant action to organize their respective local Black communities.

In the early years of the SLP, the development of an effective political strategy that addressed African Americans' issues was discouraged by precise historic circumstances, such as small African American populations in the SLP's urban strongholds in the North and Midwest (New York, Detroit, and Chicago) and the relative weakness of the socialist party in the cities where the African American community was larger (St. Louis and Cincinnati). But, on a more profound intellectual level, only rarely did SLP members manage to go past their implicit tendency to prioritize economic citizenship for white workers over the respect of social and political rights for African Americans. The attempted alliance between the SLP and the GLP in 1880 could have changed this scenario. However, differences over political strategy led to the failure of this project, sounding the death knell on the attempt to translate the diversity of opinions within the early socialist movement into a firmer commitment toward racial equality.

CHAPTER 5

Savage Capitalists, Civilized Indians

The SLP and Native Americans, 1876–1890

In June 1876, newspapers across the country brought news from the West: George A. Custer, lieutenant colonel of the Seventh Cavalry, had been killed at Little Bighorn. Five companies had died with him, in an assault led by a coalition of Native American warriors. Critiques of Custer's irresponsible behavior were soon replaced by posthumous glorification. Custer went down in public debate as a fallen hero defending his country.[1] Outgoing president Ulysses S. Grant struck a dissonant chord when he was quoted in the *New York Herald* months later: "I regard Custer's massacre as a sacrifice of troops, brought on by Custer himself, that was wholly unnecessary—wholly unnecessary."[2] Fourteen years later, news of another massacre took the American media by storm. Once again, the protagonist was the Seventh Cavalry, yet this time as the assaulter. The *Omaha Bee* wrote of a "bloody battle" at the Pine Ridge Reservation, in which some three hundred Native Americans were killed, two-thirds of them women and children. Despite the clashes between the U.S. army and the Lakota Indians reported in the weeks running up to Pine Ridge, the violence of this confrontation seemed totally incongruous. Historians now recognize the Wounded Knee Massacre as one of the most infamous pages in the history of U.S.-Native American relations.[3]

Little Bighorn and Wounded Knee bookend the first phase of the history of the Socialist Labor Party (SLP). A week after Custer and his company died in Montana, socialists met in Philadelphia to found the Workingmen's Party of the United States. Fourteen years later, socialists debated the events of Wounded Knee while preparing to Americanize the party and start a new phase in the socialist movement in the United States (as chapter six will detail). During the Gilded Age, the history of Native Americans and that of American socialism run in parallel without much apparent interaction. Yet while firsthand contact between socialists and American Indians was minimal, the dramatic events unfolding on the western frontier shaped socialist thinking. It is high time to acknowledge that history.

Frederick Jackson Turner identified the frontier as "the meeting point between savagery and civilization." In Turner's opinion, in the far West, American men and women were forging a distinctive mentality that set the United States apart from the rest of the world: individualist, self-sufficient, free. The arrival in North America of colonists and traders had laid the foundations for the United States to prosper. And if that adventure was now drawing to a close with the closing of the frontier, contended Turner, still the experiment had been successful. The frontier was "the line of most rapid and effective Americanization."[4]

Socialists framed their analyses in the same language of "savagery" and "civilization" used by Turner. The "frontier thesis" provided an unmatched clarification of America's own cultural image, and Turner's thinking was heavily reliant on contemporary theories of evolutionism, anthropology, and race.[5] Yet despite the shared premises, Turner's and the socialists' conclusions could not be further apart. For SLP members, westward advancement revealed the moral and political bankruptcy of the American capitalist system. The SLP thought that the reiterated failure of the federal government on the frontier was the inevitable outcome of a problem that could not be solved. For the socialists, the annihilation of Native Americans served the interests of the American bourgeoisie. Furthermore, the greediness, immorality, and egotism of the frontiersmen clearly revealed that the American capitalist ideology was rotten to its core. The frontier may have been the place where "savagery" and "civilization" met, but the socialists insisted that the terms of this meeting should be reversed. In the encounter between different cultural, political, and social systems on the frontier, American capitalism played the role of the savage against an indigenous population whose humanity was obliterated by white colonialism.

While socialists had no trouble seeing the link between capitalism and settler colonialism, things got more complicated when it came to envisioning an alternative future for Native Americans that was compatible with their own socialist ideology. Part of these problems stemmed from broader shifts happening in the conversation on race and evolution happening in Europe and the United States in which socialists were enmeshed, where phrenology and other pseudoscientific approaches were being replaced by newly professionalized social scientific disciplines, such as anthropology. The "Indian Question" steered the SLP away from scientific racialism to more comprehensive ways of conceptualizing and understanding racial distinctions grounded on an analysis of social and cultural differences. Most commonly, socialists discussing Native Americans rejected the idea that Indians were inferior from a physical or biological point of view, while at the same time, they contended that Native Americans had less developed social and economic structures.[6]

Within the specifically German American socialist intellectual world, however, this broad shift was complicated by a drive to combine anthropological accounts with Marxist historical materialism. In the same period when the SLP debated the "Indian question" in the United States, founder of historical materialism, Karl Marx, dedicated much effort studying modern anthropological theories. Marx spent the last years of his life glossing works from the most important anthropologists of the day, in particular the American Lewis Henry Morgan. His *Ancient Society*, an encyclopedic collection of anthropological discoveries on non-capitalist peoples, enormously fascinated Marx. In Marx's opinion, this material proved that ancient peoples and peoples living in non-capitalist societies were not "backward" or "primitive." Contesting Morgan's own argument, Marx cautiously came to doubt the idea that the human species developed along a mono-linear stadial path—a concept that was the foundation of much scientific racialist and evolutionist thinking of the day.[7]

The full complexity of Marx's reflections on anthropology would not become known to the large public until decades later.[8] As a result, debates on the subject published in the SLP press were not influenced by Marx's point of view. At the same time, the analyses of SLP members on the "Indian question" reveal parallels with Marx's own thinking on the subject. American socialists struggled to reconcile their own critiques of capitalist settler colonialism with a socialist analysis of the problem because they used Western-centric conceptions of "modernity" and "progress" tied to simplistic, mono-linear notions of human development. Yet, at times, the discussions on the position of Native Americans within contemporary American society pushed American socialists to think creatively on the subject. Socialists saw American Indian societies as social environments that were not touched by capitalism, and therefore in need of being preserved and safeguarded. Moving past a biological definition of racism, socialist analyses of the "Indian question" led to questioning their own positionality as a "superior" race and culture in a way that was absent in the conversations on Chinese immigration and Black labor.[9]

Socialists debated the "Indian question" in a moment when the vast majority of Indian nations were being forced onto reservations, under full control of the U.S. government, with their youth taken away from them through newly established "assimilation programs." The last independent Indian nations adopted guerilla tactics to safeguard their remaining pockets of autonomy.[10] Surprisingly, to a certain extent, socialists missed much of the very material consequences that this work of displacement had for American capitalism. Railroad construction and land selling provided the material infrastructure that financed capitalist expansion in the Gilded Age and the Progressive Era.[11] At the same time, their critical voices furnished an arsenal of anti-colonial arguments grounded on materialist analysis and showed how socialists formulated original methods to attack capitalism and reject a bourgeois critique of civilization based on capital accumulation.

Early German Understandings of Native Americans

Before mass German immigration to the United States began in the 1820s, images of the American Indian populated German culture. According to historian H. Glenn Penny, across the nineteenth and twentieth centuries, Germans developed an "elective affinity" for Native Americans, a fascination that created a connection between the two peoples.[12] The favorable image Germans had of Native Americans led them to identify themselves with American Indians. Penny explained that, in the early nineteenth century, Germans used the literary production of a "triumvirate" of authors—Cornelius Tacitus, Alexander von Humboldt, and James Fenimore Cooper—to form their ideas of Native Americans.

Tacitus became a popular author thanks to Romantic nationalists such as Richard Wagner and Johann G. Herder. Tacitus's *Germania* described the German tribes as fierce opponents of the Roman empire, a representation that worked to provide the nascent German nation with a glorious history. Crucially, according to Penny, Germans made a connection between the anti-imperial struggle of the German tribes against Rome and the Native American resistance against U.S. aggression. In this way, Germans became supporters of the Native American cause.[13] With regard to Humboldt, Penny stressed that the German naturalist took a strong stance against the excesses of imperialism and spoke in favor of the Indian. He also set a key precedent by personally visiting South America and writing of his explorations. Other German intellectuals followed suit and visited the Great Plains in the United States in the 1820s and 1830s. In particular, the diary of Maximilian von Wied-Neuwied, *Travels in Inner North America in the Years 1832–1834*, codified "the image of the noble plains warrior." Illustrated by the Swiss painter Karl Bodmer, the book was published in German, French, and English from 1839 onward. Finally, Cooper's novels furnished material to inspire the imagination of the German reader. Cooper's *Leatherstocking Tales* centered on the adventures of the Indian-educated white Natty Bumppo and became the most frequently translated American book in Germany. Its countless reproductions played a key role in popularizing the image of Native Americans.[14]

Across the nineteenth century, this romantic image of the Native American competed with political and sociological considerations. Historian Jens-Uwe Guettel explained that German elites used the United States as a role model for their idealized projections of a unified imperial Germany. German intellectuals and political leaders were fascinated by the ability of the United States to mix republican ideals and an imperialist policy. In Guettel's words, for them, "America was living proof that empire and liberty were by no means mutually exclusive."[15] In this framework, Native Americans came to embody a vestige of the past threatened by the spread of "civilization" westward. Positions varied, from the rigid white supremacism of Immanuel Kant to the benevolent and moral fatalism of Friedrich List. But the bottom line remained the same: It was just a matter of time before Indians would become a thing of the past.[16]

Socialist sources reflected these fluctuations between benevolent Romanticism and disenchanted politics-driven social evolutionism. Penny spoke of a "disjuncture of cultural structures" to explain how favorable images of Native Americans clashed with the violence experienced by German American settlers on the frontier in the mid-1860s. He mentioned the example of a group of socialist members of a Turner club who moved from Cincinnati to the colony of New Ulm, Minnesota. Penny stressed that these socialist German Americans harshly criticized the inefficient and corrupt policy of the U.S. federal government toward Native Americans but failed to realize that their own presence on Indian lands was odious to the local Dakota groups. After the tensions turned to violence between the Indians and white settlers, the German immigrants silenced their criticisms of the federal government and realigned their position along racial lines.[17]

Articles written for socialist papers in the 1860s reveal further discrepancies between theory and practice when it came to the "Indian question" ("*die Indianer frage*"). The *Arbeiter Union*, the official paper of the Allgemeine Deutsche Arbeiter-Verein (United German Workers' Association) edited after September 1869 by Adolph Douai, offered a comprehensive analysis of U.S.–Native American relations.[18] The labor paper engaged the "Indian question" soon after the election of Ulysses S. Grant. Though it was an unsuccessful effort, Grant had been elected on a mandate to reduce the deployment of the Union army on the frontier and to end the policy of international treaties with Indian tribes that had shaped the federal approach since the eighteenth century.[19]

The *Arbeiter Union* shared many of the critiques that would lead to the changes introduced by Grant's administration. According to the German American labor paper, the treaty system was flawed, inefficient, and contradictory. For one, individual white traders were not allowed to interact with Native Americans, and the relationships between entire Native American nations and the United States were entrusted to a handful of "Indian agents" from the Bureau of Indian Affairs. These agents focused more on enriching themselves than on enforcing the terms of the treaties that Native Americans signed with Washington. "Indians . . . understand their contractual relationship quite correctly in terms of international law," wrote the *Arbeiter Union*. In this situation, it was not the alleged violent nature of the Native Americans to provoke episodes of violence against white settlers. Rather, it was the systematic violation of treaty terms by the American government. "When the patience [of Native Americans] is exhausted, they declare war on the faithless Union government in their traditional way. They threaten hostility. In the end, just like civilized belligerents, they hold themselves harmless against those whites who fall into their hands because they cannot fight the Union otherwise."[20]

The *Arbeiter Union* defended Native Americans from the accusation of savagism. Yet, at the same time, like the vast majority of the American public opinion, it envisioned for them a future of assimilation. The rejection of international treaties was part of a broader strategy for the gradual integration of Native Americans in the American society. "The [present] system is fundamentally wrong because it gives Indians sustainment without work, encourages them in their laziness, and is culture-adverse," wrote the *Arbeiter Union*. Invoking the example of the Six Nations in upstate New York and the Massachusetts Indians, "who learnt to practice agriculture, animal husbandry and trade," the article intoned that "Indians can and want to work, if they have no alternative but to fully abandon their wild habits and become useful citizens." Native Americans should receive "full civil rights under the ordinary civil jurisdiction" so that they are protected from "the arbitrary acts of violence" of white settlers. This approach, concluded the article, would bring peace on the frontier.[21]

In another article, different from the previous in content and tone, the *Arbeiter Union* introduced an argument about the cost of the government's policy toward the native population as a way to support the acculturation of the Indians of the Great Plains.[22] "This handful of wilds costs us a few million a year on annuities . . . the maintenance of at least two thirds of our standing army, which is around 20 million, plus other expenses every now and then if an Indian war begins." On top of these expenses, there were the "hundreds of lives and millions of stolen property that fall victim to these savages. This is what the wild Indians cost us."[23] To stop what they saw as a waste of federal money, the *Arbeiter Union* mentioned a policy of allotment. The article specified the size of the allotment each individual should receive (forty acres), adding that all tribes should be concentrated into one single territory ("an area to watch as big as one of our smaller states") and that their only contact with whites should be with teachers and "friends of the civilization of red-skins."[24]

Grant's attempts to pacify the frontier ended in failure. Under his watch, international treaties were abandoned in favor of creating reservations. Grant made use of representatives belonging to Christian religious communities to implement his Indian policy. They approached the Indian from a benevolent if paternalistic point of view, thinking that the way to prevent the extermination of Native Americans was by promoting their "civilization." But the presence of zealous Methodist or Quaker agents did not reduce the problem of endemic corruption within the Bureau of Indian Affairs; the cunning of the newly appointed agents often worsened the situation. Furthermore, despite its commitment to pacification, placing people on reservations relied on the use of the army, especially against those Indians who did not comply. Therefore, the period of the so-called peace policy was actually characterized by continued armed engagements on the frontier in a guerrilla-style confrontation that continued well into the 1880s.[25]

In this period, socialists shared some parts of the paternalistic approach of Grant's religious reformers. They disagreed on what policy would achieve their aim. Grant's philanthropists wanted to educate Native Americans to Christian precepts, and the reservation policy fit well with this intention. To have Native Americans organized in neatly defined areas, under the direct control of a single person, was ideal for weakening tribal societies and promoting new values and cultural systems. This policy went together with educational programs for Native American children, who were relocated to the East and educated according to "moral" and "civilized" standards of behavior, defined by the white man.[26] Conversely, socialists focused on a simplistic policy of allotment—a strategy that the federal government ultimately embraced in the 1880s.

At the heart of these policy differences were the fundamental philosophies adopted by Christian philanthropists on the one hand and socialists on the other. The former believed that change should be imposed on Native Americans through social and moral reeducation. Socialists, meanwhile, held that a change in Native American's economic structures—from hunting to farming—would be decisive. The priority accorded to economics reflected the socialists' historical materialist approach, here deployed in a simplistic, mono-linear fashion. They believed that if American Indians changed their systems of goods production, "acculturation" according to "civilized" standards would naturally follow. This was a necessary passage for a future progression toward socialism. In the early 1870s, socialist German Americans were observers of the Indian problem, even though their proposals differed only vaguely from those of the reformers in Washington, DC.

The SLP in the 1870s: Savage Capitalism

By the end of the decade, when socialists began again to discuss the problems of Indian integration and settlement, American politics had changed considerably. The president at the time, Rutherford B. Hayes, had to acknowledge the failure of the reservation policy, which had not eliminated armed conflicts or delivered the desired result of integration. Furthermore, Hayes needed to stop corruption in the Bureau of Indian Affairs, which was devouring public funds without yielding any significant outcomes.[27] The *New York Times* labeled the situation at the bureau "a disgrace to the Nation," based on an analysis of a damning report commissioned in 1877 by the newly appointed secretary of the interior, Carl Schurz.[28] That investigation, which lasted over six months, sparked a national crisis. Through intense lobbying and political pressure, Schurz prevented the move of the Bureau of Indian Affairs from the secretary of the interior to the minister of war—a measure that had been insistently called for in Washington.[29]

Socialist papers joined the chorus of voices attacking federal Indian policy. The so-called Indian question was arguably the most glaring example of the failure of the ruling class, consistent with the SLP's constant accusation against the rich for building economic prosperity on the backs of American workers. The bankruptcy of the federal plan showed the limits of an economic system based on greed and immorality. For socialists, debating the "Indian question" was a way to sharpen their arguments against the failure of industrial capitalism as a whole.

August Otto-Walster's *Volksstimme des Westens* was a leading voice on Native American affairs. The *Volksstimme* was the only socialist newspaper based in a frontier city, St. Louis, a place that felt the immediate consequences of the Indian wars fought on the Great Plains during the 1870s. Moreover, the *Volksstimme*'s heyday overlapped with Schurz's tenure as secretary of the interior (1877–1881). Schurz was a prominent political presence in Missouri; the state had elected him to the senate in the early 1870s, and he was one of the editors of the Republican daily *Westliche Post*. Schurz's central role in the reorganization of the Bureau of Indian Affairs made him an immediate political target for a socialist movement seeking to make inroads in the German American communities dominated by the Republican Party.[30]

The *Volksstimme des Westens* picked up the topic when Schurz nominated former Union army general O. O. Hammond as inspector of the Missouri Indian Bureau in June 1878. The nomination gave the *Volksstimme* a chance to educate its socialist readership on the extent of the corruption in the Bureau of Indian Affairs. Based on information revealed in the report of the Department of the Interior, the *Volksstimme* noted that bureau agents had been assigned a budget to purchase goods for the Native Americans. "Just imagine [General O.O. Hammond's] astonishment when he came to control the objects purchased for the Indians, and he found them not by the dozens, but by the thousands, stored in the basement, in the agent's office, in the dispensary, even in caves under the ground." Hundreds of items had been found, "unopened packages with knives, sabers, spoons . . . axes, files, hammers, saws, large bales of red and blue cloth, flannel, calico, blankets, shawls, large packages of twine, knitting and scissors, countless caps and hats, the finest fat man's suits, a thousand pounds of tobacco," all purchased to satisfy the avarice of the agents and never handed to Native Americans. The article explained that agents often interacted with Indian chiefs who could not read and write. They signed lists of requested materials in good faith, sometimes with the help of interpreters that bureau agents bribed in advance with a share of the ordered goods.[31] The *Volksstimme* was not surprised by the calls to move the Indian bureau away from the secretary of the interior, given the levels of corruption.[32] Socialists went as far as to side with the Democrats, who openly rejected Schurz's request for more funding to continue the Indian wars in the West. "There could hardly be more hideous wickedness than publicly demanding that millions of dollars more be spent on soldiers to shoot the poor Indians, killed by mischievous Republican officials under the prospect of the great Reform minister Karl Schurz."[33] A direct link between the violence against Native Americans on the frontier and the repression of workers' strikes in the American cities was drawn by socialists. In "inviting" Schurz to abandon his post and go back to running the editorial board of the *Westliche Post*, the *Volksstimme* referred back to when the paper had called for "the shooting of workers who fight for their rights," a method not far from the one proposed to solve the "Indian problem."

For socialists, the corruption in the Indian office was only part of the problem. Even if corruption were to disappear, the strategies proposed by the federal government—from appeasement to the use of reservations—were destined to fail for one reason and one reason only: capitalism. Socialists made this point by flipping the conversation as presented in the mainstream liberal and conservative press. If the objective of the federal government was to "civilize" savage Indians so they could join white society, the goal of socialists was to show that the capitalist system for which the Native Americans were being tamed was not "civilized" at all. In an article in the *New Yorker Volkszeitung*, the socialists did not hesitate to label as "dreadful" the atrocities perpetrated by the Apache and Chiricahua in Arizona and New Mexico.[34] Furthermore, they said that it was "very understandable" that citizens had directed a letter to the U.S. president asking him to act against the Indians. "But," continued the article, "one should not forget how the outbreak of the American Indian anger came into existence." Indian violence was caused by the repeated invasions of the reservation by white miners seeking to extract charcoal found on the Apache and Chiricahua's territory. Was it "any wonder if the wild original owners of the land lost patience and seized their arms?"

The story of a Native American scout and interpreter for the Union army, reprinted in the *Volksstimme* from the columns of the *Chicagoer Presse*, furthered the point. The interpreter belonged to the Union army battalion led by General Nelson A. Miles, who chased Nez Perce Indians across North Dakota and Oregon in the summer of 1877.[35] After that campaign was over, he traveled deep into Indian territory to find his daughter, who had been kidnapped by the Nez Perce during their precipitous attempt to reach Canada. He found her in the camp of Sitting Bull and brought her back unharmed. "They [the Indians] looked after them even without knowing the teachings of the 'Christian civilization.'"[36] The problem, continued the article, started when the interpreter and his daughter passed the "white borders." They were attacked and severely wounded by white settlers, and the woman was raped before her father's eyes. "This is the way in which the man was rewarded for being a loyal friend of the whites and the government . . . Is it any wonder why such civilization aspirations are not that understandable to Indians?"[37] This final passage, which recalled almost word for word the point made in the *New Yorker Volkszeitung*, captures why socialist activists contested the logic of "civilization" put forward by the federal government. White settlers' behavior revealed that they, not the Native American victims, were "savages." The essentialist racial and cultural hierarchies were turned upside down.

The socialists also used private property, another foundation of the capitalist system, to explore the contradictions of the federal approach toward Native Americans. The *Volksstimme* wrote that "the poor Indians are quite unlucky not to have conceived of and adopted the European culture and justice before. Had their native lands assured to themselves as legitimate landlords, how nicely they could live off their interests now, rather than being driven as homeless from place to place and deprived of one right after another."[38] The *Volksstimme* pointed to the contradiction of those middle-class reformers who, on the one hand, defended the "holiness" of private property, and on the other, did not recognize the property of the original inhabitants of the American continent. "Who were the first owners of the land before the Europeans came? . . . You fool Indian, why did you not hire pettifogging lawyers to arrange your real estate, or why did not you defend with your own life every inch of ground against those robbers who steal today where and what they can, instead of allowing [them] to deport you eternally westward with smooth words and contracts full of broken promises?"[39] In fact, Native Americans did defend every inch of their lands with their own lives. That was precisely what brought war and devastation to their communities.

The official SLP paper, *Sozialist,* put it bluntly in its July 18, 1885, issue: "For the Americans, the treatment of the Indians was simply a matter of expediency: if their lands were needed, they were driven out, regardless of contracts or promises, regardless of their (the Indians) rights or interests. No wonder that the Indians did not become 'peaceful' and steadfast, that they took every opportunity that seemed to provide an opportunity to destroy or chastise the hated intruders."[40] In an analysis that started with colonial America and went up to the present time, the socialist weekly wrote of the pattern of exploitation endured by Native Americans. They said that considering colonial America and then Jackson's removal of the civilized tribes and finally the policy in the late 1800s of placement on reservations (a policy widely undermined by railroad barons and western ranchers), the different outcome was unlikely to happen. The government "does provide Indians with means of subsistence as far as necessary, it pays many civil servants and grants funds to civilize the Indians, laws on laws are passed for their protection and for their elevation: futile efforts as long as there are capitalists, civil servants and chiefs that bribe and cheat the law with impunity."[41]

In July 1881, right after the end of his tenure as secretary of the interior, Carl Schurz published a long article on the Indian problem in the *North American Review.* Schurz immediately confessed "a fact too well known to require proof or to suffer denial," namely, "that the history of our Indian relations presents, in great part, a record of broken treaties, of unjust wars, and of cruel spoliation."[42] Searching for the origins of this situation, Schurz drew a distinction between the behavior of the federal government and that of white settlers. "It is also a fact that most of the Indian wars grew, not from any desire of the Government to disturb the Indians on the territorial possession guaranteed to them, but from the restless and unscrupulous greed of frontiersmen."[43] Schurz suggested that the government had its hands tied by the unstoppable force of settler colonialism. "In spite of all its good intentions and its sense of justice, the forces of the Government will find themselves engaged on the side of the white man. The Indians will be hunted down at whatever cost."[44] Schurz suggested that the choice for Native Americans was hard but inevitable: They could embrace white civilization and find a place in the Anglo-American society or face extermination. The conclusion of the July 1885 *Sozialist* article responded directly to Schurz's point. "The utter extermination is the tendency of the *civilization* method that has been practiced on the original inhabitants of this land."[45] Schulz presented the choice between civilization or extermination, but the *Sozialist* argued that this was a false alternative because capitalist civilization meant, by its very operation, the obliteration of Native Americans.

The Place of Native Americans in Socialist Teleology

Political commentary was not the only way in which Native Americans were featured in the socialist press during the Gilded Age. In the intellectual context of the time, the socialist community also wanted to take part in the widespread academic debate on Native Americans and race. Across Europe and the United States, the study of Native American cultures advanced the scientific conversation on human difference. The theories of racial differentiation produced by naturalists like Samuel Morton and Josiah C. Nott in the mid-nineteenth century, based on pseudoscientific measurements of crania and other body parts, were being overtaken. On the one hand, loose interpretations of Darwin's theories favored the growth of social doctrines that used evolution to interpret social, political, and economic interactions. On the other, an increased focus on social and cultural differences among human groups led to the birth of new scientific disciplines. In the United States, Lewis Henry Morgan distinguished himself as a pioneer in a field that adopted this second approach and was rapidly achieving intellectual independence and prestige: anthropology.[46]

Morgan became an anthropologist by chance. Early in his career as a lawyer in New York, he came in contact with the Seneca, a nation belonging to the Iroquois tribe. During his business trips to the tribe, he gathered evidence on the societal and cultural structures of that community. Across three decades of direct observation and study of the subject, Morgan built a theory of social evolution that he presented in his landmark publication,

Ancient Society, or Researches in the Lines of Human Progress from Savagery, through Barbarism to Civilization, published in 1877.[47] *Ancient Society* presented a system that divided the process of human evolution into three main stages—savagery, barbarism, and civilization. Morgan's categories were carefully constructed according to a series of principles, which included kinship and family systems, technology, institutions of government, property, and economic development. His work became the canon for the first generation of academically trained American anthropologists. His system was highly successful because it insisted on a rigid, scientifically determined taxonomy to classify human groups according to their cultural and social habits. It did not rely on arbitrary physical measures or other imprecise categorizations. At the same time, it incorporated evidence from other fields into a coherent whole. In the words of Steven Conn, "Morgan's theories married developments in geology, paleontology, and Darwinian evolution to human culture, and made the development of culture a natural process embracing the whole family of man."[48]

Karl Marx was among the intellectuals deeply impressed by Morgan. Upon receiving *Ancient Society*, Marx embarked upon a penetrating study and analysis of the book.[49] Historian Franklin Rosemont examined why, at the end of his life, the German philosopher dedicated so much time reading anthropological works and especially why he privileged Morgan's. According to Rosemont, "It was not mere 'anthropology' . . . that Marx found so appealing in Lewis Henry Morgan's *Ancient Society* but rather . . . the merciless critique and condemnation of capitalist civilisation that so well complements that of Charles Fourier." According to Rosemont, "*Ancient Society*, and especially its detailed account of the Iroquois, for the first time gave Marx insights into the concrete *possibilities* of a free society *as it had actually existed in history.*"[50] Morgan, in other words, with an impressive quantity of new information, brought to life what Marx and Engels called "primitive communism." He gave Marx food for thought about what a future communist society might resemble. Marx saw in Morgan's theory not only alternative examples of development but real models, existing in history, that worked better than contemporary capitalism.

A second generation of American anthropologists, led by Franz Boas, strongly criticized Morgan's work for its implicit ethnocentrism. Despite the richness of his data, Boas and others argued, Morgan had designed a mono-linear scale of progress, which misrepresented the diversity of human groups and ultimately put whites at the top of human evolution.[51] Marx did not see things this way. Rather, he stressed the ways in which Morgan's teleological schema contradicted itself and revealed the progress of allegedly "primitive" societies—societies which Marx saw as essentially superior, "in human terms, to the degraded civilisation founded on the fetishism of commodities," as Rosemont put it. As a result, Marx saw Morgan's work as a powerful scientific tool against those who identified the notion of progress with industrial capitalism.[52]

For a long time, the extent of the multilinearity of Marx's thought has remained obscure. Immediately after Marx's death in 1883, Engels took the extensive notes Marx had written on Morgan and published them under the title *The Origin of the Family, Private Property, and the State*. This book elevated Morgan's *Ancient Society* to the status of a core text of Marxist ideology, conferring on the American anthropologist a "strange posthumous career" amongst Marxist thinkers.[53] Only after the publication of a critical edition of Marx's notes by Lawrence Krader in 1971, however, did it become clear that Engels's book only partially reproduced the complexity of Marx's ideas. Engels's work actually favored a mechanistic interpretation of Morgan, which meshed more readily with Engels's own understanding of *Ancient Society* than it did with Marx's annotations. Kevin B. Anderson, building on Raya Dunayevskaya's reflections on the subject, fully reconstructed Marx's vision of a non-linear pathway to socialism—one that acknowledged specific social, economic, and political circumstances across the world.[54]

SLP members in their party press in the late 1870s and early 1880s were not cognizant of Marx's notes on Morgan nor did they have familiarity with Engels's *The Origins of the Family*, which was published in 1884. Yet the socialist press' theoretical explorations on the future of Native Americans in the United States allowed the SLP readership to tap into a problem whose significance was crucial not only in the United States but across the western socialist world. Was the socialist commonwealth the inevitable final step of a mono-linear evolution that started with savagism and continued with barbarism and capitalism? Or could socialism be achieved through different paths and in different ways according to specific economic, social, and cultural features? While many Second Internationalists writing in the 1890s and early twentieth century embraced a rigid mono-linearism, revealing a problematic Eurocentrism approach to the issue, when the SLP press published on the topic, things were hardly settled.[55]

An article published in the *Chicagoer Vorbote* in 1882 discussed the "civilization skills" (*zivilisationsfähigkeit*) of Native Americans and showed that socialists had an interest in adopting modern scientific racialism in discussing the issue of Native Americans. "From a scientific point of view, the question of the civilization skills of Indians is judged differently than what can be done from the standpoint of philanthropy," claimed the opening words of the article.[56] Samuel Morton's phrenology was the main polemical target. Morton had used cranial measurements to make a case for a physiologically determined inferiority of Native Americans. The socialist article rejected the premise that physiology had any use as a standard for judging levels of "civilization." The article outlined the many contradictions in Morton's data: Peruvians and Mexicans, who had produced the most advanced pre-Colombian societies, had an average skull size of 72 cubic inches, while the "wild" Indians averaged 82 cubic inches. Creeks, Iroquois, and Inuits averaged 87 to 88, like Caucasians, but the Cherokees, the "most gifted" among the civilized Indian tribes, did not go past 75 cubic inches, which was less than the average cranic size of African Americans (78). But these contradictions did not matter, sarcastically quipped the article, as "those who believe in phrenology, like Morton, always have their answers to such questions ready in advance." In other words, that Morton's own data contradicted his theories was irrelevant because his ideas on Native Americans were based on prejudices, not facts.

The socialist article maintained that assessing the "civilization skills" of Native Americans was simply impossible. It would require "centuries" in which they lived in the same social, political, and economic situation as Europeans and Anglo-Americans before being able to judge. Without considering, added the article, the fact that certain Native American nations had already proven their capability to adopt "civilized" institutions in the 1830s—attempts that were mercilessly crushed by President Jackson, in whose eyes "Indians had no rights. They were red people, not people."[57]

The *New Yorker Volkszeitung* suggested that a "passage" through capitalism was pointless for Native Americans, who had already adopted a "superior" form of social organization based on collectivism. A piece in the *Volkszeitung* discussed Indian policy in 1882, right after Samuel J. Kirkwood had replaced Carl Schurz as secretary of the interior. The article raised several objections against the policy of allotment, recently introduced by the government. One such objection contested the idea that introducing private property among Native Americans would favor their already full-blown "civilization." "We should rather ask ourselves whether they are more advanced [than us] in the path towards civilization." The article pointed out that in several states, Native Americans had already embraced agriculture, trade, stock-raising, and arts and crafts—all without abandoning the practice of common lands. "What compel or seduce the Indians to become accustomed to the vices of capitalism? . . . Why stimulate them to give up the feeling of mutual commitment (solidarity) for one another, in which there is more genuine religion than in all the official Christianity?" Faithful in the near advent of socialism, the article saw no reason to ask Native Americans to embrace a social model that "will probably not survive the end of the century anywhere in the accultured world."[58]

The debate on allotment, which continued for years in the early 1880s as the federal government sought to put its policy into practice, gave socialists endless occasions to comment on the controversial issue of how to "civilize" Native Americans. While some hinted at the idea that no work of civilization was needed, as Native Americans were already "free" of the nefarious influence of capitalism, others in the movement disagreed. In 1884, the *New Yorker Volkszeitung* reported on the military campaign against the Apaches in the Southwest, led by General George Crook. Crook had decades of experience on the frontier, having fought the Snake Indians in the 1864–1868 Snake War, and the Sioux in the Great Sioux Wars of 1876–1877. The socialist newspaper clearly showed its admiration for the general, who was renowned for treating Indians fairly and justly.[59] On this occasion, the *Volkszeitung* endorsed the general's proposal to grant allotments to individuals and not tribes as a whole. Their argument defending this policy was in stark contrast to the position the newspaper had defended two years prior: "The Indian communism looks like that of the ancient people—it needs to go through a preliminary stage of private property, to fork out the earthy inertia, the lack of independence and the tribal ferocity, and later to be allowed to upgrade to the higher level of the scientific communism anticipated by the whites."[60]

Here, the *Volkszeitung* posited scientific communism as a future stage of human development, confirming its adhesion to a mono-linear version of Marxian historical materialism. What is significant here is that scientific communism was given a racial connotation and became the evolutionary stage of "whites." Anthropology was used to define "Indian communism's" positive aspects as something that could be reclaimed after a passage through private property had relieved the native people of their savagery. Scientific communism, then, was not only the future stage of human development in a historical materialist sense; it was also the pinnacle of the evolutionary scale from an anthropological point of view. This implied that only whites, namely, those who lived in advanced industrial economies, could access the level of evolution that came after capitalism. Native Americans, conversely, had yet to go through the entire process of "evolution."

The *Sozialist* concurred in a November 1885 article. The issue arose in the discussion on the impact of allotment on the civilization of wild Indians. The article gave an extensive description of the doubts President Cleveland and secretary of interior Lucius Lamar had and then went on to attack Lamar's belief that Christianization was a key element in advancing the process of Indian integration. The article recalled the failure of Grant's Christian agents. "How is it possible that a Christian . . . mind, who holds his doctrine of 'eternal truth' that must remain valid under all circumstances, at all times and in all nations, can be an effective teacher?!"[61] The journalist who wrote the article did not jettison the whole of Christianity, conceding that it had useful principles that could be used to promote the civilization of Indians. But relying on anthropology and the dynamics of social evolution, he explained that it was naïve to think Native Americans could turn into Christians in the blink of an eye. "Indians are asked to develop in a couple of decades of training courses what the humanity earned in millennia of culture." The positive elements of the Christian religion would need time to flourish according to the slow dynamics of social evolution, and furthermore, an "individualist phase" was necessary. Ultimately, the *Sozialist* agreed with the allotment plans discussed by Cleveland and Lamar. "That private property, individualism and the competitive economy have been a good school for humanity and would also be for the Indians, this is unmistakable." These words written by a socialist, as strange as they may be to read, show just how engrained social evolutionism was within German American socialist thought. Individualism was seen as nothing more than "a transition to socialist communism," and, in fact, it was necessary to set Native Americans on this correct path.

A final thought expressed in poetic terms concluded this dense article. "Following the poet's words: 'the tree of humanity urges its flowers to bloom.' The Indian, like the Semite, the Asian and the Negro, is a variety of the human flowering."[62] Therefore, even if the Native American communist culture had to be abandoned, their extermination was not acceptable. Native Americans had a place in the future socialist society. It is important to understand the intellectual tension behind these words. The *Sozialist* author was not rejecting the anthropological tenets that held that Native Americans were inferior to whites nor did he want to stop the social and cultural development of what he categorized as white culture. What he did maintain was that this development must include *all* human "flowers." The socialist thinker formulated this opinion in a pre-Boasian framework. He did not consider that to assimilate Native Americans within white society was already to obliterate their cultural diversity—and, to some extent, was an uprooting of human "flowers." Even if he lacked sensitivity with regard to the survival of Indian culture, this journalist writing in the socialist press wanted to make sure that the Indian human group was seen as part of the future of humanity.

Conclusions

After the Wounded Knee massacre in 1890, the conservative *New Yorker Staats Zeitung* revisited the distinction between extinction and civilization to analyze the event. "The great majority of the remaining indigenous people of this country will only become 'good' at all if they are either exterminated or if they are forced to earn their daily bread through honest work in the sweat of their brow." Socialists were stunned by what they read. "The exterminated Indians will be 'good!'" Indeed, that was "an ingenious capitalist solution to the problem," wrote the *Volkszeitung*.[63] In 1893, Frederick Jackson Turner declared that the frontier was closed. In reality, clashes in the West continued well into the twentieth century. The problem was not solved. It was just that whites had stopped paying attention to it.[64] By then, socialists had perfected their anti-capitalist message with regard to the Native American problem. Calls for "extermination" were invoked in the capitalist press to stop Native American violence—a violence that was produced by the infamous conditions in which the federal government forced Native American nations. "And this worthless faithless and rapacious scum of civilization grumbles about the faithlessness and greed of the barbarians and savages!" erupted the *Volkszeitung* after Wounded Knee.

In parallel with this perfecting of an anti-capitalist message, the evidence analyzed in this chapter sheds light on the ways in which socialists progressively replaced scientific racialist discourses of racial inferiority with analyses focused on levels of civilization, i.e., social and economic development. They abandoned theories such as Morton's and replaced them with authoritative contemporary sciences, such as anthropology and historical materialism. In doing so, they forged new discourses on race that went beyond simplistic forms of biological racism. But the hesitations and contradictions of SLP members show that the passage from one approach to the other was not smooth and immediate. While rejecting scientific racialism, at times, socialists continued to replicate the same tendencies of racial "essentialization" proper of mid-nineteenth century American racist thinkers; they kept ascribing social and cultural attitudes to the "nature" or innate essence of each racial group, going back to languages and approaches born in the first part of the century with the deliberate objective of proving the inferiority of certain racial groups. Sometimes, socialists celebrated Native American communities as free from the nefarious influence of capitalism. In so doing, the SLP walked the same path that Karl Marx moved along in his explorations of Morgan's theories. Ultimately, the socialist debate on the "Indian question" captured a phase of development within socialist thought, with trends that started in the 1880s and fully matured only in the 1890s, when the SLP entered a new phase of its history under the leadership of Daniel De Leon.

CHAPTER 6

The SLP in the 1890s

Americanization and Socialist Evolutionism

In 1899, the Socialist Labor Party (SLP) celebrated International Workers' Day with a special edition of its English-language weekly, the *People*. On the cover, they put the image of a woman representing liberty and equality, descending from her throne to help men and women break the chains that bind them. In a smaller image below, a group of individuals holds aloft a banner with the word "unity" emblazoned on it. The line of figures was notable for its racial diversity and included, from left to right, an African American man (with the aesthetic features of the slave Gordon in the famous 1863 image from *Harper's Weekly*), two white women, a Native American man, three white men, and a Chinese man.[1] The special edition was designed to celebrate the achievements of the organization and to galvanize its activists. The number of party sections had more than tripled in the previous five years, and the party had received a record 80,000 votes in the 1898 elections. At the end of the century, the SLP was going through arguably one of the most successful periods in its history.[2]

The celebratory issue of the *People* attested to the changes in the party's racial policy. The cover image, an explicit celebration of interracial and international solidarity, and the articles throughout the paper made it clear that the socialist organization had formulated a new way to understand racial diversity in the 1890s, an approach based on the centrality of class solidarity among workers of different racial and ethnic backgrounds. The SLP had always focused on class exploitation as a key category of analysis rather than racial discrimination. Members of the party had repeatedly, if inconsistently and with varied perspectives, acknowledged and addressed certain aspects of race and ethnicity as factors in their thinking and their politics. But the ideas conveyed in the special issue of the *People* represented

FIGURE 6. *The People*, May 1, 1899.

a decisive consolidation of the party's focus on class while acknowledging racial diversity.[3]

The SLP's emergence as a national organization played a crucial role in this transition. The 1890s saw the SLP become more directly involved in organized labor on a national level. In the transition from the composite radical movement of the early Gilded Age to the American Federation of Labor's (AFL) "prudential unionism," socialists proposed alternative (if unsuccessful) strategies to reinvent labor unionism, expand workers' rights, and change American capitalism.[4]

In parallel ways, the ethnic outlook of the American socialist movement also changed, opening up prospects for growth in the twentieth century. For many scholars, it was not until the founding of the Socialist Party of America (SPA) in 1901 that the United States had a distinctively American socialist tradition, with an American membership and a significant (if short-lived) presence on the American political scene. Scholars of U.S. socialism regularly dismiss the SLP for its ethnic composition. Theodore Draper, for example, contended that the SLP "was never more than an American head on an immigrant body." Despite a small presence of American activists at the top of the organization, suggested Draper, the SLP never managed to extend its influence beyond a few ethnic enclaves. Similarly, Gary Marks and Seymour Martin Lipset argued that "for many years the SLP 'was a small Turnverein whose members hassled over old world politics'" and in which "early meetings were conducted in German." The birth of the SPA works well as the jumping-off point for a history of the socialist movement that organically developed within the "American century."[5] At times, when the narrative on American socialism stretches back to include precursors of the movement, two intellectuals, authors of bestselling English-language socialist books, are mentioned: Laurence Gronlund, author of *The Cooperative Commonwealth*, and Edward Bellamy, author of *Looking Backward: 2000–1887*. The success of their two books confirms that Gronlund and Bellamy could translate socialism into a language comprehensible to the American working class—something that foreign socialists had failed to do up to that point.[6]

This narrative rests on making a distinction between "American" and "foreign" socialism that was hard to recognize at the time and was already being contested when the SPA was founded. It is beyond doubt that the socialist movement had grown organically in immigrant communities and that this sometimes complicated the movement's advance. At the same time, one should not forget the size of the immigrant community in America's northern and midwestern cities at the end of the nineteenth century nor the extent to which immigrant and native workers interacted. Political activism overcame ethnic barriers, especially in radical movements. Through political activism, immigrants carved out a space for themselves in American society, often "Americanizing" the movements that had originally been so "foreign."[7]

The SLP in the 1890s provides an example of just such a trend. Socialists relied on large German American and Jewish trade union federations whose influence came to full maturation in the final decade of the century. The links between the SLP and the unions put the party in the condition to flourish in this period, while the crisis of 1893 reignited labor activism across the country. The party further contributed to its relaunch through a new leadership and party organization. Under the controversial Marxist thinker Daniel De Leon, a polyglot and cosmopolitan intellectual who was at ease both among foreign and English-speaking workers, the party completed a bold plan of "Americanization" while bridging the distance between the various ethnic communities that animated it.[8]

De Leon also presided over the consolidation and clarification of the party's approach toward race. In the 1890s, the *People*—the official English-language paper that replaced the *Workmen's Advocate* in 1891—articulated a Marxist theory firmly rooted in social evolutionism. Unlike German American socialists in the 1880s, De Leon's SLP rejected biology-based scientific racialism and denounced Spencerism, calling it a bourgeois doctrine that justified inhumane social and economic policies by distorting Darwinism. Lewis Henry Morgan became the guiding light who had given American workers the key to interpret American society. But the 1890s SLP abandoned the flirtation with non-linear stadial thinking that had characterized their reflections on Native Americans in the 1880s. Instead, the SLP embraced a plan that tied historical materialism to Morgan's anthropology in a coherent if simplistic evolutionist theory that placed socialism as the inexorable future of world history. In this theoretical scheme, racism was an evil that would disappear along with the other injustices suffered by American workers. In this way, in the 1890s, the SLP resolved the contradictions that had characterized its approach in the previous decades.

But the strengths of the renewed SLP also contained seeds of its weaknesses. The clarity that had made the SLP's political message intelligible to so many workers across ethnic barriers was gained by oversimplifying Marx's historical materialism to the point where it was almost unrecognizable. In the SLP's propaganda, Marx's capacious and evolving critical method became an infallible theory predicting the course of social events with precision—socialists had nothing to do but to prepare to govern the impending change. Animated by an unshakeable faith in the advent of socialism, the SLP squandered the countless occasions that arose in this conflict-ridden decade—from cooperating with the People's Party in the early 1890s to steering the AFL away from its conservative turn. But the most important and most egregiously neglected opportunity that the SLP missed was the chance to build a multiracial and multiethnic coalition to support its socialist program. While distancing itself from social racialism and biology-based racial theories, the NYC-based group that led the party did not clearly tackle racial inequality nor did they offer support to racial minorities. In fact, ultimately the aggressive policy of Americanization proposed by De Leon shattered the multiethnic coalition that had supported the socialist movement up to that point. By embracing a socialist version of evolutionism, the SLP mounted a principled defense of racial equality and laid the foundations for a conversation on race that could continue into the twentieth century. But the political opportunities opened by this shift were not met, and instead, a disastrous split in 1899 turned the SLP into an irrelevant political sect.

Americanization and Evolutionism in Daniel De Leon's SLP

In the 1890s, two shifts linked to the ethnic and racial makeup of the SLP took place. First, the party began a process of Americanization of its structures and membership. From the 1890s on, party documents were available exclusively in English, and there were also changes in the composition of the membership, the party strategy, and its perspective on the future. Second, the party's racial platform embraced a mixture of evolutionism and historical materialism, thus easing many of the tensions that had previously existed in socialist racial policy. This shift transformed the socialists' political message, though it rarely translated into viable policies. Both of these developments were already evident in the political trajectory and works of Danish American leader Laurence Gronlund in the 1880s. They came to fruition under Daniel De Leon in the 1890s.

Gronlund's personal and political trajectory embodied the hybrid nature of American socialism of the period. Historian Howard H. Quint called Gronlund's 1884 *The Cooperative Commonwealth* the first attempt by an American socialist writing in English to provide "a comprehensive yet simplified analysis of Marxism for the man of the street."[9] Gronlund himself described his book as the first exposition of "socialism—*modern* Socialism, *German* socialism, which is fast becoming *the* Socialism the world over" as presented "by a writer possessing the American bias towards the practical."[10] Gronlund wanted to Americanize socialism, but by default, he did it as an immigrant from the ranks of the SLP. Gronlund was born in Denmark in 1848. He studied law in Copenhagen and Milwaukee, was admitted to the Illinois bar in 1868, and practiced law until the late 1870s. Mark Pittenger suggested that Gronlund, under the name of Peter Lofgreen, resurfaced in 1877 when he took part in the St. Louis general strike as a member of the WPUS strike committee. This circumstance is disputed in a document written by the real Peter Lofgreen, a Swedish Mormon who briefly joined the labor movement in 1877 before returning to Utah that same year.[11] Who took part in the 1877 St. Louis strike is still unclear. What is certain is that Gronlund authored the pamphlet *The Coming Revolution*, which the SLP used as its chief propaganda tool in the English language across the 1880s (the pamphlet was eventually turned into the last chapter of *The Cooperative Commonwealth* in 1884).[12] After a brief sojourn in the U.K., Gronlund was back to the United States in 1886. Between 1886 and 1890, he was a proactive party member, joining the National Executive Committee (NEC) in 1888.[13]

In the preface to the 1890 edition of *The Cooperative Commonwealth*, Gronlund claimed that "one of the happiest effects of my book is that it has led indirectly, and perhaps unconsciously, to Mr. Bellamy's *Looking Backward*."[14] While Bellamy never corroborated this claim, it is entirely plausible that he took inspiration from the most important explanation of socialism in the English language available at the time. Gronlund's book was popular, with 100,000 copies sold between the United States and the United Kingdom across several editions. But it could not compete with the enormous success of Bellamy's novel, which topped 400,000 copies in the United States alone and was translated into all the main European languages.[15] *Looking Backward* effectively translated socialism into a story that anyone could relate to. Denouncing the social problems caused by capitalism, the book pictured a futuristic utopia in which a national system solved all issues through centralized planning and organization. Gronlund so warmly embraced Bellamy's book that he even denied permission for any more reprints of his own work to clear the way for the sale of Bellamy's book.[16] Perhaps it was Gronlund's presence on the SLP's NEC that made the socialists embrace the Nationalist Clubs in the late 1880s. The *Workmen's Advocate* regularly reported on the initiatives of the Nationalist Clubs scattered around the country. At the end of the 1880s and in the first years of the 1890s, the SLP and the Nationalist Clubs insistently sought ways to cooperate. Gronlund was an open supporter of these attempts.[17]

It was through these connections that De Leon eventually moved from the nationalist movement to the SLP in 1890. In the late 1880s, when various factions of the party were embroiled in a ruthless fight for control of the organization, the socialist press took close note of De Leon's frequent speaking tours around the country, undertaken in support of Bellamy's nationalist movement. In early 1890, De Leon took part in a meeting to organize a mass protest against the school policy proposed by the city of New York, chaired by the SLP's Lucien Sanial and attended, amongst others, by Florence Kelley. Both De Leon and Kelley represented Nationalist Clubs. At the event, De Leon replaced an incapacitated Bellamy and read his address to the crowd. Amongst the speakers were Samuel Gompers and Peter J. McGuire. In the summer of 1890, the SLP and the nationalists tried to forge a national coalition without success. After that failed attempt, some areas continued to fill joint candidates or have joint sections.[18] In October

1890, De Leon still "spoke on behalf of the Nationalists" and turned down an offer to head a joint nationalist-SLP ticket for New York City mayor.[19]

In 1891, after the group publishing the *New Yorker Volkszeitung* emerged as the leading faction of the SLP, De Leon was given the important role of vice editor of the newly founded English-language the *People*. One year later, when Lucien Sanial stepped down from the editorship of the paper for health reasons, De Leon took his place. Through this position as editor of the English-language weekly of the organization, he turned the paper into the main propaganda tool of the party and swiftly gained control over the politics of the SLP. He retained this position without interruption until his death in 1914.[20]

One may wonder why the German American socialist leadership, accustomed to quarreling over Marxist orthodoxy and jealously guarding its organization from external influence, allowed a new convert like De Leon to scale the hierarchy of the party so quickly. Several factors converged to make De Leon the right person in the right place at the right time. For one, De Leon had an intellectual and personal background that sparked the interest of the immigrant SLP leadership. The son of a well-off Sephardic family, De Leon had a prestigious academic record from German schools and Dutch academia.[21] Once he arrived in the United States, he had nearly gotten a tenured academic job at Columbia—only to see it denied for political reasons.[22] De Leon spoke fluent German, French, Portuguese, and, of course, English. He was trained in classics, law, history, and sociology. After his espousal of Marxism in 1890, he immersed himself in the study of historical materialism. De Leon was a cosmopolitan intellectual with an unshakable commitment to the cause of workers' rights—seemingly the perfect person to lead the multiethnic working-class communities the SLP sought to organize.[23]

In addition to his prestigious background, De Leon had a strong personality and imposing leadership style that connected perfectly with the SLP. Abraham Cahan, a leading figure in the NYC Jewish socialist community, second only to the German American community in terms of size and importance, recorded his first impressions of De Leon, saying he was "a supremely brilliant speaker and lecturer, being a highly educated and capable person possessing powerful faculties of oratory. His addresses were at all times profound, crystal clear, and scrupulously logical and interesting." Cahan recalled the first lecture on Marx's theory delivered by De Leon and claimed that "perhaps this was the best exposition on Marxian ideas that had ever been heard in New York." For Cahan, De Leon "was an important acquisition. Since [Sergei E.] Schevitsch we had no one with as forceful a personality."[24] Jewish writer Leon Kobrin shared Cahan's opinion, writing that "none of the Socialist leaders [were] for a time so adored among the

Socialists, and particularly by the Jewish socialists, as he . . . De Leon, broad and middle height, with a dark-bronzed oriental face, a beard of soft white down and the eyes of a 20-year-old impassioned youth."[25]

Thanks to the trust earned among the notables of the party, De Leon pressed ahead with the Americanization of the SLP—a process often announced but never before put into practice. In 1888, the SLP had adopted a platform whose opening words recalled Thomas Jefferson's Declaration of Independence: "The Socialist Labor Party of the United States, in convention assembled, reasserts the inalienable right of all men to life, liberty, and the pursuit of happiness."[26] Under De Leon's leadership, words were followed by deeds, ranging from political aspects to cultural and theoretical ones. While the German-language *Sozialist* moved outside the party, becoming the weekly edition of the *New Yorker Volkszeitung*, the English-language

FIGURE 7. Portrait of Daniel De Leon. 1900. Library of Congress, George Grantham Bain Collection, Prints and Photographs Division, LC-B2-1304-2.

the *People* became the SLP's leading organ.[27] Through the party press, the new leadership set its chief political goal straight: to "bore from within" and turn into recruiting pools the two largest union federations existing in the United States, the AFL and the Knights of Labor. While previous generations of SLP members had split between trade unionists and party ballot activists, in this period, the socialists' strategy was coordinated. De Leon, exercising tight control of the New York City sections, led the attempt to infiltrate the Knights of Labor via the District Assembly 49 and the United Hebrew Trades. Members of the Chicago sections moved independently to lead the assault on the AFL.[28]

In the meantime, the *People* became a consistent and articulated compendium of socialist pedagogy, where the theories of Marx were used to illustrate to American workers the reasons for their exploitation. Week by week, the *People* offered expositions on the key tenets of historical materialism, the theory of salaries, and Marx's law of value. As well, the *People* hosted many English-language translations of Marxian classics, and the SLP established a party publishing house, the New York Labor News Company.[29] The SLP did not simply limit himself to translating Marx; it strove to frame the doctrine in American cultural language. An example of this effort is the "Uncle Sam and Brother Jonathan" series written by De Leon. This weekly column featured fictional debates between Uncle Sam, the personification of the United States but also a scholarly and opinionated expert on Marx, and Brother Jonathan, an American worker unfamiliar with the dynamics of the American economy and organized labor. It is perhaps too facile to identify Uncle Sam with De Leon himself, the "red pedagogue" devoted to the education of the naïve American worker. But the fact that he chose Uncle Sam to represent his own recasting of the SLP reveals the most profound objective of the series. The leader of the SLP aimed to link the socialist point of view with the pillars of American culture, permanently departing from the idea that socialism was an imported ideology.[30]

The Americanization of the SLP coexisted with the party's consolidation of a solid multiethnic base. In fact, the two apparently contradictory processes reflected the broader developments of the decade. Socialists continued significant recruitment in the immigrant population, even though the composition of the immigrant influx into the party changed over time. While the number of socialists arriving from Germany slowed down as a result of the abolition of the anti-socialist laws in 1890, other immigrant groups grew in size and significance, especially the Jewish, Bohemian, Scandinavian, and Italian communities. Adopting the socialist movement became a means through which immigrants could integrate into American society. So Americanization and ethnicization of the party continued in parallel: While De Leon and the NYC leadership perfected the translation into American vernacular of Marx's ideology in the *People*, immigrant communities strengthened their ties with unions across the country and started their own socialist language papers.[31]

Alongside the change in the ethnic outlook—and look—of the party, clarity on the intellectual foundation of the SLP's racial policy also took place in the 1890s. The *People* offered a version of Marxian socialism that relied on social evolution. This had straightforward consequences for the party's approach to race. This shift toward evolutionist historical materialism started with Laurence Gronlund in the 1880s and continued with De Leon in the 1890s. Gronlund's *The Cooperative Commonwealth* fused Marxism and social evolutionism. Gronlund's embrace of historical materialism was rooted in the political economy of David Ricardo and Adam Smith. At the same time, he replaced Marx's Hegelian dialectic with a teleological and progressive evolutionism nurtured in Spencerian organicism. Gronlund believed that the class conflict between labor and capital would solve itself when the trusts, grown to an incontrollable size, were replaced by a national trust led by the people—the cooperative commonwealth. Mark Pittenger stressed that "the trust epitomized the concentration of capital and socialization of production that would mark the end of private ownership." It was the triumph of the "organic over the individual," with the cooperative commonwealth representing a positive monopoly that would guarantee harmony among the various part of the society.[32] "*The Coming Revolution is strictly an Evolution*" wrote Gronlund in the introduction of his book, stressing the teleological and evolutionist nature of his socialism.[33]

De Leon shared Gronlund's outlook but brought it more in line with his own intellectual background, which was a mix of positivism, anti-Spencerism, and materialist teleology. De Leon created a rigid identification between "natural laws" and "social laws," and more precisely, between "biology" and "sociology." In "Reform or Revolution," a programmatic speech delivered in 1896, De Leon declared that "the laws that rule sociology run upon lines parallel with and are the exact counterparts of those that natural science has established in biology."[34] As a biologist studies the laws of nature to understand the evolution of living beings, so the sociologist studies the laws of social interaction to understand the evolution of society:

> In the first place, the central figure in biology is the species, not the individual specimen. In sociology, the economic classes take the place of the species in biology. Consequently, that is the central figure on the field of sociology that corresponds to and represents the species on the field of biology. In the second place, struggle, and not piping peace; assimilation

> by the ruthless process of the expulsion of all elements that are not fit for assimilation, and not external coalition—such are the laws of growth in biology, and such are and needs must be the laws of growth in sociology.

Through this straightforward analogy, De Leon identified class struggle as the organizing principle of social conflict, in the same way as "assimilation" governed biological processes. "Socialism," continued De Leon, "recognizes in modern society the existence of a struggle of classes, and the line that divides the combatants to be the economic line that separates the interests of the property-holding capitalist class from the interests of the propertiless class of the proletariat."[35]

De Leon's repudiation of Herbert Spencer ran along lines of class. While Spencer continued to influence De Leon, an editorial published in the inaugural issue of the *People*, likely written by De Leon, indicated that Spencer's middle-class upbringing was the reason his theory was "illogical" and incompatible with a convincing analysis of social evolution. De Leon attacked Spencer's assault on socialism, which had started in the mid-1880s and was updated in the American context in the 1890s.[36] Without abandoning Spencer's fundamental intuition—that evolution regulated not just the development of animals and the humankind but human social interaction as well—De Leon contested the way in which Spencer applied his theory to the present society. "Survival of the fittest," the editorial insisted, ought to be replaced by class struggle operating according to the "social laws" that a Marxist, logical, and rigorous analysis made evident. Spencer may have been gifted with a "broad mind" and a "great heart," yet his views were "more or less narrowed by the limited horizon of [the middle class], which selfishly considers itself the whole world and identifies the progress of mankind with its own progress." One of the missions of the newborn *People* was to reply to the intellectuals of the Spencer school and show "the actual course of social evolution."[37]

Along with this rejection of Spencerism came a wholehearted endorsement of Lewis Henry Morgan's anthropological theories. In the words of Paul Buhle, "DeLeon had been converted to Socialism by reading in tandem Engels's *Anti-Dühring* and Lewis Henry Morgan's anthropology." De Leon's enthusiasm for the American anthropologist came through in his speeches and articles. As Marxist sociology explained the latest phase of human evolution, so Morgan's anthropology clarified the evolutionary passages that had led to the current stage. Seneca Indians popped up in De Leon's lectures on reform, revolution, and anarchism and offered simplified examples of the origins of private property and capitalism.[38] In the meantime, De Leon rearticulated socialism as the final stage of a process of social and cultural development that was tightly related to the specifics of American history. In an article significantly titled "The Philosophy of the History of Political Parties," De Leon sketched his theory of the immediate future of American society. The socialist leader divided American history into three phases and contended that each was intimately connected to the "historical mission" of a party. The Democratic Party, "born by the democratic breath of Thomas Jefferson," had contributed to the history of the country by defeating the elitist tendencies of Hamilton and identifying freedom as the leading American value. The Republican Party, "born of a people's determination to abolish chattel slavery; inspired by Lincoln's great motto 'this country must be either all slave or all free,'" had the mission of establishing liberty for all after the Civil War. The third phase—yet to come—would be led by the socialist movement. The Democratic and the Republican Parties would soon disappear. De Leon maintained that the SLP was the one most likely to pick up the torch of freedom and lead the United States toward universal emancipation.[39]

In many ways, De Leon's ideology resolved the intellectual tensions observed in socialist literature in previous decades. German American intellectuals of the 1870s and 1880s debated which one between scientific racialism, geographic determinism, Darwinism, or Spencer's "survival of the fittest" was the best approach to understand human differences. De Leon cut the Gordian knot by firmly tying the party's approach the social evolutionism, where social and cultural explanations of human differences replaced biology-based theories. He did it while offering an overall coherent and articulated version of Marxian socialism.

This move had multiple effects on the SLP's racial policy. On the one hand, it meant the consolidation of the party's stance on a position of principled egalitarianism rooted in a class analysis of economic and social relations. In a moment when scientific racialism was on the rise, spread by the likes of influential intellectuals such as William Z. Ripley, who published *The Races of Europe* in 1899, this meant for the socialists severing the connections with an intellectual area that would soon underpin some of the most exclusionary and reactionary immigration and social policies in the history of the country. On the other hand, though, this switch to social evolutionism limited the socialists' ability to develop an egalitarian racial politics. Socialists debating the "Indian question" in the 1880s offered a problematized version of the relationship between evolution and historical materialism. They questioned their belonging to a "superior" race or culture and sought original ways to address the problem of racial diversity. The embracing of a more rigidly structured social evolutionism, linked to an Americanized version of Marxist historical materialism, closed the door to further reflection—as a focus on the SLP and African Americans in the 1890s aptly shows.

"A Special Division in the Ranks of Labor": The SLP on African Americans in the 1890s

During the 1890s, one of the circumstances that had limited the diffusion of the SLP among African Americans up to that time underwent change as the party started to recruit more members in the South. By the end of the century, the SLP had representatives in Texas, Georgia, Louisiana, Alabama, and Maryland. The Carolinas and Florida remained beyond their reach. But this moderate expansion in numbers allowed them to discuss the problems faced by African Americans, and local militants were now present to provide firsthand information on how to gain members in the South.[40] At the same time, the rigid social evolutionism through which Daniel De Leon interpreted issues of race did not leave much room for individualized and group-specific analyses. This led to a contradictory situation. On the one hand, the SLP leadership guided by De Leon stood for racial equality, but they did not articulate the matter further nor did they formulate specific measures to support African American demands. On the other hand, the SLP membership widely discussed the problem, offering a selection of analyses and proposals that easily surpassed anything they had done prior to 1890.

De Leon defended racial equality but wavered on the idea that African Americas represented a "special" section of the American working class. In 1897, De Leon responded to New York's Black newspaper the *Age*, when it denounced the lack of African Americans in William McKinley's newly formed cabinet. De Leon disagreed that racial discrimination had caused that lack of representation. If African Americans "look more closely at facts, they will discover that the neglect of which they complain is in no way attributable to their color, but is closely akin to the treatment which the Republican party bestows on the WORKING CLASS, regardless of 'race, creed or previous condition of servitude' . . . it is not as BLACKS that the Republican party turns its back upon them but as PROLETARIANS."[41] De Leon was right to suggest that since the Civil War, Republicans had lost their interest in the Black electorate. Yet he missed one of the key reasons why that had happened: The Democrats were succeeding in disenfranchising Black voters and the Black vote had become nearly nonexistent, thus, unimportant. The 1896 presidential election was the moment when most of the southern states began to put in place rules that legally disenfranchised African Americans. This crucial detail was lost on De Leon.[42]

In another circumstance, De Leon attacked the famous African American leader Frederick Douglass, who remained in the folds of the Republican Party despite its reduced commitment to African American rights.[43] While eulogizing Douglass for an article he published in the *A.M.E. Church Review*, De Leon denounced the economic exploitation of Black workers and deprecated African American leaders for not "realiz[ing] that the plight of the Negro is the plight of Labor in general. . . . That the present cause of the one is the cause of both; and that their salvation depends upon the abolition of present slavocracy—the capitalist class or plutocracy of the land."[44] Douglass, continued De Leon, "can today be looked upon as a striking monument of the impotence of the warm heart unguided by intelligence. If he possessed the knowledge requisite to guide his feelings . . . he would be today in the ranks of the Socialists, instead of in those of the very ones whose systems keeps the Negro in degradation."[45]

When clearly presented with the opportunity, De Leon stated his principled support for racial equality. An occasion came in 1904, during the Amsterdam congress of the Socialist International. During the congress, a group of American socialists belonging to the Socialist Party of America signed a proposed resolution that limited immigration on the basis of race, referring specifically to "workingmen of backward races (Chinese, Negroes, etc.)." Commenting on an early draft of the resolution, in which the word "inferior" was used instead of "backward," De Leon wrote, "Where is the line that separates 'inferior' from 'superior' races? . . . Socialism knows not such insulting, iniquitous distinctions as 'inferior,' and 'superior' races among the proletariat."[46] De Leon pointed to the tendency in capitalism to foster and exploit racial and national divisions, a concept that scholars Elizabeth Esch and David R. Roediger labeled in 2012 "the production of difference." "To the native American proletariat, the Irish [were] made to appear an 'inferior' race; to the Irish, the German; to the German, the Italian; to the Italian—and so down the line . . . It is for capitalism to fan the fires of such sentiments in its scheme to keep the proletariat divided."[47]

On some occasions, De Leon acknowledged the social impact of racial discrimination, in particular on labor relations. Commenting on the outcome of a meeting in Boston of an African American society, De Leon wrote that "the negro constitutes, by reason of the special history back of him, a special division in the ranks of Labor." De Leon added that "in no economic respect" was the Black worker "different from his fellow wage slaves of the other races . . . yet by reason of his race, which long was identified with serfdom, the rays of the Social Question reached his mind through such broken prisms that they were refracted into all the colors of the rainbow, preventing him from appreciating the white light of the Question."[48] To a limited degree,

De Leon recognized that race created a unique and exceptional set of circumstances. Rather than deepening the implications of this idea, however, De Leon placed the burden on the Black worker, who he said must change their attitude and embrace the right path established by the socialist doctrine.

Party members filled the void left by the timid and underdeveloped approach of the party leadership, as exemplified by De Leon. And while the SLP never reached a coherent or full-fledged position on the topic, its membership carried forward a sustained conversation toward that goal. Writing from various parts of the South, socialists shared information and exchanged details on practical and theoretical problems. They offered to lead efforts to organize the Black electorate. Members in the North debated and articulated comprehensive analyses on the race question.

How to establish contact with Black workers was a significant challenge for socialists. Among those who wrote from the South, none underestimated the significance of race. S. M. White, writing from Atlanta, detailed the depth and significance of Black disenfranchisement.[49] S. H. D. McTier from Virginia defined the race question "a great obstacle" in the spread of socialism. "So powerful is that race weapon, and so well used by our political fakirs, that when on various occasions a reform party has flashed forth which threatened to overthrow the power that be, it was smashed by no other argument than that of the cry of: 'Nigger; Nigger!' at the sound of which the poor ignorant white slaves fled in terror back to their master to hug and kiss their chains with more fervent love than ever."[50] Harry R. Engel from Alabama openly attacked the southern white workers as "belligerent and blinded by race prejudice."[51]

At the same time, socialists from the Deep South were skeptical of gaining a foothold in the area. They said that the collapse of the populists after the 1896 elections had opened up opportunities, yet the prospects looked grim.[52] Distributing party propaganda among Black workers was rarely considered, and on some occasions the socialists' own racial prejudice stood in the way. Harry R. Engel, who opened his article by criticizing the racism of white southern workers, cited "the widespread illiteracy due to a woeful lack of schools and the impervious minds of the negros [*sic*]" among the "well-nigh insurmountable" barriers encountered. He added that "our literature and mode of reasoning is abstruse to people who use only a monosyllabic dialect or the patois of the negro."[53]

Militants from Texas and Maryland showed more optimism about socialism in the South. Frank Lellner from San Antonio noticed that unemployment caused by the mechanization of agriculture and the expansion of big ranches had created social conditions for socialist propaganda to succeed.[54] Baltimore's Henry McAnarney called for men and funds to help re-organize the Maryland party sections in Baltimore and surrounding coastal areas where the United Mine Workers no longer had a presence.[55] In both cases, however, racial relations did not feature as a prominent topic of interest.

A different and more detailed point of view came from J. Howard Sharp, an SLP member located in Greenfield, Tennessee. Initially, Sharp cited ignorance as "the greatest obstacle" to socialist propaganda. Yet he rapidly moved on to a lengthy description of the system of sharecropping, calling it another element that stood in the way of socialist interaction with Black workers. "Despite the freedom the emancipation proclamation was supposed to confer, the ex-slaves are now almost as much dependent upon the property owners as they were before the war." He stated that the Black worker had to give over "his life" to white landowners.[56] Sharp then analyzed the working conditions of Black laborers. He detailed how African Americans worked in rural environments where they were subjected to unfair contractual conditions, many on the same plantations they had worked before the Civil War. The dynamic that tied them to their employer was paternalistic at best. "The negro is in a measure loyal to his employer, and the hold of the whites is strong upon him."[57] What is more, the prejudice of white southerners made it impossible to interact socially with African Americans. "White men and women who have come from the North have been frequently forced to leave. Even Southern white Republicans who have organized the negroes have been boycotted and socially ostracized." Sharp's conclusion was pessimistic: "Northern comrades can judge from this what must be the moral courage of him who attempts to organize Socialist Sections among the negroes." Given these circumstances, Sharp contended that the only possibility available for socialists was to "make converts among the more intelligent and honest negroes, furnish them with means and literature, and leave it to them to carry on the work among their race."[58]

Sharp's 1897 article is arguably the most comprehensive analysis of the possibilities of the SLP organizing in the South ever published in the *People*. In a number of ways, it is comparable to the articles published by Adolph Douai and August Otto-Walster in the socialist press in the late 1870s. Yet Sharp's view had its shortcomings. At times, he was hesitant to condemn white southerners as perpetrators of Black inequality. On education, for example, he timidly stated that "whether [Black ignorance] results from the negro's ineptitude or from a deliberate and concerted effort on the part of the ruling class to prevent his enlightenment, opinions will differ," before adding that southern legislators' response to the Blair education bill, a measure defending Reconstruction-era civil rights legislation, "would support the latter belief."[59] At the same time, Sharp gave a wide ranging and accurate description of working conditions and racial relations in the South, concluding his article with a proposal that was more detailed and plausible than the ones offered by the two German American leaders in the 1870s. By 1898, the SLP could celebrate a small success that moved the party in the direction advocated by Sharp. When the *People* reported problems with the attempt by white Virginia socialists to bring in Black members, socialists from Pocahontas, Virginia, wrote to report that they had successfully opened the first Black-only section of the party.[60]

While Southern socialists engaged more regularly with the peculiarities of southern politics and tried to turn theory into practice, the "Negro question" became the object of dedicated attention for northern members as well. In 1898, the New Jersey activist Robert Windon titled his contribution in the *People*, "What Will Socialism Do for the Negro?" According to Windon, socialism would improve the living conditions of Black Americans in two ways. First, it would "abolish competition" in the workplace and "establish the public ownership of the means of production." This would end discrimination against Black workers by employers as "the negro will be a part owner with his white neighbor in all the nation's capital." Second, Windon argued that socialism, by "bring[ing] about universal education," would sweep away prejudice against Blacks because "race prejudices cannot exist with true enlightenment."[61] With these suggestions, Windon claimed that the abolition of capitalism created the foundation for the disappearance of racism. Once the material conditions that produced racial hatred in the workplace changed, education would wipe racism from the face of the world.

Windon's piece clearly articulated what African Americans could expect in the future socialist commonwealth and how the internationalist philosophy of socialism planned to address racial discrimination. When compared with vague socialist analyses of the 1870s and 1880s, his article represented a step forward in the conceptualization of the relationship between socialism and race. Nevertheless, the content, once again, focused on an abstract future without engaging present conditions. What was the immediate plan of the SLP for the advancement of the African American community? What could Black workers hope for if they voted socialist in a local election? Windon was silent on these aspects.

By comparing socialist approaches of the 1890s with those of the 1870s and 1880s, it becomes clear that much of the diversity (and confusion) that had characterized the early phase of the SLP had disappeared. To some extent, the SLP's focus on class promoted by its leadership contributed to that outcome, leading the party away from any sort of theory of racial differentiation based on essentialist, scientist, or biologist arguments. This may appear paradoxical, given the value De Leon placed on the connection between biology and sociology. But, in fact, the strict focus on class was the core of De Leon's analytical framework. The class-first position defined by De Leon and embraced by American socialists in this period did not use Darwinism or scientific racialism to explain differences between human races. It rejected the idea that human groups with different biological features competed in a perennial struggle for existence. In particular, it rejected the idea that different human groups existed at all. De Leon used "race" only as a social concept, to explain the history of certain groups. In so doing, De Leon and his followers severed any connection with those who defended essentialist points of view. While there were exceptions to this trend, as the articles by Sharp and Engel show, as a general rule, the adoption of a race-neutral position closed the theoretical gaps that had given rise to racism within the socialist ranks in the 1870s and 1880s.

In the end, however, the position advocated by De Leon and his followers led American socialists to misunderstand the role of race in America. De Leon was arguably the first socialist leader to write explicitly that "there is no race question, nor color question . . . What there IS is the Humanity Question—the SOCIAL QUESTION."[62] This well-intended attempt of De Leon and his followers to shift the conversation away from racial differences and focus on economic inequalities carried the undesirable consequence of making socialists tone deaf to the ways in which race shaped social and economic circumstances across the country.

The Fall of the Multiethnic SLP

In the 1890s, the SLP simultaneously achieved its period of peak influence and laid the foundations for its ultimate demise. The Americanization of the party, its further penetration into ethnic communities, and its closer link with local trade unions (especially in New York and Chicago) made it a healthier and more proactive organization. The SLP ran its first presidential ticket in 1892. While in 1892 the party was present on the ballot in five states, that number grew to twenty-one in 1896, a reflection of the fact that the number of party sections had increased to around 200 in those four years; numbers of votes grew accordingly. The SLP went from polling 30,000 votes in 1896 to 80,000 in the 1898 midterms.[63] Party's leader Rudolph Katz, with some blandishment, wrote that by 1895, "the Socialist Labor Party had grown to be a factor to be reckon[ed] with."[64]

Meanwhile, controversial political decisions sowed dissent that soon violently revealed itself. Contention had characterized De Leon's leadership from its inception. Months after taking over the *People*'s editorship, De Leon started a reckless war against the People's Party. His strategy was to establish an independent political profile for the SLP, but his move curtailed any possibility that the two movements would cooperate on the ground against corporate parties. In 1895, after the SLP's tactic to "bore from within" the AFL and the Knights of Labor failed, De Leon set up an independent socialist federation, the Socialist Trade and Labor Alliance (STLA). The STLA was born to nurture the socialist presence in organized labor, yet it made the lives of socialist workers more complicated by forcing them to have a double affiliation or make a painful choice between the different federations. Finally, De Leon and his followers distinguished themselves by their rigid and uncompromising attitude toward party discipline, an approach that provoked mounting resentment against the New York sections under the control of De Leon's circle.[65]

Tension in the SLP reached the breaking point in the summer of 1899. After years of friction and cross accusations in the party press, a group gathered around the *New Yorker Volkszeitung* and organized a coup to oust De Leon and the National Executive Committee. The group's attempt to physically occupy the party's headquarters rapidly escalated into a violent clash, with the two factions fighting over membership lists and printing equipment. It took a year-long legal battle to determine that De Leon and his followers could retain the party name and its membership list. In the interim, two versions of the *People* were published, completely confusing the party membership outside New York and delighting the anti-socialist press. Eventually, the anti-Deleonite faction joined Eugene Debs's Social Democratic Party and founded the Socialist Party of America (SPA) in 1901. The SLP started its slow transformation into a cradle of De Leon's acolytes.[66]

Historians and left-leaning activists have exhausted the discussion on the political reasons of this split. Instead, the significance of the debate on the Americanization of the socialist movement undertook in 1899 remains unexplored, especially considering it was the beginning of a conversation that continued in socialist and communist parties until the 1930s, at least. Daniel De Leon's insistence on erasing ethnic markers in the SLP had a crucial role in causing the split. On the other side of the argument, leaders of the Jewish and the German American communities were reacting to the leadership's attempt to crush the particular form of political militancy they had created—a militancy that was practiced within ethnic circles but was ideologically tied to the broader socialist cause.

De Leon's idea that the party needed to Americanize itself was not initially seen as a problem by the immigrant groups within the organization. In fact, in the 1890–1895 period, De Leon could rely on the support of ethnic-based organizations such as the *New Yorker Volkszeitung* and German American trade unions, as well as the United Hebrew Trades, a Jewish federation of trade unions founded in New York in 1888. These groups embraced with enthusiasm the plan of expanding among English-speaking workers and threw their support behind it. But the situation changed quickly. At the ninth convention of the party in 1896, a clause stating that "no section or subdivision [of the party] shall be designated by race or nationality" was inserted into the SLP constitution. There could be no doubt of the new direction the party was taking.[67] The convention also discussed the problems within the Jewish socialist community of New York. Jewish immigrants had contributed significantly to the expansion of the party, opening twenty-five sections between 1889 and 1897. They also pioneered two of the most successful newspapers in the socialist movement, the *Arbeter Tsaytung*, a weekly started in 1890, and *Dos Abend Blat*, a daily launched in 1895. By the time of the convention, there was internal strife in the cooperative publishing association that controlled both publications, with arguments over the relations between the association and the SLP. Some wanted to sever the connection with the socialist party; others wanted to remain loyal and influence its policy from within. The SLP convention dismissed the problem as something that Jewish members should solve themselves and approved a resolution that determined that the political line of the publishing association should be controlled by the NEC of the party. This decision made clear the distance the party leadership had traveled from the problems of its militants. By unilaterally imposing SLP control of the publishing association, the convention weakened the position of the SLP supporters and accelerated the secession from the party of a lively group of intellectuals, led by Abraham Cahan and Louis Miller. In 1897 they founded a new daily, the *Forverts*, and cut ties altogether with the party.[68]

But the main challenge to De Leon's activities came from the German American community. The *Volkszeitung* group included many of the militants who had led the SLP until 1890 and had initially favored De Leon's rise. Secure in their historical role and their popularity among German American workers, still a core constituency of the party, these leaders did everything in their power to end De Leon's leadership. De Leon had no hesitation in counterattacking. His arguments against his former political sponsors demonstrate that ethnicity played a central role in shaping the internal debate in the SLP. In a series of articles published against the *Volkszeitung* leadership, De Leon pointed to the failure of the German American leadership to abide by the party's mission of spreading socialism among American workers. Disclosing the opinions of his internal enemies during a party debate, De Leon wrote that "as a matter of course, THE PEOPLE came in for a full share of abuse, although most of its assailants do not and cannot read [English], and none knows enough English to judge."[69] Elsewhere, De Leon expanded his argument, this time having recourse to the theme of Americanizing the party. Speaking of the representatives of the *Volkszeitung* faction, he wrote:

> It is no accident that among these spokesmen is a Schlüter—only a temporary sojourner in this land, awaiting the expiration of the sentence against him to return to his home in Germany; it is no accident that among these spokesmen is a Dr. Halpern . . . a gentleman, whose jovial countenance we may at any time miss from our midst, his heart being in Russia, whither he pants to return as soon as it may be safe to do so; it is no accident that amongst these spokesmen is a Feigenbaum—a member who only the other day was seeking the perfect arrangements whereby he could fall on his feet back to Europe.[70]

By 1899, De Leon conceived of the immigrant leadership, with their stubborn refusal to learn English and their attachment to their motherland, as an obstacle to the success of socialism. On the opposite site of the barricade, German and Jewish leaders understood precisely the issue at stake. "For some years we have heard a great deal, from high quarters within the party, as to the necessity of an 'American socialist movement,'" wrote the anti-Deleonite the *People* after the split. "The Socialist Labor Party in America will never be 'American' in the sense of being anti-foreign."[71]

This article in the anti-De Leon press reveals the central role played by ethnic hatred in the 1899 split. The clash in the party was a battle for the ethnic identity of American socialism. De Leon's insistent attacks on his adversaries' immigrant status were clearly linked to his understanding of race and ethnicity. Paul Buhle, one of the most astute commentators of De Leon's political trajectory, wrote that "De Leon could not help reducing workers to The Worker, a being without any discernible secondary characteristics."[72] As De Leon was fundamentally unable to understand race as an independent variable in shaping American working conditions, so he could not see ethnic identity as a crucial ingredient for the success of the political movement that he led. Within the inability of De Leon's SLP to understand the significance of ethnic and racial identity in the social, personal, and cultural reality inhabited by American workers lies the ultimate reason why the party broke apart, as well as why it failed to develop a strategy to include members from the least privileged racial minorities in the country.

Conclusions

The 1899 split ended the period in which the SLP was a key incubator of ideas about race and ethnicity within the American socialist movement.

Right from its founding in 1876, the socialist party had brought together radicals who sought out original ways to apply the tenets of socialism to the problems created by racial inequality in the United States. The 1890s was a time when many tendencies that had become apparent in the earlier years reached final maturity. With a class-focused approach based on the synthesis of anthropology and historical materialism, in the 1890s, the SLP resolved the tension between opposing theories of race that had been used for years to approach the conversation on racial and economic equality. The columns of the *People* provided an interpretation of Marx's historical materialism that was based on social evolutionism and the prioritizing of class.

At the same time, while upholding a clearer position on racial equality, in this decade, the SLP also embraced a systematic denial of the importance of race relations in the country. This produced a paradox: On the one hand, the SLP grew in members and voters, expanded its reach in the South and found itself in a better position to recruit African Americans; at times, socialists worked out viable strategies to approach Black workers. On the other hand, the constant tendency to downplay the importance of race relations and the vagueness of the political proposals put forward by the party prevented any significant interracial cooperation. De Leon's writings were telling. Not only did he lack sophistication in his understanding of the role of race and ethnicity but his insistence on a simplistic and mechanistic version of historical materialism made it impossible for the improved conversation on race in the South to coalesce into party politics.

These developments in racial politics happened alongside a ruthless battle for the "immigrant soul" of the movement. A powerful block of German American and Jewish socialists in control of the most proactive workers' communities that animated the SLP accused De Leon and his followers of imposing a strategy to Americanize the party; the De Leonites criticized their opponents for their inability to break from their ethnic communities. The factions' inability to find a compromise marked the end of the SLP as the prime leader of American socialism.

Ultimately, the events of the 1890s revealed how important race and ethnicity were in this phase of the socialist movement. In spite of minor successes, De Leon's SLP struggled to find a way to defend workers' rights in America's multiethnic and multiracial society. De Leon's class-focused approach solved the theoretical tension between the fight for economic justice and the defense of racial equality, but it failed to find ways to put this theory into practice.

CONCLUSION

The Past and the Future of Racial Socialism

> "You can't have capitalism without racism. And if you find a person without racism and you happen to get that person into a conversation and they have a philosophy that makes you sure they don't have this racism in their outlook, usually they're socialists or their political philosophy is socialism."
>
> —Malcolm X

In 1901, representatives of the Social Democratic Party, led by Eugene V. Debs and former members of the Socialist Labor Party (SLP) who had lost their legal battle against the De Leonists to control the party, met in Indianapolis to establish the Socialist Party of America (SPA). The proceedings of the convention made clear that in the last years of the 1890s, the SLP had become more of a hindrance than a boon for the creation of an interracial socialist movement. Three Black members attended the convention: William Costley, Cal John H. Adams, and Edward D. McKay. The *Worker*, a socialist weekly from New York City, emphasized the importance of their contribution to the convention. They were "fine orators," showing "a firm grasp of Socialism and of the Socialist conception of the race question . . . They used the language of the great abolitionist [Wendell Phillips] to give utterance to the teachings of Karl Marx," wrote the *Worker*'s correspondent with enthusiasm.[1]

The extensive debate on a clause about Black workers in the SPA made the presence of Costley, Adams, and McKay central. Initially, a resolution demanding "equal rights for all human beings without distinction of color, race or sex" and recognizing that Black workers suffered "under direct exploitation and oppression by the ruling class" was submitted to the resolutions committee. Several white socialists, including former SLP member Morris Hillquit, objected to this resolution, arguing that there was no more reason "for singling out the negro race especially . . . than for singling out the Jews or Germans or any other nationality, race or creed here present." However, one of the three Black delegates, William Costley, insisted that the SPA platform must include a stance on Black labor. He penned a new document that stated that "the Negro as part of the great working class occupies a distinct and peculiar position in contradiction to other laboring elements in the United States" and went as far as openly denouncing "lynching, burning and disenfranchisement" of Black Americans in the South.[2] While discussions of racism and racial violence had come up in socialist newspaper articles and lectures before, a reference to lynching would have been a departure from anything ever seen in an American socialist official document.

Once again, political expediency stood in the way of what would have been a significant step toward an open commitment to racial equality by the socialist movement. Editor Algie M. Simons was the most explicit, openly stating that the resolution, if adopted, would have made "a great deal of trouble in the South." Many spoke in favor of passing the resolution with no changes. Reverend George D. Herron emphatically declared that he "would prefer that we lost every white vote in the South than to evade the question which is presented today in that resolution." But when the plank was reproposed at the end of the convention after some pruning to the language (made by Herron himself), the reference to "lynching, burning and disenfranchisement" was no longer there.[3]

Philip S. Foner contended that, despite this omission, the platform was an exceptional document that "went far beyond the old cliché urging equality 'without distinction of color, race, sex or creed' so typical of socialist resolutions from 1879 to the turn of the century."[4] Foner's assessment is slightly off target because he did not consider the resolution adopted by the SLP in 1879 in which an interracial alliance between northern and southern labor was openly invoked. The 1879 SLP resolution and the 1901 SPA platform had striking similarities in the ways in which they were framed, from the inference that the interests of capitalists in the North and the South fostered racial animosity among workers, to the final invitation toward Black workers to join the socialist movement. But the SPA resolution read like an upgrade of the SLP's document: It was longer, more detailed, more exhaustive.[5] In the twenty years that had passed between the two documents, the movement had become more diverse, solid, and articulated. This made a significant difference in its capacity to respond to racial inequality.

In the SPA, many of the trends that had been initiated in the 1890s came to full maturation. The socialist movement perfected its balance between pursuing an aggressive strategy of Americanization and retaining its links with powerful non-English-speaking communities, which continued to animate socialist and communist parties well within the twentieth century. While expanding its membership and multiplying its votes among English-speaking workers, the SPA continued to welcome new immigrants who kept flowing in the country until the early 1920s. Immigrant leaders who constituted the backbone of the SLP immigrant leadership—like Morris Hillquit, Hermann Schlüter, and Abraham Cahan—retained their key positions in the SPA. They were joined by a new generation of leaders who added new constituencies to the party, from the midwestern editor of the *Appeal to Reason* Julius Wayland to the German American leader of the Socialist Party of Oklahoma, Oscar Ameringer, and trade unionist leaders like Mother Jones and Bill Haywood. It should not be a surprise that the main driving force behind this development was Eugene V. Debs, a second-generation French American and champion of American radicalism who was named after Eugène Sue and Victor Hugo.[6]

In the same vein, the racial politics of the SPA developed along lines that had been traced at the end of the nineteenth century. Like the SLP, the SPA adopted a class-first position that would be accompanied with a principled defense of racial equality. Yet many conflicting voices found room in the broad tent that the American socialist movement built in the early twentieth century. The SPA membership spanned the open segregationist of its Louisiana and Texas sections to the arch-defender of Black enfranchisement Oscar Ameringer. It briefly enrolled Black intellectuals like W. E. B. Du Bois and Hubert Harrison while sending the white supremacist Victor Berger to congress. Two of the founders of the National Association for the Advancement of Colored People, William English Walling and Mary White Ovington, stood in the SPA, alongside the author of the pamphlet "Nigger Equality," Kate Richards O'Hare. In this variety of opinions, socialist evolutionism remained the standard framework for conversation on race. Even more than in the Gilded Age, in the Progressive Era, debates on social evolution, "savagism," and "civilization" intertwined with the analysis of the patterns of industrialization and progress of the country.[7]

Historian Paul Heideman argued that in the 1910s, the SPA was in the process of solving some of its contradictions and adopting a firmer commitment to racial equality. "Slowly, but perceptibly, the party was beginning to take the task of opposing racism more seriously."[8] The process of defining a position that kept together class struggle and the defense of racial equality did not start in the early twentieth century with the foundation of the SPA but at least half a century prior. This approach—a straightforward application of the internationalist and class-based philosophy of Karl Marx and Friedrich Engels, sensibly adapted to the American context—was initially formulated in the United States by internationalists like Joseph Weydemeyer, Friedrich A. Sorge, and Joseph P. McDonnell.

In the Gilded Age, the relationship between socialism and race was the subject of a long debate between opposing factions. Some of them were accommodating to the existence of racial inequality, either for political reasons, intellectual proclivities, or the defense of personal interests. A class-first and racial-conscious position started to emerge as the leading doctrine at the end of the century, although in the context of a socialist organization, like De Leon's SLP, that made it impossible for socialism to advance in the country. This position breathed to new life in the SPA, in the declaration of Eugene V. Debs that the party "would be false to its historic mission, violate the fundamental [principles] of Socialism, deny its philosophy and repudiate its own teachings if, on account of race considerations, it sought to exclude any human being from political equality and economic freedom."[9]

World War I and the Russian Revolution cut short the debate on the subject in the SPA. After 1918, in a left-wing world that was now bitterly divided among a socialist and a communist camp, the process took parallel routes. Among the communists, the exchange between the U.S.S.R. and the United States went both ways. While at the beginning of the 1920s, Black activists and intellectuals like Otto Huiswoud and Claude McKay advised the Communist International on how to tackle the "Negro question" in the context of Lenin's anti-imperialist framework, in 1928 the Comintern shaped the Communist Party of the USA's line on Black emancipation through the detailed Black Belt thesis, a document establishing the African American working class as an anti-capitalist and anti-imperialist bastion both in the U.S. and in Africa. Among the socialists, leaders like A. Philip Randolph used socialist doctrine to build a trade unionist movement specifically catered for Black workers. The dialectic between socialists, communists, and its sectarian spinoffs characterized much of the 1920s and the early 1930s. But the New Deal era opened new possibilities for collaboration. Although differences were never obliterated, in the 1930s, both communists and socialists put the fight against racism at the very center of their political action.[10]

In the process, and in collaboration with the liberal wing of the Democratic Party, the American Left built the foundations on which the civil rights movement was built. The Cold War would make it impossible for activists inspired by socialism and communism to claim their allegiance, but the actions of leaders like Ella Baker, Bayard Rustin, Stanley Levison, and A. Philip Randolph speak for themselves. The "sudden" explosion of the civil rights movement in the 1950s was not sudden at all—it relied on the social and political infrastructure laid down by communist, socialist, and popular front activism in prior decades. Domestic policy, strategic priorities, and international circumstances pushed the civil rights movement to focus on legal rights over the broader goal of achieving human rights for African Americans and racial minorities. But class and economic issues came back to the fore in the second half of the '60s. Black Power movements worked in continuity with the long-term mission of achieving full equality for African Americans in the country. Finding a solution to the intertwined problems of class and racial exploitation was their ultimate goal.[11]

During the protests of the '60s, patriarchy, sexism, and gender discrimination joined class and racial inequality among the core polemical targets of protest movements on the left. The organized Left had a long-standing problem with gender equality in its ranks. The First International and the Workingmen's Party of the United States carried the gender-exclusivist label "workingmen" in their official denominations. Across their history, the SLP, the SPA, and the CPUSA, while including women's groups who proactively sought to promote the fight for gender equality, persisted with a male-centered point of view. The civil rights movement featured groups that started to take gender equality more seriously, but they were exceptions rather than the norm. The New Left spearheaded second-wave feminism but only when its female leaders abandoned sexist organizations like the Students for a Democratic Society. The Black Panther Party relied on the groundwork of Black women while framing its public image around a muscular, male-centered imagery.[12]

Out of the frustration for the inability of civil rights, New Left, and feminist movements to conceive of a politics that addressed racial, class, and gender oppression simultaneously grew arguably the most lucid manifesto against intersectional oppression ever written in the twentieth century: the "Combahee River Collective Statement." "We believe that sexual politics is as pervasive in Black women's lives as are the politics of class and race," wrote the authors. "We also often find it difficult to separate race from class from sex oppression because in our lives they are most often experienced simultaneously."[13] As stressed by Keeanga-Yamahtta Taylor, the Combahee River Collective was not "writing against Marxism, but, in their own words, they looked to 'extend' Marxist analysis to incorporate an understanding of the oppression of Black women."[14] As the statement puts it, "We are not convinced . . . that a socialist revolution that is not also a feminist and antiracist will guarantee our liberation." With its inclusivist, internationalist, anti-imperialist approach, the "Combahee River Collective Statement" represents an intellectual pinnacle of a tradition of intersectional Marxist analyses with a long, venerable, and distinctively American history.

Reconstructing the fraught origins of this long path toward an intersectional, inclusivist, and egalitarian socialism gives new insight on the history of radicalism and race both in the United States and across the world. Against a backdrop still set on the idea that socialism "did not happen" in the United States, it is time to recognize the presence of a socialist movement that *did happen* and developed in accordance with specific American circumstances. The extent and significance of the socialist conversation on race in the Gilded Age reconstructed in this book make this reality evident. Socialists like Joseph Weydemeyer, Adolph Douai, Paul Grottkau, Abraham Cahan, or Daniel De Leon were neither "German" nor "Dutch" nor "Jewish" in their exposition of socialism. They were not "native" Anglo-Americans, either. Instead, their approaches were a mixture, a patchwork, a synthesis of ideas traveling across continents, applied to eminently American circumstances. The immigrant origins of American socialism are what made it peculiar, and this mixture remained present in the movement during the Progressive Era. Across the twentieth and twenty-first centuries, American socialism grew even more multiethnic and multiracial, when Black, Latinx, Asian, and Native American people either joined the movement or embraced socialist ideas to support their political activism. If anything exceptional has to be found in American socialism, then, it is the proximity that socialist ideas had with the analysis of racial and ethnic diversity in the country, from its very inception in antebellum America to the present day.

But this proximity hardly meant a smooth ride toward a race-conscious, egalitarian socialism, as the early history of the SLP so clearly attests. German radical immigrants arrived in the United States in the 1850s with no clear understanding of the relationship between socialism and race. It was the Civil War that dragged them into a debate in which the achievement of Black emancipation went along with hopes for a new season of working-class activism across the country. Yet the aftermath of the war was a disappointment, not just for the failure of these expectations but also for the fracturing of the multiracial effort that had brought about the end of slavery. The Gilded Age saw many trends unfolding together. While the white-dominated public debate pushed the issue of African American equality to the background, the conversation on race broke down into many overlapping and contradictory facets, among which were the future of Native Americans, the closure of the frontier, and the place of immigrants from

Europe and Asia in the American society. For the American socialist movement, the search for a coherent way to jointly address class and racial inequality was a constant feature of the period.

The victory of class-conscious racial egalitarianism over white supremacist racialism was not a forgone conclusion. One only needs to look at the concurrent developments taking place in the Australian and South African labor movement or in the American Federation of Labor, which embraced approaches that openly prioritized the white majority, to understand that things could have easily been otherwise.[15] At the same time, still at the end of the nineteenth century, socialists failed to offer a fully acceptable articulation of the problem. The SLP never developed a proactive racial policy that put the fight against racism at the center of its political action nor did it promote special measures to defend the equality of its members in the organization from racial prejudice. This mixed legacy was the platform upon which the American Left developed in the twentieth century.

Notes

Introduction

1. David O. Stowell, ed., *The Great Strikes of 1877* (Urbana: University of Illinois Press, 2008); Brian Greenberg, *The Dawning of American Labor: The New Republic to the Industrial Age* (Hoboken: Wiley and Sons, 2018), 1–10.

2. "The Great Meeting. The Organized Workingmen of New York Throng the Great Hall of the Cooper Union," *Labor Standard*, August 4, 1877. On Joseph P. McDonnell, see Herbert G. Gutman, "Joseph P. McDonnell and the Workers' Struggle in Paterson, New Jersey," in *Power and Culture: Essays on the American Working Class*, ed. Ira Berlin (New York: The New Press, 1987). At the time of writing, McDonnell and the *Labor Standard* were in the middle of a political battle for the control of the WPUS. See *Labor Standard*, "Weekly Review," June 2, 1877. See infra chapter two.

3. "Die Indianer, Neger und Chinesen in Nord-Amerika," *Volksstimme des Westens*, November 2, 1877. The article was signed with the initials "R. M." The positions expressed in the article allowed me to identify the author as R. J. Mills, a regular correspondent of the *Labor Standard*. See R. Mills, "To the Editor of the *Labor Standard*," *Labor Standard*, July 8, 1876; R. J. Mills, "A Voice from Chinese America," *Labor Standard*, July 22, 1876. The article was published in German. Unless otherwise noted, all translations from German are my own.

4. "Nord-Amerika," *Volksstimme des Westens*.

5. On the passage from property capitalism to corporate capitalism, the weakening of democratic structures, and labor ideologies, see Nancy Cohen, *The Reconstruction of American Liberalism, 1865–1914* (Chapel Hill: University of North Carolina Press, 2002); Rosanne Currarino, *The Labor Question in America: Economic Democracy in the Gilded Age* (Urbana: University of Illinois Press, 2011); Leon Fink, *The Long Gilded Age: American Capitalism and the Lessons of a New World Order* (Philadelphia: University of Pennsylvania Press, 2015). On urbanization and the depopulation of

the countryside, see Rebecca Edwards, *New Spirits: Americans in the "Gilded Age," 1865–1905* (New York: Oxford University Press, 2006); Charles W. Calhoun, ed., *The Gilded Age: Perspectives on the Origins of Modern America* (Lanham: Rowman and Littlefield Publishers, 2007).

6. Historians have abundantly investigated the racialization of American capitalism. See Heather Cox Richardson, *The Death of Reconstruction: Race, Labor, and Politics in the Post-Civil War North, 1865–1901* (Cambridge, MA: Harvard University Press, 2001); Najia Aarim-Heriot, *Chinese Immigrants, African Americans, and Racial Anxiety in the United States, 1848–82* (Urbana: University of Illinois Press, 2003); Bruce E. Baker and Brian Kelly, eds., *After Slavery: Race, Labor, and Citizenship in the Reconstruction South* (Gainesville: University Press of Florida, 2013); Martin Ruef, *Between Slavery and Capitalism: The Legacy of Emancipation in the American South* (Princeton, NJ: Princeton University Press, 2014); Edlie L. Wong, *Racial Reconstruction: Black Inclusion, Chinese Exclusion, and the Fictions of Citizenship* (New York: New York University Press, 2015); Walter Johnson, *The Broken Heart of America: St. Louis and the Violent History of the United States* (New York: Basic Books, 2017).

7. Philip S. Foner, *The Formation of the Workingmen's Party of the United States: Proceedings of the Union Congress, Held at Philadelphia, July 19–22, 1876* (New York: American Institute for Marxist Studies, 1876); Socialistic Labor Party, *Platform, Constitution, and Resolutions*, Adopted at the National Congress of the Workingmen's Party of the United States, held at Newark, NJ, December 26, 27, 28, 29, 30, 31, 1877 (Cincinnati: Ohio Volks-Zeitung Print, 1878).

8. David Montgomery, "Labor and the Republic in Industrial America: 1860–1920," *Le Mouvement Social*, no. 111 (April–June 1980): 201–15, https://doi.org/10.2307/3778016. See also Montgomery, *Citizen Worker: The Experience of Workers in the United States with Democracy and the Free Market During the Nineteenth Century* (Cambridge: Cambridge University Press, 1993), 130–37.

9. Fink provided an updated historical survey of the concept of labor republicanism, which he called "the American ideology," in *Long Gilded Age*, 12–33. Alex Gourevitch offered an investigation of the concept from the perspective of a political theorist in *From Slavery to the Cooperative Commonwealth: Labor and Republican Liberty in the Nineteenth Century* (Cambridge: Cambridge University Press, 2015). For an analysis of the concept in the context of the historiography on American socialism, see Michael Kazin, "Introduction: Daniel Bell and the Agony and Romance of the American Left," in Daniel Bell, *Marxian Socialism in the United States* (Ithaca: Cornell University Press, 1995), xxiv-xxv.

10. Rosanne Currarino discussed a dichotomy between two opposing ways of understanding the "labor question" during the Gilded Age, one based on republican values and one based on economic rights, that recall the distinction made here. See Currarino, *Labor Question in America*, 3–10.

11. See "The Union Complete," *Labor Standard*, October 21, 1876.

12. The party did not keep regular lists of members. It is, therefore, difficult to reconstruct the precise dimension of the different ethnic groups within the party.

However, scholars agree on placing the percentage of German Americans between 80 and 90 percent. See Morris Hillquit, *History of Socialism in the United States* (1903; repr., New York: Russell and Russell, 1965), 213; Hartmut Keil, "German Working-Class Immigration and the Social Democratic Tradition of Germany," in *German Workers' Culture in the United States, 1850 to 1920*, ed. Keil (Washington, DC: Smithsonian Institution Press, 1988), 7. On German American socialism in the 1890s and beyond, see Dorothee Schneider, *Trade Unions and Community: The German Working Class In New York City, 1870–1900* (Urbana: University of Illinois Press, 1994), 209–18.

13. On the fundamental importance of the labor press during the Gilded Age, see Elliott Shore, Ken Fones-Wolf, and James P. Danky, eds., *The German-American Radical Press: The Shaping of a Left Political Culture, 1850–1940* (Urbana: University of Illinois Press, 1992); Kim Moody, "A Gilded-Age Social Media: John Swinton, Joseph Buchanan, and the Late Nineteenth-Century Labor Press," *Labor* 15, no. 1 (2018): 11–24, https://doi.org/10.1215/15476715-4288638.

14. The American historian Philip S. Foner has contended that in its first fifteen years of existence, the SLP's treatment of race was scarce, if almost nonexistent—a situation that slowly improved during Daniel De Leon's leadership in the 1890s. See Philip S. Foner, *American Socialism and Black Americans: From the Age of Jackson to World War II* (Westport, CT: Greenwood Press, 1977), 59–62; 70–78. See infra chapters four and six.

15. T. Thomas Fortune and Ida B. Wells were amongst the most vocal African American journalists of the Gilded Age, incessantly denunciating episodes of racial discrimination against African Americans across the country. See Shawn Leigh Alexander, ed., *T. Thomas Fortune, the Afro-American Agitator: A Collection of Writings, 1880–1928* (Gainesville: University Press of Florida, 2008); James West Davidson, *"They Say": Ida B. Wells and the Reconstruction of Race* (New York: Oxford University Press, 2009); Lori Amber Roessner and Jodi L. Rightler-McDaniels, eds., *Political Pioneer of the Press: Ida B. Wells-Barnett and Her Transnational Crusade for Social Justice* (Lanham: Lexington Books, 2018).

16. The term "science" here is not meant to imply legitimacy. Rather, "modern racial science" refers to the vast group of pseudosciences that developed between Europe and the United States whose aim was to demonstrate authoritatively the existence of a hierarchy between different human groups. For general contextualization, see George M. Fredrickson, *Racism: A Short History* (Princeton, NJ: Princeton University Press, 2002), 49–96; Peter J. Bowler, *Evolution: The History of an Idea* (Berkeley: University of California Press, 2003); Francisco Bethencourt, *Racisms: From the Crusades to the Twentieth Century* (Princeton, NJ: Princeton University Press, 2014). Chapters two, three, and five offer a more in-depth discussion of the topic.

17. Werner Sombart, *Why Is There No Socialism in the United States?* (1906; repr., London: Palgrave Macmillan, 1976).

18. Selig Perlman, *A History of Trade Unionism in the United States* (1922; repr. New York: Augustus M. Kelley, 1950); Selig Perlman, *A Theory of the Labor Movement* (1928; repr., New York: Augustus M. Kelley, 1949); John H. M. Laslett and

Seymour Martin Lipset, eds., *Failure of a Dream? Essays in the History of American Socialism* (Garden City, NY: Anchor Press/Doubleday, 1974); Mike Davis, *Prisoners of the American Dream: Politics and Economy in the History of the US Working Class* (London: Verso, 1986); Seymour Martin Lipset and Gary Marks, *It Didn't Happen Here: Why Socialism Failed in the United States* (New York: W. W. Norton, 2000); Robin Archer, *Why Is There No Labor Party in the United States?* (Princeton, NJ: Princeton University Press, 2007); Kim Moody, *Tramps and Trade Union Travelers: Internal Migration and Organized Labor in Gilded Age America, 1870–1900* (Chicago: Haymarket Books, 2019).

19. The most straightforward example of this approach is Michael Kazin, *American Dreamers: How the Left Changed a Nation* (New York: Vintage Books, 2012).

20. Hillquit, *History of Socialism*; Timothy Messer-Kruse, *The Yankee International: Marxism and the American Reform Tradition, 1848–1876* (Chapel Hill: University of North Carolina Press, 1998).

21. According to Foner, the problem was that "the socialism question rests on a number of assertions that may not survive careful analysis," among them the undemonstrated premise, stemming from Marx's theory, that a country with a capitalist economy was meant to develop a socialist political movement. More recently, Leon Fink has built on Foner's argument to further dismantle the inner logic of exceptionalist arguments. Fink observed that once research led to the abandonment of "the ideal-typical 'class-conscious' proletariat of classic Marxism," a category that "didn't seem to exist anywhere," the need for comparisons between the United States and Europe disappeared. See Eric Foner, "Why Is There No Socialism in the United States?" *History Workshop*, no. 17 (Spring 1984): 73; Fink, *Long Gilded Age*, 6.

22. Others studies of American socialism and American communism focused on the specificity of conditions in the United States include Nick Salvatore, *Eugene V. Debs: Citizen and Socialist* (Urbana: University of Illinois Press, 1983); James R. Green, *Grass-Roots Socialism; Radical Movements in the Southwest, 1895–1943* (Baton Rouge: LSU Press, 1978); Mari Jo Buhle, *Women and American Socialism, 1870–1920* (Urbana: University of Illinois Press, 1983); Robin D. G. Kelley, *Hammer and Hoe: Alabama Communists during the Great Depression* (Chapel Hill: University of North Carolina Press, 1990).

23. James R. Barrett and David R. Roediger, "In between Peoples: Race, Nationality and the 'New Immigrant' Working Class," *Journal of American Ethnic History* 16, no. 3 (Spring 1997): 14.

24. Shelley Fisher Fishkin, "Crossroads of Cultures: The Transnational Turn in American Studies: Presidential Address to the American Studies Association, November 12, 2004," *American Quarterly* 57, no. 1 (March 2005): 20.

25. Bruce Levine, *The Spirit of 1848: German Immigrants, Labor Conflict, and the Coming of the Civil War* (Urbana: University of Illinois Press, 1992), 10.

26. Standing on the shoulders of Levine and other historians of the New Labor History school, a younger generation of scholars has produced fine analyses of ethnic radical groups. In particular, this book has been inspired by the following works:

Tony Michels, *A Fire in Their Hearts: Yiddish Socialists in New York* (Cambridge, MA: Harvard University Press, 2005); Tom Goyens, *Beer and Revolution: The German Anarchist Movement in New York City, 1880–1914* (Urbana: University of Illinois Press, 2007); Kenyon Zimmer, *Immigrants against the State: Yiddish and Italian Anarchism in America* (Urbana: University of Illinois Press, 2015).

27. Paul Buhle, *Marxism in the United States: A History of the American Left* (London: Verso, 1987).

28. Kathleen Cleaver, "Introduction," in David R. Roediger, *The Wages of Whiteness: Race and the Making of the American Working Class* (London: Verso, 2007), xxiv.

29. Besides Roediger's *Wages of Whiteness*, these are the works that have come to be identified as canonical: Alexander Saxton, *The Rise and Fall of the White Republic: Class Politics and Mass Culture in Nineteenth-Century America* (London: Verso, 1990); Theodore Allen, *The Invention of the White Race* (London: Verso, 1994–1997); Noel Ignatiev, *How the Irish Became White* (New York: Routledge, 1995); Ruth Frankenberg, *White Women, Race Matters: The Social Construction of Whiteness* (Minneapolis: University of Minnesota Press, 1993); Matthew Frye Jacobson, *Whiteness of a Different Color: European Immigrants and the Alchemy of Race* (Cambridge, MA: Harvard University Press, 1998). Roediger has offered an analysis of the origins of the approach and of the relationships between its most important proponents in his *Class, Race, and Marxism* (London: Verso, 2017), 47–72. Not everyone agrees on the utility of whiteness studies for the investigation of working-class racial ideologies. The most direct attack to the discipline remains Eric Arnesen, "Whiteness and the Historians' Imagination," *International Labor and Working-Class History*, no. 60 (Fall 2001): 3–32, with replies from James R. Barrett, David Brody, Barbara J. Fields, Eric Foner, Victoria C. Hattam, and Adolph Reed Jr. Analyses that attempt to formulate a balanced assessment of whiteness studies include Peter Kolchin, "Whiteness Studies: The New History of Race in America," *The Journal of American History*89, no. 1 (June 2002): 154–173, https://doi.org/10.2307/2700788; Andrew Hartman, "The Rise and Fall of Whiteness Studies," *Race and Class* 46, no. 2 (October 2004), https://doi.org/10.1177/0306396804047723: 22–38; John Munro, "Roots of 'Whiteness,'" *Labour/Le Travail* 54 (Fall 2004): 175–192, https://doi.org/10.2307/25149509.

30. James R. Barrett, "Whiteness Studies: Anything Here for Historians of the Working Class?" *International Labor and Working-Class History* 60 (October 2001): 38.

31. Anna Pegler-Gordon, "Debating the Racial Turn in U.S. Ethnic and Immigration History," *Journal of American Ethnic History* 36, no. 2 (Winter 2017): 40, https://doi.org/10.1017/S0147547901004392.

32. George J. Sanchez, "Race, Nation, and Culture in Recent Immigration Studies," *Journal of American Ethnic History* 18, no. 4 (Summer 1999): 69, https://doi.org/10.5406/jamerethnhist.36.2.0005.

33. John J. Bukowczyk, "The Racial Turn," *Journal of American Ethnic History* 36, no. 2 (Winter 2017): 5. On the 1999 debate between George J. Sanchez and Rudi Vecoli

and its historical relevance, see also Erika Lee, "A Part and Apart: Asian American and Immigration History," *Journal of American Ethnic History* 34, no. 4 (Summer 2015): 28–42.

34. Michael C. Dawson, *Blacks in and Out of the Left* (Cambridge, MA: Harvard University Press, 2013), ix.

35. On the Progressive Era, see the next footnote. On the Left in the 1930s, see footnote 50 and the conclusion of this book.

36. This description of the limits of early socialists on race is based on Munro, "Roots of 'Whiteness,'" 176–77. Eugene V. Debs's quote comes from "The Negro in the Class Struggle," *International Socialist Review* IV, no. 5 (November 1903). The only available analysis of Gilded Age socialist racial thinking is Foner, *American Socialism and Black Americans*. The Progressive Era period is better served. Sally M. Miller's pioneering work has recently been integrated by Paul Heideman. See Sally M. Miller, *Race, Ethnicity, and Gender in Early Twentieth-Century American Socialism* (London: Garland, 1996); Sally M. Miller, "For White Men Only: The Socialist Party of America and Issues of Gender, Ethnicity and Race," *The Journal of the Gilded Age and Progressive Era*, 2, no. 3 (July 2003): 283–302; Paul Heideman, "Introduction," in *Class Struggle and the Color Line: American Socialism and the Race Question, 1900–1930*, ed. Heideman (Chicago: Haymarket Books, 2018). Richard Iton touched on the SPA in the context of his broader argument that race prevented the creation of a left-wing party in the United States. See Richard Iton, *Solidarity Blues: Race, Culture, and the American Left* (Chapel Hill: University of North Carolina Press, 2000).

37. Cedric J. Robinson, *Black Marxism: The Making of the Black Radical Tradition* (Chapel Hill: University of North Carolina Press, 2000), 45–68. The idea of "racial capitalism" has recently been rediscovered and is now used for analyses of race and capitalism in the United States and across the world, both in the context of the "New History of Capitalism" but not only. See Sven Beckert and Christine Desan, eds., *American Capitalism: New Histories* (New York: Columbia University Press, 2018); Gargi Bhattacharyya, *Rethinking Racial Capitalism: Questions of Reproduction and Survival* (London: Rowman and Littlefield International, 2018); Destin Jenkins and Justin Leroy, eds., *Histories of Racial Capitalism* (New York: Columbia University Press, 2021).

38. Kevin B. Anderson, *Marx at the Margins: On Nationalism, Ethnicity, and Non-Western Societies* (Chicago: University of Chicago Press, 2016). On Marx and colonialism, authors that expand Anderson's point include Lucia Pradella, "Marx and the Global South: Connecting History and Value Theory," *Sociology* 51, no. 1 (2016): 146–61, https://doi.org/10.1177/0038038516661267; Sandro Mezzadra and Ranabir Samaddar, "Colonialism," in *The Marx Revival: Key Concepts and New Interpretations*, ed. Marcello Musto (Cambridge: Cambridge University Press, 2020), 247–65; Marcello Musto, *The Last Years of Karl Marx: An Intellectual Biography* (Stanford: Stanford University Press, 2020).

39. Geoff Eley, *Forging Democracy: The History of the Left in Europe, 1850–2000* (New York: Oxford University Press, 2002), 17–46.

40. Richard Hofstadter, *Social Darwinism in American Thought* (1944; repr., Boston: Beacon Press, 1992).

41. George W. Stocking Jr., *Race, Culture, and Evolution: Essays in the History of Anthropology* (New York: Free Press, 1968), 42–59; Robert C. Bannister, *Social Darwinism: Science and Myth in Anglo-American Social Thought* (Philadelphia: Temple University Press, 1979); Mike Hawkins, *Social Darwinism in European and American Thought, 1860–1945: Nature as Model and Nature as Threat* (Cambridge: Cambridge University Press, 1997); Thomas C. Leonard, "Origins of the Myth of Social Darwinism: The Ambiguous Legacy of Richard Hofstadter's Social Darwinism in American Thought," *Journal of Economic Behavior and Organization* 71, vol. 1 (July 2009): 37–51; Daniel E. Bender, *American Abyss: Savagery and Civilization in the Age of Industry* (Ithaca: Cornell University Press, 2009).

42. The only work on socialism and social evolutionism covering both the Gilded Age and the Progressive Era is Mark Pittenger, *American Socialists and Evolutionary Thought, 1870–1920* (Madison: University of Wisconsin Press, 1993). While unique and groundbreaking in its focus, Pittenger embraced too simplistic a notion of evolutionism, which he equated with Spencerism, and left out German-speaking socialists such as Friedrich A. Sorge and Adolph Douai. Progressive Era socialism is more thoroughly discussed but on no occasion with a specific focus on social evolutionism. See footnote 18.

43. Lorenzo Costaguta, "Before Baku: The Second International and the Debate on Colonialism (1900–1920)," in *The Comintern and the Global South: Global Designs / Local Encounters*, eds. Anne Garland Mahler and Paolo Capuzzo (London: Routledge, 2022).

44. The German socialist movement was divided between a Marxist and a Lassallean component, the trade unionist Social Democratic Workers' Party, and the electoral politics-focused General German Workers' Association. Distinctions were blurred and the two organizations partially overlapped in political strategy, while having a different geographical focus. Distances were bridged in 1875, when the two groups fused in the Socialist Labor Party of Germany (from 1890, Social Democratic Party of Germany). This is the event that inspired the creation of the WPUS. Selig Perlman, "Upheaval and Reorganisation (since 1876)," in John Commons et al., *History of Labour in the United States* (New York: Macmillan Company, 1935–1936), 269–301; Philip S. Foner, *History of the Labor Movement in the United States: From the Founding of the American Federation of Labor to the Emergence of American Imperialism* (New York: International Publishers, 1956), 32–47; W. L. Guttsman, *The German Social Democratic Party, 1875–1933: From Ghetto to Government* (London: George Allen and Unwin, 1981), 45–50.

45. On Chinese immigrants in the United States, see Madeline Y. Hsu, *Dreaming of Gold, Dreaming of Home: Transnationalism and Migration between the United States and South China, 1882–1943* (Stanford: Stanford University Press, 2002); Erika Lee, *At America's Gates: Chinese Immigration during the Exclusion Era, 1882–1943* (Chapel Hill: University of North Carolina Press, 2007); Beth Lew-Williams, *The Chinese Must Go: Violence, Exclusion, and the Making of the Alien in America* (Cambridge, MA:

Harvard University Press, 2018). On Native Americans, Richard White, *Railroaded: The Transcontinentals and the Making of Modern America* (New York: W. W. Norton, 2011). On the aftermath of the Civil War, with an emphasis on labor, Richardson, *The Death of Reconstruction*; Eric Arnesen, ed., *The Black Worker: Race, Labor, and Civil Rights since Emancipation* (Urbana: University of Illinois Press, 2007); Baker and Kelly, *After Slavery*; Matthew Hild and Keri Leigh Merritt, eds., *Reconsidering Southern Labor History: Race, Class, and Power* (Gainesville: University Press of Florida, 2018). For a broad list of the literature used in the book, please see the references in chapters three, four, and five.

46. Wendy Kline, *Building a Better Race: Gender, Sexuality, and Eugenics from the Turn of the Century to the Baby Boom* (Berkeley: University of California Press, 2001); Jonathan Peter Spiro, *Defending the Master Race: Conservation, Eugenics, and the Legacy of Madison Grant* (Burlington: University of Vermont Press, 2009).

47. William P. Jones, "'Nothing Special to Offer the Negro': Revisiting the 'Debsian View' of the Negro Question," *International Labor and Working-Class History* 74, no. 1 (Fall 2008): 212–24, https://doi.org/10.1017/S0147547908000252.

48. Miller, "For White Men Only."

49. Vladimir Ilyich Lenin, *Imperialism, the Highest Stage of Capitalism: A Popular Outline* (1917, repr., London: Lawrence and Wishart, 1934); Marilyn Lake and Henry Reynolds, *Drawing the Global Colour Line: White Men's Countries and the International Challenge of Racial Equality* (Cambridge: Cambridge University Press, 2012); Oleksa Drachewych and Ian McKay, eds., *Left Transnationalism: The Comintern and the National, Colonial and Racial Questions* (Montreal: McGill-Queen's University Press, 2019); David Featherstone and Christian Høgsbjerg, eds., *The Red and the Black: The Russian Revolution and the Black Atlantic* (Manchester: Manchester University Press, 2021).

50. On the period leading up to the "Black Belt Thesis," the resolution approved by the Comintern in 1928 on African Americans in the U.S., see Jacob A. Zumoff, *The Communist International and U.S. Communism, 1919–1929* (Leiden: Brill, 2014), 249–351; Heideman, *Class Struggle and the Color Line*. On interracial organizing in the 1930s in the U.S., Kelley, *Hammer and Hoe*; Mark Solomon, *The Cry Was Unity: Communists and African Americans, 1917–1936* (Jackson: University Press of Mississippi, 1998).

Chapter 1. "Freedom for All"

1. Karl Marx to Friedrich Engels, January 11, 1860, in *The Civil War in the United States*, ed. A. Zimmerman (New York: International Publishers, 2016), 17.

2. Karl Marx, *Capital: A Critical Analysis of Capitalist Production* (London: Swan Sonnenschein, 1887), 287.

3. "Karl Marx, on Behalf of the International Workingmen's Association, to Abraham Lincoln, November 22, 1864," in Marx and Engels, *The Civil War*, 153–54. On the relationship between Karl Marx and Abraham Lincoln, see Robin Blackburn, *An Unfinished Revolution: Karl Marx and Abraham Lincoln* (London: Verso, 2011).

4. Historian Angela Zimmerman traced a line of continuity in Marx's idea of revolution that went from the failed revolts of 1848 and 1849 to the successful struggle against slavery in the United States in the 1860s. The American Civil War was a wake-up call for European workers to take up that revolution from the point where they had left it in 1849. See A. Zimmerman, "From the Second American Revolution to the First International and Back Again: Marxism, the Popular Front, and the American Civil War," in *The World the Civil War Made*, eds. Gregory P. Downs and Kate Masur (Chapel Hill: University of North Carolina Press, 2015), 308. The Civil War offered an occasion to Marx and Engels to sharpen their analysis on capitalism, race, and class, as shown by August H. Nimtz Jr. and Kevin B. Anderson, among others. August H. Nimtz Jr., "Marx and Engels on the US Civil War: The 'Materialist Conception of History' in Action," *Historical Materialism* 19, no. 4 (2011): 175–98, https://doi.org/10.1163/156920611X592409; Kevin B. Anderson, "Marx's Intertwining of Race and Class during the Civil War in the United States," *Journal of Classical Sociology* 17, no. 1 (2017): 28–40, https://doi.org/10.1177/1468795X17691387.

5. Carl Wittke, *Refugees of Revolution: The German Forty-Eighters in America* (Philadelphia: University of Pennsylvania Press, 1952); Stanley Nadel, "From the Barricades of Paris to the Sidewalks of New York: German Artisans and the European Roots of American Labor Radicalism," *Labor History* 30, no. 1 (1989): 47–75, https://doi.org/10.1080/00236568900890021; Bruce Levine, *The Spirit of 1848: German Immigrants, Labor Conflict, and the Coming of the Civil War* (Urbana: University of Illinois Press, 1992); Mark A. Lause, *Long Road to Harpers Ferry: The Rise of the First American Left* (London: Pluto Press, 2018).

6. Levine, *Spirit of 1848*; Mischa Honeck, *We Are the Revolutionists: German-Speaking Immigrants and American Abolitionists after 1848* (Athens: University of Georgia Press, 2011); Alison Clark Efford, *German Immigrants, Race, and Citizenship in the Civil War Era* (Cambridge: Cambridge University Press, 2013).

7. Freidrich A. Sorge, "Joseph Weydemeyer un sein Anteil an der deutschen Bewegung der vierziger Jahre und an der amerikanischen Bewegung der fünfziger Jahre," *Pionier Illustrierter Volks-Kalender*, New York, 1897. For an extensive analysis of this fascinating yearly supplement published by the German American socialist community of New York City between 1882 and 1933, see Carol Poore, "The *Pionier* Calendar of New York City: Chronicler of German-American Socialism," in *The German-American Radical Press: The Shaping of a Left Political Culture, 1850–1940*, eds. Elliott Shore, Ken Fones-Wolf, and James P. Danky (Urbana: University of Illinois Press, 1992), 108–21.

8. Wilhelm Weitling expounded his doctrine in *Guarantees of Harmony and Freedom* (1842). For critical analyses of Weitling's role in the European socialist movement, see Carl Wittke, *The Utopian Communist: A Biography of Wilhelm Weitling, Nineteenth-Century Reformer* (Baton Rouge: LSU Press, 1950); Lothar Knatz and Hans-Arthur Marsiske, eds., *Wilhelm Weitling, ein deutscher Arbeiterkommunist* (Hamburg: Ergebnisse, 2000).

9. Jonathan Sperber, *Karl Marx: A Nineteenth-Century Life* (New York: Liverlight Publishing Corporation, 2013), 149–52. The 2017 movie *The Young Karl Marx* vividly

(if a bit dramatically) reconstructs the meeting. *The Young Karl Marx,* directed by Raoul Peck (Agat Films and Cie, 2017).

10. On Hermann Kriege in the United States, see Hermann Schlüter, *Die Anfänge der Deutschen Arbeiterbewegung in Amerika* (Stuttgart: J. W. W. Dietz, 1907), 29–50. The circular against Kriege was the only document the Communist Correspondence Committee ever produced. See Sperber, *Karl Marx,* 132; "Circular against Kriege," in Karl Marx and Friedrich Engels, *Collected Works* (London: Lawrence and Wishart, 2010), 6:35. In 1847, the Communist Correspondence Committee joined forces with the League of the Just and became the Communist League. In 1848, Marx and Engels wrote the program of the new organization: *The Communist Manifesto.* See B. Nicolaevsky, "Towards a History of 'the Communist League' 1847–1852," *International Review of Social History* 1, no. 2 (1956): 234–52.

11. James McPherson, *Battle Cry of Freedom: The Civil War Era* (New York: Oxford University Press, 1988), 78–112.

12. On Evans and the NRA, see Mark A. Lause, *Young America: Land, Labor, and the Republican Community* (Urbana: University of Illinois Press, 2005).

13. Quoted in Schlüter, *Die Anfänge der Deutschen Arbeiterbewegung,* 189; see also Levine, *Spirit of 1848,* 151–52.

14. At the beginning of his time in the United States, Weitling edited the *Volk-Tribun* and took part in Kriege's Social Reform Association. After Kriege's sudden death in 1850, Weitling started his own association and paper—the Arbeirterbund and the *Republik der Arbeiter,* respectively.

15. "Etwas für die Schwarzen," *Republik der Arbeiter,* October 1850. In the same issue, see also "Flecken im Sternenbanner."

16. "Die elementaren Richtungen der Zeit," *Republik der Arbeiter,* May 27, 1854. The *Republik der Arbeiter* published a wealth of antislavery material, including correspondence from German immigrants in the South. Evidence from Weitling's paper contradicts Marxist historian Hermann Schlüter, who wrongly claimed that "throughout his career Weitling treated slavery in a completely superficial way." Schlüter, *Die Anfänge,* 190; Hermann Schlüter, *Lincoln, Labor, and Slavery: A Chapter from the Social History of America* (New York: Socialist Literature, 1913), 72–73. A complete edition of the *Republik der Arbeiter,* with tables of contents and an introduction by Gian Mario Bravo, is available in *Die Republik der Arbeiter, New York 1850–1855* (Vaduz: Topos Verlag, 1979).

17. Quoted in Levine, *Spirit of 1848,* 150.

18. Levine, *Spirit of 1848*; August H. Nimtz Jr., *Marx, Tocqueville, and Race in America: The 'Absolute Democracy' or 'Defiled Republic'* (Lanham: Lexington Books, 2002), 41–86; Honeck, *We Are the Revolutionists*; Efford, *German Immigrants,* 53–66.

19. Born in 1818 in Münster, an early attempt to conduct a military career in the Prussian army had rapidly turned Weydemeyer into a fierce enemy of the Prussian autocratic regime. Weydemeyer became close friends with Marx in the mid-1840s while working as editor of the *Trierische Zeitung* in Marx's hometown, Trier. See Karl Obermann, *Joseph Weydemeyer: Pioniere del socialismo in America, 1851–1866* (Milano: Edizioni Pantarei, 2002); David Herreshoff, *The Origins of American Marxism, from*

the Transcendentalists to De Leon (New York: Monad Press, 1973), 62–68; Justine Davis Randers-Pehrson, *Adolf Douai, 1819–1888: The Turbulent Life of a German Forty-Eighter in the Homeland and in the United States* (New York: Peter Lang, 2000), 285.

20. Karl Marx, "The Eighteen Brumaire of Louis Bonaparte," *Die Revolution*, December 1851–March 1852 (repr. New York: Mondial, 2005); Obermann, *Joseph Weydemeyer*, 50–81.

21. Levine, *Spirit of 1848*, 92, 102; Richard T. Ely, *The Labor Movement in America* (New York: Thomas Y. Crowell, 1886), 221–23; Herreshoff, *Origins of American Marxism*, 60–62; Sorge, "Joseph Weydemeyer."

22. *Turn-Zeitung*, September 1, 1852; Obermann, *Joseph Weydemeyer*, 91; Herreshoff, *Origins of American Marxism*, 61.

23. On Marx and Engels's writings on slavery, see Marx and Engels, *The Civil War*.

24. Levine, *Spirit of 1848*, 148–58.

25. Philip S. Foner and Brewster Chamberlin, eds., *Friedrich A. Sorge's Labor Movement in the United States: A History of the American Working Class from Colonial Times to 1890* (Westport, CT: Greenwood Press, 1977), 94–95.

26. "German Anti-Nebraska Demonstration," *New York Times*, March 2, 1854; Obermann, *Joseph Weydemeyer*, 172.

27. Henry Matzner, *A Brief History of the American Turnerbund*, trans. by Theodore Stempfel Jr. (Pittsburgh: Executive Committee of the American Turnerbund, 1924), 13.

28. Eric Foner, *Free Soil, Free Labor, Free Men: The Ideology of the Republican Party before the Civil War* (New York: Oxford University Press, 1995), 301–17.

29. Joseph Weydemeyer, "Zur Tariffrage," *Illinois Staats-Zeitung*, n.d. An undated clipping of Weydemeyer's article is available in the Joseph Weydemeyer Papers, International Institute of Social History, Amsterdam, Folder 339. Weydemeyer's series was also used by Friedrich Kapp in his book on slavery in the United States. See Friedrich Kapp, *Geschichte der Sklaverei in den Vereinigten Staaten von Amerika* (New York: L. Hauser, 1860), 184–85. Kapp and Weydemeyer presented in different evenings during a talk series organized by the Mercantile Library Association of New York. See Obermann, *Joseph Weydemeyer*, 176–78. A copy of Weydemeyer's speech on the economic situation in the South is available in Weydemeyer's archive at the International Institute of Social History, Folder 334. Weydemeyer also wrote on the subject in the *Westliche Post*. See Joseph Weydemeyer, "Die Finanzzustand im Süden: Die Operationen des Schatzsecretärs Cobb," *Westliche Post*, December 15, 1860.

30. Adolph Douai, *Autobiography of Dr. Adolf Douai: Revolutionary of 1848, Texas Pioneer, Introducer of Kindergarten, Educator, Author, Editor, 1819–1888*, trans. and ed. Richard H. Douai Böker, 1959, Adolph Douai Papers, Briscoe Center for American History at the University of Texas, Austin, Folder 2, 65.

31. Robert A. Calvert, Arnoldo De Leon, and Gregg Cantrell, *The History of Texas* (Hoboken: Wiley-Blackwell, 2013), 85–95, 127–30.

32. Calvert, De Leon, and Cantrell, *History of Texas*, 112, 118.

33. W. Darrell Overdyke, *The Know-Nothing Party in the South* (Gloucester, MA: Pater Smith, 1968).

34. Douai, *Autobiography of Dr. Adolf Douai*, 26.

35. As for the plan of being a farmer, after a few excursions in the New Braunfels outskirts, that idea was immediately dropped. Douai, *Autobiography of Dr. Adolf Douai*, 100–105.

36. Douai, *Autobiography of Dr. Adolf Douai*, 112.

37. Adolph Douai, "Ein Labensbild. Sclavenhälter und Sclaven," *San Antonio Zeitung*, August 27, 1853.

38. Adolph Douai, "Die freiein Farbigen in den Nicht-Sclaven Staaten," *San Antonio Zeitung*, August 12, 1854.

39. "Free Labor and Slave Labor," *San Antonio Zeitung*, May 5, 1855.

40. Adolph Douai, "The South and the Middle Class," *San Antonio Zeitung*, January 6, 1855.

41. This is the letter that Thomas Jefferson sent to Edward Coles in August 1814. See Thomas Jefferson to Edward Coles, August 25, 1814, Thomas Jefferson Papers at the Library of Congress, Manuscript Division, Library of Congress.

42. Adolph Douai, "A Letter of Thomas Jefferson," *San Antonio Zeitung*, December 2, 1854.

43. Douai, "A Letter of Thomas Jefferson."

44. Carl Wittke, *Against the Current: The Life of Karl Heinzen (1809–80)* (Chicago: University of Chicago Press, 1945), 94.

45. Thomas Alter II, *Toward a Cooperative Commonwealth: The Transplanted Roots of Farmer-labor Radicalism in Texas* (Urbana: University of Illinois Press, 2022), 37–40. Honeck, *We Are the Revolutionists*, 43; "Die Platform der freier Männer," *San Antonio Zeitung*, April 15, 1854.

46. Honeck, *We Are the Revolutionists*, 43–46.

47. "A Last Word," *San Antonio Zeitung*, December 8, 1855.

48. Loyd David Easton, *Hegel's First American Followers: the Ohio Hegelians: John B. Stallo, Peter Kaufmann, Moncure Conway, and August Willich, with Key Writings* (Athens: University of Ohio Press, 1966), 159–70; David T. Dixon, *Radical Warrior: August Willich's Journey from German Revolutionary to Union General* (Knoxville: University of Tennessee Press, 2020). Like Kriege and Weitling, Willich picked up a fight with Karl Marx, in this case involving a challenge to a duel, which Marx refused, opting for a more familiar challenge on paper. See Karl Marx, "The Knight of Noble Consciousness," in Marx and Engels, *Collected Works*, 12:479.

49. Easton, *Hegel's First American Followers*, 180; Honeck, *We Are the Revolutionists*, 20.

50. August Willich, "Was geht uns der Nigger an? Wir wollen mit uns selbst anfangen!" *Cincinnati Republikaner*, October 3, 1859.

51. Willich, "Was geht uns."

52. August Willich, "Die Rubicon ist vollbracht! Die Racherhat vollbracht! +John Brown+," *Cincinnati Republikaner*, December 3, 1859.

53. The details of the meeting are taken from Honeck, *We Are the Revolutionists*, 71–73, 94–97; see also August Willich, "Die Todesfeier John Browns," *Cincinnati Republikaner*, December 5, 1859.

54. August Willich, "Die Todesfeier John Browns."

55. Mischa Honeck, "An Unexpected Alliance: August Willich, Peter H. Clark, and the Abolitionist Movement in Cincinnati," in *Germans and African Americans: Two Centuries of Exchange*, eds. Larry A. Greene and Anke Ortlepp (Jackson: University Press of Mississippi, 2010), 31.

56. August Willich, "Zur Frage: sind die Farbigen Menschen oder nicht? Der Deutsche, der Amerikaner, der Afrikaner," *Cincinnati Republikaner*, December 27, 1859.

57. Joseph R. Reinhart, ed., *August Willich's Gallant Dutchmen: Civil War Letters from the 32nd Indian Infantry* (Kent, OH: Kent State University Press, 2006), 22–23.

58. Reinhart, *August Willich's Gallant Dutchmen*, 142.

59. Zimmerman, "Second American Revolution," 313; Obermann, *Joseph Weydemeyer*, 209–50.

60. "Platform," *San Antonio Zeitung*, August 27, 1853.

61. Obermann, *Joseph Weydemeyer*, 171–181; Foner and Chamberlin, *Friedrich A. Sorge*, 95–97; Schlüter, *Die Anfänge*, 194.

62. Nimtz, *Marx, Tocqueville, and Race*, 72–74.

63. Obermann, *Joseph Weydemeyer*, 225; Efford, *German Immigrants*, 118–19; David T. Burbank, City of Little Bread: The St. Louis General Strike of 1877 (Unpublished microcard, 1957), 22–25.

64. On St. Louis in the aftermath of the Civil War, see Walter Johnson, *The Broken Heart of America: St. Louis and the Violent History of the United States* (New York: Basic Books, 2020), 239–44; the debate on Black suffrage in Missouri after the Civil War has been accurately described in Efford, *German Immigrants*, 87–114. The quote on St. Louis as "imperial capital of the 'white man's country'" is from Johnson, *Broken Heart of America*, 243.

65. Eric Foner, *A Short History of Reconstruction, 1863–1877* (New York: Harper and Row Publishers, 1990), 23–28.

66. *Westliche Post*, September 1, 1865.

67. *Westliche Post*, September 1, 1865. Weydemeyer was referring to the so-called Port Royal Experiment, a successful attempt to distribute lands to freed African Americans that started in 1861. See Willie Lee Rose, *Rehearsal for Reconstruction: The Port Royal Experiment* (Athens: University of Georgia Press, 1999).

68. *Westliche Post*, September 1, 1865. Weydemeyer's analysis anticipates W. E. B. Du Bois's point of view, who in *Black Reconstruction in America* identified the "Black worker" as the protagonist of the Civil War and Reconstruction. See W. E. B. Du Bois, *Black Reconstruction in America, 1860–1880* (New York: The Free Press, 1932); Brian Kelly, "W. E. B. Du Bois, Black Agency, and the Slaves' Civil War," *International Socialist Review*, no. 100 (Spring 2016). Historians have thoroughly documented the repeated and insisted attempts of free Blacks to educate themselves and use their civil rights in the immediate aftermath of Civil War. See Bruce E. Baker and Brian Kelly, eds., *After Slavery: Race, Labor, and Citizenship in the Reconstruction South* (Gainesville: University Press of Florida, 2013); Heather Andrea Williams, *Self-Taught: African American Education in Slavery and Freedom* (Chapel Hill: University

of North Carolina Press, 2007); David Williams, *I Freed Myself: African American Self-Emancipation in the Civil War Era* (Cambridge: Cambridge University Press, 2014).

69. *Westliche Post*, September 8, 1865.

70. *Westliche Post*, September 8, 1865. See also David R. Roediger, *Seizing Freedom: Slave Emancipation and Liberty for All* (London: Verso, 2014), 105–46.

71. Richard White, *The Republic for Which It Stands: The United States during Reconstruction and the Gilded Age, 1865–1896* (New York: Oxford University Press, 2017), 194–95.

72. David Montgomery, *Beyond Equality: Labor and the Radical Republicans, 1862–1872* (New York: Knopf, 1967), 176–77; Philip S. Foner and David R. Roediger, *Our Own Time: A History of American Labor and the Working Day* (London: Verso, 1989), 81–120.

73. Labeled by some historians "labor republicanism," this set of values continued to characterize the American working class in the 1870s and 1880s, becoming the cornerstone upon which some of the most important workers' organizations of the Gilded Age (such as the Knights of Labor in the 1880s) were built. See Leon Fink, *Workingmen's Democracy: The Knights of Labor and American Politics* (Urbana: University of Illinois Press, 1983); Joseph Gerteis, *Class and the Color Line: Interracial Class Coalition in the Knights of Labor and the Populist Movement* (Durham: Duke University Press, 2007). A critical treatment of the category of republicanism can be found in Daniel T. Rodgers, "Republicanism: The Career of a Concept," *The Journal of American History* 79, no. 1 (June 1992), 11–38, https://doi.org/10.2307/2078466.

74. Hermann Schlüter, *Die Internationale in Amerika: Ein Beitrag zur Geschichte der Arbeiter-Bewegung in den Vereingten Staaten* (Chicago: Deutsche Sprachgruppe der Sozialist. Partei der Ver. Staaten, 1918), 80–98; David Montgomery, *Citizen Worker: The Experience of Workers in the United States with Democracy and the Free Market during the Nineteenth Century* (Cambridge: Cambridge University Press, 1993), 142; Dorothee Schneider, *Trade Unions and Community: The German Working Class In New York City, 1870–1900* (Urbana: University of Illinois Press, 1994), 45. On the Communist Club: Statuten des Kommunisten Klubs in New York, Reel 2, International Workingmen's Association Papers, Microfilmed edition, International Institute of Social History, Amsterdam. August H. Nimtz emphatically defined the Communist Club as "the first Marxist organization in the Western hemisphere." See Nimtz, *Marx, Tocqueville, and Race in America*, 68. He probably misquoted Philip S. Foner, who offered a more moderate assessment of its Marxist inclination: "On October 25, 1857, some former members of the European Communist League in the New York metropolitan area formed the Communist Club, the first one in the Western Hemisphere. The club corresponded with Marx and with members of utopian settlements in America." Philip S. Foner, *American Socialism and Black Americans: From the Age of Jackson to World War II* (Westport, CT: Greenwood Press, 1977), 5. Other sources seem to suggest that the links with the European movement were limited, to say the least. In 1868, Weydemeyer sent a letter to Karl Marx introducing

the vice president of the club, Albert Komp, and mildly suggesting that Marx established a connection with the group ("Something good might come out of it," wrote Weydemeyer). It is not clear whether Marx ever picked up the suggestion. The Club gathered radicals of various inspirations, including utopian socialists, freethinkers, and atheists. It is unclear why this group picked "communist" as its defining feature. See Herreshoff, *American Disciples*, 68–69; letter by Weydemeyer quoted in Obermann, *Joseph Weydemeyer*, 181.

75. Roediger, *Seizing Freedom*, 111. On the foundation and early history of the IWA, see Marcello Musto, ed., *Workers Unite! The International 150 Years Later* (London: Bloomsbury, 2014).

76. Samuel Bernstein, *The First International in America* (New York: August M. Kelley, 1965), 26–34; Timothy Messer-Kruse, *The Yankee International: Marxism and the American Reform Tradition, 1848–1876* (Chapel Hill: University of North Carolina Press, 1998), 61. Sorge suggested that the task of this delegate was to study "emigrant conditions and make appropriate contacts," which could imply attending the IWA congress. Foner and Chamberlin, *Friedrich A. Sorge*, 140.

77. Lorenzo Costaguta and Johannes S. Lotze, "Multilingualism and Transnationalism in the Study of Socialist Movements: A Letter from Friedrich A. Sorge to Karl Marx," *RSA Journal* 31 (2020), 227–52; Karl Marx to Hermann Meyer, July 4, 1868, in Karl Marx and Friedrich Engels, *Letters to Americans: 1848–1895* (New York: International Publishers, 1953), 74–75. Philip S. Foner and Timothy Messer-Kruse argued that Section 1 received credentials in 1867. This is not correct. The Communist Club voted to join the IWA in 1867, but its entrance was not approved until 1869, as specified by Bernstein and Schlüter. See Philip S. Foner, "Friedrich Adolph Sorge: 'Father of Modern Socialism in America,'" in Foner and Chamberlin, *Friedrich A. Sorge*, 15; Messer-Kruse, *Yankee International*, 72–73; Bernstein, *First International in America*, 31; Hermann Schlüter, *La Prima Internazionale in America: Un contributo alla storia del movemimento operaio negli Stati Uniti* (Milano: Edizioni Lotta Comunista, 2015), 8.

78. "Die Internationale Arbeiter Association and die National Arbeiter-Union der Vereinigten Staaten," *Arbeiter Union*, June 2, 1869; Foner and Chamberlin, *Friedrich A. Sorge*, 155; Montgomery, *Beyond Equality*, 165–68; Selig Perlman, "Upheaval and Reorganisation (from 1877)," in John Commons et al., *History of Labour in the United States*, (New York: Macmillan Company, 1935–36), 2:223–24; Stan Nadel, "The German Immigrant Left in the United States," in *The Immigrant Left in the United States*, eds. Paul Buhle and Dan Georgakas (Albany: State University of New York Press, 1996), 53–54.

79. *Statuten des Kommunisten Klubs in New York*, Reel 2, International Workingmen's Association Papers, Microfilmed edition, International Institute of Social History, Amsterdam.

80. Foner, *American Socialism*, 37.

81. Messer-Kruse, *Yankee International*, 192; Schlüter, *La Prima Internazionale*, 10; Foner, *American Socialism*, 37.

82. "Die weißen und die schwarzen Arbeiter," *Arbeiter Union*, December 1869.

83. See Costaguta and Lotze, "Multilingualism and Transnationalism." An extensive biographical profile of Sorge is Foner, "*Friedrich Adolph Sorge*," 3–41. See also Herreshoff, *American Disciples*, 68–72; Stanley Nadel, "The Forty-Eighters and the Politics of Class in New York City," in *The German Forty-Eighters in the United States*, ed. Charlotte Brancaforte (New York: Peter Lang, 1989), 52–53.

84. Quoted in Messer-Kruse, *Yankee International*, 183.

85. Friedrich Engels claimed that Karl Marx said this phrase in two different letters. See Friedrich Engels to Eduard Bernstein, November 2–3, 1882, in Marx and Engels, *Collected Works*, 46:353; Engels to Conrad Schmidt, August 5, 1890, Marxists.org, https://www.marxists.org/archive/marx/works/1890/letters/90_08_05.htm.

86. Ellen Meiksins Wood, "Democracy," in *The Marx Revival: Key Concepts and New Interpretations*, ed. Marcello Musto (Cambridge: Cambridge University Press, 2020), 51–69.

87. Sorge never published works of political analysis in which he explicitly described his approach. In the sole pamphlet he authored, he offered a broad description of what socialism was without going into significant details on strategy. See Friedrich A. Sorge, *Socialism and the Worker* (London: Justice Printery, 1890, repr. on Marxists.org, https://www.marxists.org/archive/sorge/1876/socialism-worker.htm). Sorge's hostility toward the ballot box clearly transpired in his memories on the American labor movement (see Foner and Chamberlin, *Friedrich A. Sorge*, 109–10, 160–61) and in his political conduct (see Foner, "*Friedrich Adolph Sorge*," 22–24; Messer-Kruse, *Yankee International*, 143–48).

88. Foner and Chamberlin, *Friedrich A. Sorge*, 156.

89. Bernstein, *First International in America*, 64.

90. On trade unionism in the IWA, see Marcello Musto, "Introduction," in *Workers Unite!*, ed. Musto, 36. On Marx, peasants and wage workers, see Marx quoted in Kevin B. Anderson, *Marx at the Margins: On Nationalism, Ethnicity, and Non-Western Societies* (Chicago: University of Chicago Press, 2016), 147–48.

91. According to the 1870 census, around 92 percent of the African American population lived in southern states (4,495,478 of 4,880,009). See from Francis A. Walker, *A Compendium of the Ninth Census* (Washington: Government Printing Office, 1872), 10–12.

92. Karl Marx to Meyer and Vogt, April 9, 1870, in Marx and Engels *Collected Works*, 43:474–75.

93. Marx and Engels, *Collected Works*, 43:474–75. Marx's letter was written in German. The word "niggers" was in English in Marx's original. Kevin Anderson noted that "again, as in several passages in his writings on the Civil War, Marx is using a racist term to make an antiracist point." See Anderson, *Marx at the Margins*, 269–70; Foner, *American Socialism and Black Americans*, 41.

94. Notebook, 1868, Reel 1, International Workingmen's Association Papers, Microfilmed edition, International Institute of Social History, Amsterdam.

95. "Die Wahl in Virginien," *Arbeiter Union*, July 9, 1869; on the 1869 vote in Virginia, see Foner, *Short History of Reconstruction*, 180–81.

96. *The Hague Congress of the First International, September 2–7, 1872, Minutes and Documents* (Moscow: Progress Publishers, 1976), 136. Messer-Kruse reported Sorge saying "niggers" instead of "Negroes" on this occasion, saying that "Engels has Sorge using the German word 'negern' in his account." *Negern* is the plural of the word *Neger* which means "Negro" in German. The English translations of the source use "Negroes." See Messer-Kruse, *Yankee International*, 180, 282 (fn. 55).

97. Bernstein, *First International in America*, 60–61; Messer-Kruse, *Yankee International*, 149–156, 180–81.

98. "Abschied von unsern Lesern," *Arbeiter Union*, September 15, 1870; Foner and Chamberlin, *Friedrich A. Sorge*, 151; Messer-Kruse, *Yankee International*, 100–106; J. Michelle Coghlan, *Sensational Internationalism: The Paris Commune and the Remapping of American Memory in the Long Nineteenth Century* (Edinburgh: Edinburgh University Press, 2016).

99. On the Woodhull sisters, see Amanda Frisken, *Victoria Woodhull's Sexual Revolution: Political Theater and the Popular Press in Nineteenth-Century America* (Philadelphia: University of Pennsylvania Press, 2004); Myra MacPherson, *The Scarlet Sisters: Sex, Suffrage, and Scandal in the Gilded Age* (New York: Twelve, 2014). On William West, see Mark A. Lause, "The American Radicals and Organized Marxism: The Initial Experience, 1869–1874," *Labor History* 33, no. 1 (1992): 55–80.

100. Messer-Kruse, *Yankee International*, 43.

101. Messer-Kruse, *Yankee International*, 11.

102. Foner, *American Socialism*, 37–38; Messer-Kruse, *Yankee International*, 195–97.

103. Messer Kruse, *Yankee International*, 201–07.

104. Herreshoff, *Origins of American Marxism*, 91.

105. On West's trip to The Hague, Lause, "American Radicals and Organized Marxism," 55–56. In his otherwise detailed history of the American labor movement, Sorge glossed over the details of these events. See Foner and Chamberlin, *Friedrich A. Sorge*, 159. A balanced reconstruction of these events can be found in Michel Cordillot, "Socialism v. Democracy? The IWMA in the USA, 1869–1876," in *"Arise Ye Wretched of the Earth:" The First International in a Global Perspective*, ed. Fabrice Bensimon et al. (Leiden: Brill, 2018), 270–81.

106. David T. Burbank, "The First International in St. Louis," in *Missouri Historical Society Bulletin* 18 (January 1962): 163–71; Michel Cordillot, *Aux Origines du Socialisme Moderne: Le Première International, la Commune de Paris, l'Exil* (Paris: Les Editions de l'Atelier, 2010).

107. John B. Jentz and Richard Schneirov, *Chicago in the Age of Capital: Class, Politics, and Democracy During the Civil War and Reconstruction* (Urbana: University of Illinois Press, 2012), 152–70; James Green, *Death in the Haymarket: A Story of Chicago, the First Labor Movement, and the Bombing that Divided Gilded Age America* (New York: Anchor Books, 2007), 49–51.

108. "Kapital gegen Arbeit oder die Weißenhetze gegen die Neger," *Vorbote*, September 19, 1874.

109. "Die Farbigen im Süden," *Vorbote*, September 26, 1874.

110. "Aus dem Süden," *Vorbote*, October 17, 1874.
111. "Die Rassenkampf im Süden," *Vorbote*, December 26, 1874.
112. Schlüter, *Lincoln, Labor, and Slavery*.

Chapter 2. "Geographies of Peoples"

1. "Frederick Engels's Speech at the Grave of Karl Marx," Marxists.org, accessed November 1, 2018, https://www.marxists.org/archive/marx/works/1883/death/burial.htm.

2. Quoted in Richard Weikart, *Socialist Darwinism: Evolution in German Socialist Thought from Marx to Bernstein* (San Francisco: International Scholars Publications, 1999), 22.

3. Margaret A. Fay, "Did Marx Offer to Dedicate *Capital* to Darwin? A Reassessment of the Evidence," *Journal of the History of Ideas* 39, no. 1 (1978): 133–46, https://doi.org/10.2307/2709077.

4. Diane Paul, "'In the Interests of Civilization:' Marxist Views of Race and Culture in the Nineteenth Century," *Journal of the History of Ideas* 42, no. 1 (1981): 115–38, https://doi.org/10.2307/2709420; Mark Pittenger, *American Socialists and Evolutionary Thought, 1870–1920* (Madison: University of Wisconsin Press, 1993); Manfred B. Steger, *The Quest for Evolutionary Socialism: Eduard Bernstein and Social Democracy* (Cambridge: Cambridge University Press, 1997), Weikart, *Socialist Darwinism*; David Stack, *The First Darwinian Left: Socialism and Darwinism, 1859–1914* (Cheltenham: New Clarion Press, 2003); Lorenzo Costaguta, "Before Baku: The Second International and the Debate on Race and Colonialism," in *Global Designs/Local Encounters: Political Imaginaries of the Third International*, eds. Anne Garland Mahler and Paolo Capuzzo (London: Routledge, forthcoming).

5. On the spread of Darwinism in the United States, see Mike Hawkins, *Social Darwinism in European and American Thought, 1860–1945: Nature as Model and Nature as Threat* (Cambridge: Cambridge University Press, 1997); Ronald L. Numbers, *Darwinism Comes to America* (Cambridge, MA: Harvard University Press, 1998). Richard Hofstadter's concept of "social Darwinism" retains some influence in the literature. This is a concept I avoid because I contend that it does not help to explain how theories of race developed during the Gilded Age. See Richard Hofstadter, *Social Darwinism in American Thought* (Boston: Beacon Press, 1955); Robert C. Bannister, *Social Darwinism: Science and Myth in Anglo-American Social Thought* (Philadelphia: Temple University Press, 1979); Thomas C. Leonard, "Origins of the Myth of Social Darwinism: The Ambiguous Legacy of Richard Hofstadter's Social Darwinism in American Thought," *Journal of Economic Behavior and Organization* 71 (2009): 37–51.

6. The literature on the diffusion of Darwinism in Germany include Sara Eigen and Mark Larrimore, *The German Invention of Race* (New York: State University of New York Press, 2006); Daniel Gasman, *The Scientific Origins of National Socialism: Social Darwinism in Ernst Haeckel and the German Monist League* (London: Macdonald, 1971); Alfred Kelly, *The Descent of Darwin: The Popularization of Darwinism in*

Germany, 1860–1914 (Chapel Hill: University of North Carolina Press, 1981); Robert J. Richards, *The Tragic Sense of Life: Ernst Haeckel and the Struggle over Evolutionary Thought* (Chicago: University of Chicago Press, 2008).

7. Carol Poore documented the significance of the 1876 centennial celebration in the German American community. However, curiously, her article does not link German American celebrations across the country with the foundation of the WPUS in Philadelphia. See Carol Poore, "Whose Celebration? The Centennial of 1876 and German-American Socialist Culture," in *America and the Germans: An Assessment of a Three-Hundred Year History*, eds. Frank Trommler and Joseph McVeigh (Philadelphia: University of Pennsylvania Press, 1985), 1:176–89. On the foundation of the WPUS, see Philip S. Foner, *The Formation of the Workingmen's Party of the United States: Proceedings of the Union Congress Held at Philadelphia, July 19–22, 1876* (New York: American Institute for Marxist Studies, 1976). Apart from the people mentioned, two other workers attended the convention: A. Gabriel, who was part of the delegation of the Social Democratic Party of North America, and Chas. Braun, representing the Socio-Political Workingmen's Society of Cincinnati. Foner, *Formation of the Workingmen's Party*, 12–13.

8. The three newspapers already existed as publications of the Social Democratic Party of North America and the Workingmen's Party of Illinois. During the founding convention, it was decided that the *Social Demokrat* would be renamed *Arbeiter Stimme* and published in New York City; that the *Socialist* would be renamed *Labor Standard* and published in New York City; and that the *Vorbote* would keep its name and be published in Chicago. Foner, *Formation of the Workingmen's Party*, 17–19.

9. Justine Davis Randers-Pehrson, *Adolf Douai, 1819–1888: The Turbulent Life of a German Forty-Eighter in the Homeland and in the United States* (New York: Peter Lang, 2000).

10. Adolph Douai, *Autobiography of Dr. Adolf Douai: Revolutionary of 1848, Texas Pioneer, Introducer of Kindergarten, Educator, Author, Editor, 1819–1888*, trans. and ed. Richard H. Douai Böker, 1959, Folder 2, Adolph Douai Papers, Briscoe Center for American History at the University of Texas, Austin, 37.

11. Douai, *Autobiography of Dr. Adolf Douai*, 144.

12. Adolph Douai, "Die Geographie der Menschen," *San Antonio Zeitung*, April 4, 1854; Adolph Douai, *Land und Leute in der Union* (Berlin: Otto Janke, 1864).

13. Adolph Douai, "Abstammung und Anpassung beim Menschengeschlecht," *Vorbote*, December 7, 1878.

14. Reginald Horsman, *Race and Manifest Destiny: The Origins of American Racial Anglo-Saxonism* (Cambridge, MA: Cambridge University Press, 1981), 45.

15. Charles Louis de Secondat de Montesquieu, *The Spirit of Laws* (1748; repr. New York: The Colonial Press, 1899), 224.

16. Peter J. Bowler, *Evolution: The History of an Idea* (Berkeley: University of California Press, 1989), 90–150.

17. Bowler, *Evolution*, 156–64.

18. Bowler, *Evolution*, 151–86.

19. It is striking that Douai did not mention the fact that Charles Darwin had applied his theory of evolution to the human species in *The Descent of Man, and Selection in Relation to Sex*, a book published in 1871. Although we have no comments from Douai himself, it is plausible to assume that the German American believed that on human evolution, more work could be done. In particular, as we will see, Douai deemed it necessary to use Darwinism in conjunction with other scientific trends of the time, such as naturalism and linguistics.

20. Adolph Douai, "Abstammung und Anpassung," December 14, 1878-January 25, 1879.

21. Douai, "Abstammung und Anpassung," December 14, 1878.

22. Douai, "Abstammung und Anpassung," December 28, 1878.

23. Douai, "Abstammung und Anpassung," December 28, 1878.

24. Horsman, *Race and Manifest Destiny*, 48.

25. Adrian Desmond and James Moore, *Darwin's Sacred Cause: Race, Slavery, and the Quest for Human Origins* (London: Allen Lane, 2009), 27–110.

26. Desmond and Moore, *Darwin's Sacred Cause*, 111–141.

27. Douai, "Abstammung und Anpassung," January 18, 1878.

28. Richards, *Tragic Sense of Life*, 271.

29. Douai, "Abstammung und Anpassung," January 18, 1878.

30. Susan Jeffords, "The Knowledge of Words: The Evolution of Language and Biology in Nineteenth-Century Thought," *The Centennial Review* 31, no. 1 (1987): 66–83.

31. August Schleicher, *Darwinism Tested by the Science of Language* (Cambridge: Chadwick-Healey, 1986); John P. Maher, "More on the History of the Comparative Method: The Tradition of Darwinism in August Schleicher's Work," *Anthropological Linguistics* 8, no. 3 (1966): 1–12.

32. Nicolaas A. Rupke, *Alexander von Humboldt: A Metabiography* (Chicago: University of Chicago Press, 2008), 1–27; Walls, *Passage to Cosmos*, 12–48.

33. Sandra Nichols, "Why Was Humboldt Forgotten in the United States?" *Geographical Review* 96, no. 3 (July 2006): 399–415.

34. Laura Dassow Walls, *The Passage to Cosmos: Alexander von Humboldt and the Shaping of America* (Chicago: University of Chicago Press, 2009), 120–29; Nichols, "Why Was Humboldt Forgotten?" 405.

35. Randers-Pehrson, *Adolf Douai*, 257–58. During the commemoration, Douai entered in a dispute with a protégé of the renowned naturalist Louis Agassiz, who had celebrated Humboldt for his religious faith. Douai, a fierce atheist, slandered his intervention on the stage and was later attacked by Agassiz himself. See Randers-Pehrson, *Adolf Douai*, 259–60.

36. Quoted in Walls, *Passage to Cosmos*, 175.

37. Quoted in Walls, *Passage to Cosmos*, 175. Humboldt's theory of human differences, with its emphasis on diversity and the impossibility of classifying human differences, was an antecedent of Franz Boas's cultural pluralism. See Matti Bunzl, "Franz Boas and the Humboldtian Tradition: From Volksgeist and Nationalcharakter

to an Anthropological Concept of Culture," in *Volksgeist as Method and Ethic: Essays on Boasian Ethnography and the German Anthropological Tradition*, ed. George W. Stocking Jr. (Madison: University of Wisconsin Press, 1996).

38. Douai, "Abstammung und Anpassung," January 4, 1878. See infra chapter 1; Adolph Douai, "The Real Number of Foreign-Born Inhabitants of the U. St.," *San Antonio Zeitung,* November 25, 1854.

39. Douai, "Abstammung und Anpassung," January 25, 1878.

40. Adolph Douai's opinions on African Americans are explored in more detail in chapter four.

41. "Darwinism," *Socialist*, September 28, 1878. The article was originally published in *The Index* (date and author n.a.).

42. Angela Zimmerman reconstructed the clash between anthropology and humanist thought. Kelly and Weikart contributed with a focus on Darwinism and socialism. A. Zimmerman, *Anthropology and Antihumanism in Imperial Germany* (Chicago: University of Chicago Press, 2001), 1–10, 63–80; Kelly, *Descent of Darwin*, 3–35; Weikart, *Socialist Darwinism.*

43. Hartmut Keil, "German Working-Class Immigration and the Social Democratic Tradition of Germany," in *German Workers' Culture in the United States, 1850 to 1920*, ed. Keil (Washington, DC: Smithsonian Institution Press, 1988), 165; John B. Jentz and Richard Schneirov, *Chicago in the Age of Capital: Class, Politics, and Democracy During the Civil War and Reconstruction* (Urbana: University of Illinois Press, 2012), 221–33.

44. Paul Grottkau, "Der Darwinismus in der ökonomischen und politischen Welt," *Vorbote*, May 11, 1878.

45. Grottkau, "Der Darwinismus."

46. August Otto-Walster, *Leben und Werk: eine Auswahl mit unveröffentlichten Briefen an Karl Marx* (Berlin: Akademie-Verlag, 1966); Hartmut Keil, "A Profile of Editors of German-American Radical Press, 1850–1910," in *The German-American Radical Press: the Shaping of a Left Political Culture*, eds. Elliott Shore, Ken Fones-Wolf, and James P. Danky (Urbana: University of Illinois Press, 1992), 21. August Otto-Walster was still in the United States when Eleanor Marx and Edward Aveling toured the country in the autumn of 1886. The book that the couple published after the tour included a glowing praise of August Otto-Walster. Marx and Aveling described him as one of "the artistic souls that, famishing in the desert of today, are making for the promised land beyond, and mark the way thither by their singing." See Eleanor Marx and Edward Aveling, *The Working-Class Movement in America* (London: Sonnenschein, 1891), 207–9. On Otto-Walster's life as politician and novelist before his move to the United States, see Klaus Mathes, *August Otto-Walster: Schriftsteller und Politiker in der deutschen Arbeiterbewegung* (Frankfurt am Main: Peter Land, 1987).

47. Zimmerman, *Anthropology and Antihumanism*, 6–7.

48. Kelly, *Descent of Darwin,* 58–61; the reaction of Ernst Haeckel to Virchow's comments has subsequently become central to a debate that still divides scholars on the connections between Haeckel and Nazism. See Gasman, *Scientific Origins of*

National Socialism; Hawkins, *Social Darwinism*; Richard Weikart, *From Darwin to Hitler: Evolutionary Ethics, Eugenics, and Racism in Germany* (New York: Palgrave Macmillan, 2004).

49. August Otto-Walster, "Darwinismus und Socialdemokratie," *Volksstimme des Westens*, October 13, 1878.

50. Quoted in Weikart, *Socialist Darwinism*, 22.

51. Quoted in Weikart, *Socialist Darwinism*, 23.

52. Weikart, *Socialist Darwinism*, 22. On Marx, Engels, and their ideas on Darwin and evolutionism, see also Pittenger, *American Socialists and Evolutionary Thought*, 15–25.

53. Herbert G. Gutman, "Joseph P. McDonnell and the Workers' Struggle in Paterson, New Jersey," in *Power and Culture: Essays on the American Working Class* (New York: The New Press, 1987), 95–98.

54. "The Necessity of International Organization," *Labor Standard*, January 18, 1877.

55. Middleton, "The International Labor Congress and American Representation," *Labor Standard*, July 7, 1877.

56. Middleton, "International Labor Congress," emphasis in the original.

57. Middleton, "International Labor Congress."

58. "The Great Meeting. The Organized Workingmen of New York Throng the Great Hall of the Cooper Union," *Labor Standard*, August 4, 1877.

59. *Labor Standard*, July 2, 16, and 23, 1877; *National Socialist*, May 11, 1878.

60. Foner, *Workingmen's Party*, 105–13.

61. Philip S. Foner and Brewster Chamberlin, eds., *Friedrich A. Sorge's Labor Movement in the United States: A History of the American Working Class from Colonial Times to 1890* (Westport, CT: Greenwood Press, 1977), 199.

62. Timothy Messer-Kruse, *The Yankee International: Marxism and the American Reform Tradition, 1848–1876* (Chapel Hill: University of North Carolina Press, 1998), 255–60.

63. On internationalism and the Knights of Labor, see Steven Parfitt, "Brotherhood from a Distance: Americanization and the Internationalism of the Knights of Labor," *International Review of Social History* 58, no. 3 (December 2013): 463–91.

Chapter 3. Must They Go?

1. "The Hoodlum at Work. Chinese Wash-houses Raided and Burned Last Night," *San Francisco Examiner*, July 25, 1877.

2. *San Francisco Examiner*, July 25, 26, 27, 28, 1877; *San Francisco Chronicle*, July 23, 24, 25, 26, 27, 28, 1877; Ira Cross, *History of the Labor Movement in California* (Berkeley: University of California Press, 1935), 88–96.

3. Already in the 1930s, Selig Perlman extensively discussed Chinese immigration in California and its impact on the American labor movement. However, one just needs to read the title of his opening section on the subject ("Class Struggle *versus*

Race Struggle," emphasis in the original) to notice Perlman's own imbibing of racial prejudice in dealing with the topic. See Selig Perlman, "Upheaval and Reorganisation (from 1877)," in John Commons et al., *History of Labour in the United States* (New York: Macmillan Company, 1935–1936), 2:252–68. Contemporary labor historians have successfully corrected this issue. See especially Alexander Saxton, *The Indispensable Enemy: Labor and the Anti-Chinese Movement in California* (Berkeley: University of California Press, 1971); Stanford M. Lyman, *Chinese Americans* (New York: Random House, 1974); Andrew Gyory, *Closing the Gate: Race, Politics, and the Chinese Exclusion Act* (Chapel Hill: University of North Carolina Press, 1998); Rosanne Currarino, *The Labor Question in America: Economic Democracy in the Gilded Age* (Urbana: University of Illinois Press, 2011). On the depth and spread of anti-Chinese sentiments, it is useful mentioning the fact that even the Knights of Labor, the most progressive labor organization of the time, did not support Chinese immigration. For a thorough reconstruction of their position, see Rob Weir, "Blind in One Eye Only: Western and Eastern Knights of Labor View the Chinese Question," *Labor History* 41, no. 4 (2000): 421–36, https://doi.org/10.1080/002365600449137.

4. *Statistics of the Population of the United States at the Tenth Census (June 1, 1880)* (Washington, DC: Department of the Interior, Census Office, 1880), Vol. 1, Table 1a, "The United States, in the Aggregate, and by Sex, Nativity, and Race," 3; Table V, "Population by Race and by Counties: 1880, 1870, 1860," 382; Vol. 6.

5. Quote from Gyory, *Closing the Gate*, 1. Historians of Asian American immigration have used the history of Chinese exclusion as a means through which understanding American immigration policies. See Shih-Shan Henry Tsai, *China and the Overseas Chinese in the United States, 1868–1911* (Fayetteville: University of Arkansas Press, 1983); Madeline Y. Hsu, *Dreaming of Gold, Dreaming of Home: Transnationalism and Migration between the United States and South China, 1882–1943* (Stanford: Stanford University Press, 2002); Erika Lee, *At America's Gates: Chinese Immigration during the Exclusion Era, 1882–1943* (Chapel Hill: University of North Carolina Press, 2007); Yucheng Qin, *The Diplomacy of Nationalism: The Six Companies and China's Policy toward Exclusion* (Honolulu: University of Hawaii Press, 2009); Lon Kurashige, *Two Faces of Exclusion: The Untold History of Anti-Asian Racism in the United States* (Chapel Hill: University of North Carolina Press, 2016).

6. Saxton focuses on Californian labor movements. The SLP is recognized as a separate political movement, but it is not the focus of attention. Gyory's lens is even larger. In the context of his broad analysis of the U.S. labor movement, the specificity of the socialist movement is inevitably lost. Saxton, *Indispensable Enemy*; Gyory, *Closing the Gate.*

7. Saxton, *Indispensable Enemy*, 161.

8. See Kurashige, *Two Faces of Exclusion*, 35–61; Wenxian Zhang, "Standing Up against Racial Discrimination: Progressive Americans and the Chinese Exclusion Act in the Late Nineteenth Century," *Phylon* 56, no. 1 (2019): 8–32. Gyory suggested the distinction between importation and immigration was the most widespread position in the American labor movement. Lyman offered convincing arguments against this

position. See Gyory, *Closing the Gate*; Stanford M. Lyman, "The 'Chinese Question' and American Labor Historians," *New Politics* (Winter 2000): 113–48.

9. The past three decades have seen an exponential growth of literature on Asian American social history. Works that furnished background for this chapter include Ronald Takaki, *Strangers from a Different Shore: A History of Asian Americans* (New York: Little Brown and C., 1990); Charles J. McClain, *In Search of Equality: The Chinese Struggle against Discrimination in Nineteenth-Century America* (Berkeley: University of California Press, 1994); Judy Yung, *Unbound Feet: A Social History of Chinese Women in San Francisco* (Berkeley: University of California Press, 1995); Benson Tong, *The Chinese Americans* (Boulder: University Press of Colorado, 2003); Birgit Zinzius, *Chinese America: Stereotype and Reality - History, Present, and Future of the Chinese Americans* (New York: Peter Lang, 2005); Peter Kwong and Dušanka Miščević, *Chinese America: The Untold Story of America's Oldest New Community* (New York: New Press, 2005); Jean Pfaelzer, *Driven Out: The Forgotten War Against Chinese Americans* (Berkeley: University of California Press, 2008); Beth Lew-Williams, *The Chinese Must Go: Violence, Exclusion, and the Making of the Alien in America* (Cambridge, MA: Harvard University Press, 2018).

10. For an early and path-breaking analysis on the image of Chinese immigrants in the United States, see Stuart Creighton Miller, *The Unwelcome Immigrant: The American Image of the Chinese, 1785–1882* (Berkeley; Los Angeles: University of California Press, 1969). I found useful critical discussion of the word "coolie" in Moon-Ho Jung, *Coolies and Cane: Race, Labor, and Sugar in the Age of Emancipation* (Baltimore: Johns Hopkins University Press, 2006); Lisa Yun, *The Coolie Speaks: Chinese Indentured Laborers and African Slaves in Cuba* (Philadelphia: Temple University Press, 2007); Edlie L. Wong, *Racial Reconstruction: Black Inclusion, Chinese Exclusion, and the Fictions of Citizenship* (New York: New York University Press, 2015).

11. Saxton, *Indispensable Enemy*, 113–37.

12. Najia Aarim-Heriot, *Chinese Immigrants, African Americans, and Racial Anxiety in the United States, 1848–82* (Urbana: University of Illinois Press, 2003), 131–33.

13. "Wendell Phillips on Kearneyism," *Socialist*, December 21, 1878.

14. Frank Roney, "Drafts—History of the Workingmen's Party of California," Frank Roney Papers, Box 1, Folder 4, Bancroft Library, Berkeley.

15. Cross, *History of the Labor Movement*, 93. On Kearney and the SLP, see "California," *Labor Standard*, July 29, 1878; "Address to the Party," *National Socialist*, September 7, 1878; the event is also commented on in Commons et al., *History of Labour*, 2:254, but the date of the *National Socialist* article mentioned there is incorrect.

16. Saxton, *Indispensable Enemy*, 117.

17. Kurashige, *Two Faces of Exclusion*, 1–8.

18. Takaki, *Strangers from a Different Shore*, 82; Mark Kanazawa, "Immigration, Exclusion, and Taxation: Anti-Chinese Legislation in Gold Rush California," *The Journal of Economic History* 65, no. 3 (September 2005): 779–805; Tong, *Chinese Americans*, 46.

19. Socialistic Labor Party, *Platform, Constitution, and Resolutions*, Adopted at the National Congress of the Workingmen's Party of the United States, held at Newark,

NJ, December 26, 27, 28, 29, 30, 31, 1877 (Cincinnati: Ohio Volks-Zeitung Print, 1878).

20. "Don't Kill the Coolie!" *Socialist*, June 3, 1876. The article was published in the newspaper of the Social Democratic Party of North America, which was founded in April 1876 as *Socialist* and changed its name to *Labor Standard* in July of the same year. See Commons et al., *History of Labour*, 2:270–71. In 1878, the SLP started a new official paper, based in Chicago, named *Socialist*. This newspaper was published from September 1878 to August 1879, alongside the *Labor Standard*.

21. "Don't Kill the Coolie!" *Socialist*.

22. "The Chinese Must Go!" *Labor Standard*, June 30, 1878. This article also appeared in *Socialist*, January 11, 1879.

23. On the overlaps between the concepts of race and nationality in this period, see James R. Barrett and David R. Roediger, "In between Peoples: Race, Nationality and the 'New Immigrant' Working Class," *Journal of American Ethnic History* 16, no. 3 (Spring 1997): 3–44.

24. Quoted in Andrew Gyory, *Closing the Gate*, 131.

25. "Protest der deutschsprechenden Sektion San Francisco," *Arbeiter Stimme*, March 24, 1878.

26. "Protest der deutschsprechenden," *Arbeiter Stimme*.

27. "Protest der deutschsprechenden," *Arbeiter Stimme*.

28. "Wendell Phillips on Kearneyism," *Socialist*, December 21, 1878.

29. An extensive treatment of the origins and functions of the Six Companies can be found in Qin, *Diplomacy of Nationalism*.

30. Rusticus, "More of the Chinese Question," *Socialist*, January 18, 1879.

31. Qin, *Diplomacy of Nationalism*, 1–12; McClain, *In Search of Equality*; Pfaelzer, *Driven Out*, 198–252; Kwong and Miščević, *Chinese America*, 75–89; Tsai, *China and the Overseas Chinese*, 32–38.

32. The Qing dynasty officially lifted the ban on overseas immigration in 1860. However, even before that date, thousands of Chinese workers migrated across the Pacific, most commonly in Southeast Asia and the Pacific islands. The United States was the recipient of a small minority of Chinese emigrant population. Tsai, *China and the Overseas Chinese*, 24–60; Craig A. Lockard, "Chinese Migration and Settlement in Southeast Asia before 1850: Making Fields from the Sea," *History Compass* 11, no. 9 (2013): 772–73.

33. Elizabeth Sinn, *Pacific Crossings: California Gold, Chinese Migration, and the Making of Hong Kong* (Hong Kong: Hong Kong University Press, 2012), 93–130.

34. See, for example, the "Memorial to President Grant" that the Six Companies wrote in response to the Democratic mayor of San Francisco, Andrew Jackson Bryant, in 1876. See Judy Yung, Gordon H. Chang and Him Mark Lai, eds., *Chinese American Voices: From the Gold Rush to the Present* (Berkeley: University of California Press, 2006), 17–25; Kwong and Miščević, *Chinese America*, 39–90; Zinzius, *Chinese America*, 11–18.

35. Tsai, *China and the Overseas Chinese*, 24–60; Shih-Shan Henry Tsai, *The Chinese Experience in America* (Bloomington: Indiana University Press, 1986), 56–65;

the Burlingame Treaty can be accessed at "Additional articles to the treaty between the United States of America and the Ta-Tsing empire, of June 18, 1858. Concluded at Washington, July 28, 1868," accessed May 24, 2019, https://academic.udayton.edu/race/02rights/treaty1868.htm.

36. Rusticus, "More of the Chinese Question."

37. Rusticus, "More of the Chinese Question."

38. In the article, Rusticus compares Chinese and Irish immigrants, suggesting that Chinese immigrants, unlike the Irish, took no part in the Civil War. It is worth mentioning the difference in the size of the two communities at the time. In 1860, the Irish community counted more than a million and six hundred thousand people; the Chinese barely reached thirty thousand. "Introduction," in *Population of the United States in 1860* (Washington, DC: Government Printing Office, 1864), XXVIII. The Chinese presence in the Union army was minimal and it is hard to pin down as a result of the fact that many Asians fought disguising their real names. See Ruthanne Lum McCunn, "Chinese in the Civil War: Ten Who Served," 1995, http://www.mccunn.com/Civil-War.pdf; Association to Commemorate the Chinese Serving in the American Civil War (website), https://sites.google.com/site/accsacw/.

39. Rusticus, "The Chinese Problem," *Socialist*, February 1, 1879.

40. Rusticus, "More of the Chinese Question."

41. Miller, *Unwelcome Immigrant.*

42. On the use of Chinese workers in the U.S. South after 1865, see Jung, *Coolies and Cane.* On Chinese workers and railroad construction, see Gordon H. Chang and Shelley Fisher Fishkin, eds., *The Chinese and the Iron Road: Building the Transcontinental Railroad* (Stanford: Stanford University Press, 2019); Gordon H. Chang, *Ghosts of Gold Mountain: The Epic Story of the Chinese Who Built the Transcontinental Railroad* (Boston: Houghton Mifflin Harcourt, 2019).

43. Anti-coolie Law, Sess. II, Chap. 27, 12 Stat. 340. 37th Congress, February 19, 1862. On the legal condition of Chinese workers in the mid-nineteenth century, see also Jung, *Coolies and Cane*, 20–25, 110; Takaki, *Strangers from a Different Shore*, 34–35; Kwong and Miščević, *Chinese America*, 35–38, Lew-Williams, *The Chinese Must Go.*

44. A further confirmation of this comes from the fact that the clear majority of American workers had close to no interaction with Chinese workers. By the time the Chinese Exclusion Act was approved, Chinese immigrants had barely crossed the Rocky Mountains at all. Around seventy thousand lived in California, ten thousand in Oregon, and ten thousand in the so-called territories (the western lands that still did not have the state status in 1880—Idaho, Montana, Arizona, Washington). The Census recorded 990 Chinese immigrants in total in the New York state, 229 in Massachusetts, 269 in Illinois. In most southern states, the Chinese population did not go past double-digit numbers. See U.S. Census, "The United States, in the Aggregate, and by Sex, Nativity, and Race," 3; Wong, *Radical Reconstruction*; Jung, *Coolies and Cane*; Yun, *Coolie Speaks.*

45. The *Volkszeitung* was a beacon for German American socialist and labor activists in the country and reflected the approach of the members of the publishing

company who produced it: a group of political exiles with a strong background in socialist theory, often former members of the German Social Democratic Party, who maintained ties with Friedrich Engels and the German socialist leaders. This group was in touch with the SLP leadership but remained independent from the party. Throughout its history, there were moments in which the two organizations worked in conjunction and moments in which they diverged. By the end of the 1870s, this new newspaper (founded in 1878) was recognized as a "friend" of the SLP by the party leadership. See Philip Van Patten, "Report of the NEC to the 2nd National Convention of the Socialist Labor Party of America, Allegheny City, PA, 26th December 1879," in Socialistic Labor Party, *Proceedings of the National Convention of the Socialistic Labor Party Held at Turner Hall, Allegheny City, PA, Commencing Dec. 26th, 1879* (Detroit: National Executive Committee, 1880), 5–17. On the significance of the *Volkszeitung* in German American socialism, see Dorothee Schneider, *Trade Unions and Community: The German Working Class in New York City, 1870–1900* (Urbana: University of Illinois Press, 1994), 46–49.

46. "Die Chinesenfrage in den Ver. Staten," *New Yorker Volkszeitung*, May 1, 1880.

47. "Die Chinesenfrage," *New Yorker Volkszeitung*.

48. "Ein Jurist bertheilt den Sozialismus," *New Yorker Volkszeitung*, April 3, 1880.

49. "Die Chinesenfrage," *New Yorker Volkszeitung*.

50. "The Chinese Question Again—Leo's Reply," *Socialist*, March 8, 1879.

51. Second International socialists ferociously debated socialism, social evolutionism and Darwinism. See Richard Weikart, *Socialist Darwinism: Evolution in German Socialist Thought from Marx to Bernstein* (San Francisco: International Scholars Publications, 1998); Lorenzo Costaguta, "Before Baku: The Second International and the Debate on Colonialism (1900–1920)," in *The Comintern and the Global South: Global Designs/Local Encounters*, eds. Anne Garland Mahler and Paolo Capuzzo (London: Routledge, 2022); infra chapter 2, fn. 5.

52. "Chinese Question Again," *Socialist*.

53. "Chinese Question Again," *Socialist*.

54. "Das Bürgerrecht der Chinesen," *New Yorker Volkszeitung*, May 8, 1880.

55. "Das Bürgerrecht für Chinesen," *New Yorker Volkszeitung*, April 1, 1882.

56. "Das Bürgerrecht für Chinesen," *New Yorker Volkszeitung*.

57. Saxton, *Indispensable Enemy*, 43–44; Frank Roney, *Frank Roney: Irish Rebel and California Labor Leader: An Autobiography* (Berkeley: University of California Press, 1931).

58. Roney, *Frank Roney*, 273.

59. Roney, *Frank Roney*, 273.

60. Roney, *Frank Roney*, 273.

61. Roney, *Frank Roney*, 266.

62. Roney, *Frank Roney*, 286.

63. *San Francisco Examiner*, May 20, 1878; Saxton, *Indispensable Enemy*, 154.

64. Saxton, *Indispensable Enemy*, 127–37.

65. "The Anti-Chinese Movement. Important Statement," *Labor Standard*, June 23, 1878.

66. Saxton, *Indispensable Enemy*, 121–27.

67. Saxton, *Indispensable Enemy*, 121–27.

68. Roney, *Frank Roney*, 309–12.

69. "The Workingmen's Victory in California," *Labor Standard*, July 7, 1878.

70. "The Workingmen's Victory," *Labor Standard*.

71. "Kearney der Californische Agitator," *Volksstimme des Westens*, August 7, 1878.

72. "Address to the Party," *National Socialist*, September 7, 1878; *Socialist*, December 21, 1878; "Aus Kalifornien," *Volksstimme des Westens*, May 20, 1879; "Socialistic Labor Party. Summary of Proceedings of Nat. Ex. Committee," *Labor Review*, March 1880; "The Political Situation," *Labor Review*, May 1880; "Dennis Kearney," *Labor Review*, May 1880. The *New Yorker Volkszeitung* had an almost weekly report on San Francisco and California. See March 3, 20, 1880; April 3, 17, 24, 1880; June 12, 1880; November 6, 13, 1880. On Kearney's coalition attempt, see Mark A. Lause, *The Civil War's Last Campaign: James B. Weaver, the Greenback-Labor Party, and the Politics of Race and Section* (Lanham: University Press of America, 2007) and infra chapter 4.

73. Socialistic Labor Party, Platform, Constitution and Resolutions, Together with a Condensed Report of the Proceedings of the National Convention held at Allegheny, Pa., December 26–31, 1879, and January 1, 1880 (Detroit: National Executive Committee, 1880), 12.

74. "The Party Congress: Proposed Amendments and Changes to the Platform and Constitution of the Socialistic Labor Party," *Bulletin of the Social Labor Movement*, November 1879.

75. Saxton, *Indispensable Enemy*, 137. See also Lew-Williams, *Chinese Must Go*, 45–49.

76. Lee, *At America's Gates*; Lew-Williams, *Chinese Must Go*, 50–53.

77. "Party News," *Bulletin of the Social Labor Movement*, May 1882.

78. "Party News," *Bulletin of the Social Labor Movement*. "John" stood for "John Chinaman," the nickname at times used in periodicals of the period to indicate Chinese immigrants.

79. "Die Chinesischen Durchgangs-Regulationen," *New Yorker Volkszeitung*, February 10, 1883; "Über die Antichinesen Bill," *New Yorker Volkszeitung*, March 1, 1884.

80. Kwong and Miščević, *Chinese America*, 107.

81. Quoted in Kwong and Miščević, *Chinese America*, 110.

82. "300 Chinesen für San Francisco," *New Yorker Volkszeitung*, February 28, 1885.

83. "Chinesen gegen Weißen," *New Yorker Volkszeitung*, November 7, 1885.

84. "Boycott gegen die Chinesen," *New Yorker Volkszeitung*, December 12, 1885.

85. "Ist die Anti-Kuli Bewegung unamerikanisch?" *New Yorker Volkszeitung*, March 20, 1886.

86. The newspaper was founded in 1883, but it did not become the official organ of the party until 1886.

87. "The Chinese Pest," *Workmen's Advocate*, August 1, 1886.

88. "Chinesischer Madchenhandel in San Francisco," *New Yorker Volkszeitung*, January 21, 1888; "Chinesische Cigarrenmacher," *New Yorker Volkszeitung*, December

3, 1887; "Chinese Vice in California," *Workmen's Advocate*, May 3, 1890, 4; "Die Chinesenhetze in Milwaukee," *New Yorker Volkszeitung*, March 23, 1889.

Chapter 4. "Regardless of Color"

1. Socialistic Labor Party, *Platform, Constitution and Resolutions*, Together with a Condensed Report of the Proceedings of the National Convention held at Allegheny, Pa., December 26–31, 1879, and January 1, 1880 (Detroit: National Executive Committee, 1880), 3.

2. See C. Vann Woodward, *Origins of the New South, 1877–1913* (Baton Rouge: Louisiana State University Press, 1951); C. Vann Woodward, *The Strange Career of Jim Crow* (New York: Oxford University Press, 1955); Jane Elizabeth Dailey, *Before Jim Crow: The Politics of Race in Postemancipation Virginia* (Chapel Hill: University of North Carolina Press, 2000); Peter Kolchin, *A Sphinx on the American Land: The Nineteenth-Century in Comparative Perspective* (Baton Rouge: LSU Press, 2003); Charles Postel, *Equality: An American Dilemma, 1866–1896* (New York: Farrar, Strauss, and Giroux, 2019).

3. Philip S. Foner, *American Socialism and Black Americans: From the Age of Jackson to World War II* (Westport, CT: Greenwood Press, 1977), 60.

4. Understanding the circumstances favoring or hampering solidarity across racial lines within the American working class is a long-standing historiographical conundrum. Literature that does not specifically deal with Gilded Age socialism but that explores the problem from several perspectives includes Steven Hahn, *A Nation under Our Feet: Black Political Struggles in the Rural South from Slavery to the Great Migration* (Cambridge, MA: Harvard University Press, 2005); Eric Arnesen, ed., *The Black Worker: Race, Labor, and Civil Rights since Emancipation* (Urbana: University of Illinois Press, 2007); Bruce E. Baker and Brian Kelly, eds., *After Slavery: Race, Labor, and Citizenship in the Reconstruction South* (Gainesville: University Press of Florida, 2013); Matthew Hild and Keri Leigh Merritt, eds., *Reconsidering Southern Labor History: Race, Class, and Power* (Gainesville: University Press of Florida, 2018). The implicit racial pact keeping African Americans in the South was not broken until World War I. See Heather Cox Richardson, *The Death of Reconstruction: Race, Labor, and Politics in the Post-Civil War North, 1865–1901* (Cambridge, MA: Harvard University Press, 2001); James N. Gregory, *The Southern Diaspora: How the Great Migrations of Black and White Southerners Transformed America* (Chapel Hill: University of North Carolina Press, 2005).

5. Socialistic Labor Party, *Platform, Constitution and Resolutions*.

6. Selig Perlman, "Upheaval and Reorganisation (from 1877)," in John Commons et al., *History of Labour in the United States* (New York: Macmillan Company, 1935–36), 2:301–6.

7. "North Carolina. Our Colored Brothers in the South," *Labor Standard*, November 26, 1877.

8. "North Carolina," *Labor Standard*.

9. "New York. Labor amongst Colored Workers," *Labor Standard*, January 9, 1878.

10. "Labor in the South," *Labor Standard*, June 23, 1878.

11. "Labor in the South," *Labor Standard.*

12. Socialistic Labor Party, *Platform, Constitution and Resolutions.*

13. Obituaries published in the aftermath of Douai's death help reconstruct his role as mediator among the many factions into which the American socialist movement were split: "Our Loss," *Workmen's Advocate*, January 28, 1888; "Adolph Douai: The Gifted and Tireless Agitator Dead," *Workmen's Advocate*, January 28, 1888. See also Foner, *American Socialism*, 15–29 and infra chapter two.

14. Adolph Douai, "Something More about the Farming Population," *Labor Standard*, May 4, 1878.

15. Adolph Douai, "Farming Population."

16. Adolph Douai, "Die Negerfrage," *Vorbote*, February 22, 1879.

17. On the social composition of the South, see Statistics of the Population of the United States at the Tenth Census (June 1, 1880) (Washington, DC: Department of the Interior, Census Office, 1880); Leslie H. Fishel Jr., "The African-American Experience," in *The Gilded Age: Essays on the Origins of Modern America*, ed. Charles W. Calhoun (Lanham: Rowman and Littlefield Publishers, 2007), 143–66.

18. Adolph Douai, "Die Negerfrage."

19. Adolph Douai, "Die Negerfrage."

20. Only recently has white southern working class been the subject of sustained scholars' interest. See Matt Wray and Annalee Newitz, eds., *White Trash: Race and Class in America* (New York: Routledge, 1997); Keri Leigh Merritt, *Masterless Men: Poor Whites and Slavery in the Antebellum South* (Cambridge: Cambridge University Press, 2017).

21. "The Negro Exodus," *Chicago Daily Tribune*, March 19, 1879; "Fleeing from Slavery," *New York Tribune*, April 11, 1879. Nell Irvin Painter, *Exodusters: Black Migration to Kansas after Reconstruction* (1986; repr., New York: W. W. Norton, 1992); Bryan M. Jack, *The St. Louis African American Community and the Exodusters* (Columbia: University of Missouri Press, 2007).

22. On working class and African American resistance after 1865: Robin D. G. Kelley, "'We Are Not What We Seem': Rethinking Black Working-Class Opposition in the Jim Crow South," *The Journal of American History* 80, no. 1 (June 1993): 75–112; Eric Arnesen, "The Quicksand of Economic Insecurity: African Americans, Strikebreaking, and Labor Activism in the Industrial Era," in *The Black Worker: Race, Labor, and Civil Rights since Emancipation*, ed. Arnesen (Urbana: University of Illinois Press, 2007); David R. Roediger, *Seizing Freedom: Slave Emancipation and Liberty for All* (London: Verso, 2014); Baker and Kelly, *After Slavery*, 199–220; Hahn, *Nation under Our Feet*; Henry Louis Gates Jr., *Stony the Road: Reconstruction, White Supremacy, and the Rise of Jim Crow* (New York: Penguin, 2019).

23. "Versammlungen der Sektionen der Arbeiter Partei der Ver. Staaten," *Vorbote*, July 1, 1877, 5; David T. Burbank, *City of Little Bread: The St. Louis General Strike of 1877* (Unpublished microcard, 1957), 33–34; David T. Burbank, *Reign of the Rabble: The St. Louis General Strike of 1877* (New York: Kelley, 1966).

24. All the figures in this paragraph come from United States Census Office, Abstract of the Twelfth Census of the United States 1900 (Washington: Government Printing Office, 1902), 40–41, 102–4.

25. "Party News," *National Socialist*, August 31, 1878.

26. "Letter," *Socialist*, July 12, 1879. Historian Elliot J. Kanter reports that the Black section was formed in the twelfth ward of the city. See Elliot J. Kanter, "Class, Ethnicity, and Socialist Politics: St. Louis, 1876–1881," *UCLA Historical Journal* 3 (1982): 56.

27. On Chicago, see Bruce Nelson, *Beyond the Martyrs: A Social History of Chicago's Anarchists, 1870–1900* (New Brunswick, NJ: Rutgers University Press, 1988), 60; Jacqueline Jones, *Goddess of Anarchy: The Life and Times of Lucy Parsons, American Radical* (New York: Basic Books, 2017), 142. On New York, see Foner, *American Socialism*, 59.

28. Statistics of the Population of the United States at the Tenth Census (June 1, 1880) (Washington, DC: Department of the Interior, Census Office, 1880), Table VI, "Population by Race, Sex, and Nativity, Table VI: Population by Race, of Cities and Towns, etc.: 1880 and 1870," 423; Twelfth Census of the United States, taken in year (Washington, DC: Department of the Interior, Census Office, 1901), Table 23, "Population by Sex, General Nativity and Color, for places having 2500 inhabitants or more," 634.

29. "Aus dem Süden," *Volksstimme des Westens*, October 12, 1878; *Vorbote*, December 28, 1878.

30. "Aus dem Süden," *Volksstimme des Westens*, October 12, 1878.

31. "Aus dem Süden," *Volksstimme des Westens*, June 19, 1879; "The New Orleans Section," *Socialist*, June 28, 1879.

32. "Correspondenz aus New Orleans," *Volksstimme des Westens*, April 25, 1880.

33. Eric Arnesen, *Waterfront Workers of New Orleans: Race, Class, and Politics, 1863–1923* (Urbana: University of Illinois Press, 1994).

34. James M. Morris, "William Haller: 'The Disturbing Element,'" *Cincinnati Historical Society Bulletin* 28 (Winter 1970): 283. I am thankful to Nikki M. Taylor, who shared with me her knowledge about the subject and pointed my attention to the material I am commenting on in this section.

35. Nikki M. Taylor, *America's First Black Socialist: The Radical Life of Peter H. Clark* (Lexington: University Press of Kentucky, 2013), 28–32.

36. Taylor, *America's First Black Socialist*; see infra chapter one.

37. Foner, *American Socialism*, 59; Taylor, *America's First Black Socialist*, 30–39, 154–55. See also Herbert G. Gutman, "Peter H. Clark: Pioneer Negro Socialist, 1877," *The Journal of Negro Education* 34, no. 4 (1965): 413–18, https://doi.org/10.2307/2294092; Philip S. Foner, "Peter H. Clark: Pioneer Black Socialist," *The Journal of Ethnic Studies* 5, no. 3 (1978): 17–35.

38. *Dayton Evening Herald*, September 2, 1873.

39. *Cincinnati Commercial*, November 27, 1875.

40. *Cincinnati Daily Enquirer*, March 27, 1877. Other chronicles of these events can be found in *Emancipator*, March 31, 1877; *Cincinnati Commercial*, March 27,

1877. For Clark's early connections with socialism, see Taylor, *America's First Black Socialist*, 30–39.

41. *Cincinnati Daily Enquirer*, March 27, 1877.

42. *Cincinnati Commercial Gazette*, August 25, 1877.

43. *Cincinnati Enquirer*, August 7, 1877.

44. Morris, "William Haller"; on Willich's People's Party, see infra chapter one.

45. Taylor, *America's First Black Socialist*, 135.

46. *Emancipator*, August 18, 1877.

47. "Citizen William Haller," *Cincinnati Commercial Gazette*, March 4, 1881.

48. *Labor Standard*, November 25, 1876.

49. Morris, "William Haller," 284–86; "A card from Wm. Haller," *Socialist*, December 12, 1879; Kanter, "Class, Ethnicity, and Socialist Politics" 46–47; J. Ehman to Philip Van Patten, January 28, February 5, 6, 1880, Incoming Correspondence, Papers of the Socialist Labor Party of America, Microfilm edition, Hallward Library, Nottingham.

50. *Cincinnati Enquirer*, July 23, 1877, 8.

51. *Cincinnati Commercial*, July 22, 1879.

52. *Cincinnati Commercial*, July 22, 1879.

53. Jeffrey B. Perry, *Hubert Harrison: The Voice of Harlem Radicalism, 1883–1918* (New York: Columbia University Press, 2009); David Levering Lewis, *W. E. B. Du Bois: Biography of a Race, 1868–1919* (New York: Henry Holt, 1993); Dan S. Green and Earl Smith, "W. E. B. Du Bois and the concepts of race and class," *Phylon* 44, no. 4 (1983): 262–72; Paul Heideman, "Introduction," in *Class Struggle and the Color Line: American Socialism and the Race Question, 1900–1930*, ed. Heideman (New York: Haymarket Books, 2018).

54. On Cincinnati's short-lived socialist success, see Commons et al., *History of Labour*, 2:282.

55. Burbank, *Reign of the Rabble*, 59.

56. Burbank, *City of Little Bread*; Burbank, *Reign of the Rabble*; Kanter, "Class, Ethnicity, and Socialist Politics," 43–44; Philip S. Foner, *The Great Labor Uprising of 1877* (New York: Pathfinder, 1977); Robert V. Bruce, *1877: Year of Violence* (Chicago: Quadrangle Books, 1970).

57. Burbank, *City of Little Bread*, 33.

58. *St. Louis Daily Tribune*, July 25, 26, 27, 1877. The interracial composition of the strike is emphasized in the works quoted by Burbank, Foner, Bruce, and Roediger. Recently, Walter Johnson has revisited the evidence presented in the English-language and German-language press, both within and outside St. Louis. See Walter Johnson, *The Broken Heart of America: St. Louis and the Violent History of the United States* (New York: Basic Books, 2020), 264–78.

59. *St. Louis Daily Tribune*, August 4, 1877.

60. *St. Louis Daily Tribune*, August 4, 1877.

61. Alison Clark Efford, *German Immigrants, Race, and Citizenship in the Civil War Era* (Cambridge: Cambridge University Press, 2014), 232–33. Efford's analysis is built on the theories of David R. Roediger, especially David R. Roediger, "'Not Only the Ruling Classes to Overcome, but Also the So-Called Mob': Class, Skill, and

Community in the St. Louis General Strike of 1877," *Journal of Social History* 19, no. 2 (1985–1886): 213–239, https://doi.org/10.1353/jsh/19.2.213; David R. Roediger, *The Wages of Whiteness: Race and the Making of the American Working Class* (London: Verso, 1991), 167–68.

62. Burbank, *City of Little Bread*, 33–34.

63. Infra chapter two.

64. James Neal Primm, *Lion of the Valley: St. Louis, Missouri, 1764–1980*. (St. Louis: Missouri Historical Society Press, 1998), 326–32; Steven Rowan, "The German Press in St. Louis and Missouri in the Nineteenth Century: The Establishment of a Tradition," *The Papers of the Bibliographical Society of America* 9, no. 3 (September 2005): 459–67; John Thomas Scharf, *History of Saint Louis City and County* (Philadelphia: Louis H. Everts and Co., 1883), 902–58. On Pulitzer, see Julian S. Rammelkamp, *Pulitzer's Post-Dispatch, 1878–1883* (Princeton, NJ: Princeton University Press, 1967).

65. Stephen Aron, *American Confluence: the Missouri Frontier from Borderland to Border State* (Bloomington: Indiana University Press, 2005); Johnson, *Broken Heart of America*.

66. Robert Mills, "Die Indianer, Neger und Chinesen in Nord-Amerika," *Volksstimme des Westens*, November 2, 1877. See infra introduction.

67. "Die Neger in der Familie als Staatsbürger und Arbeiter," repr. *Volksstimme des Westens*, November 12, 1877.

68. "Die Neger in Süden," *Volksstimme des Westens*, November 20, 1877.

69. "Ein Nothschrei," *Volksstimme des Westens*, April 26, 1879.

70. "Sind die Neger im Süden frei?" *Volksstimme des Westens*, February 16, 1880.

71. "Warum die Neger jetzt demokratisch stimmen," *Volksstimme des Westens*, May 2, 1878.

72. Eric Foner, *A Short History of Reconstruction, 1863–1877* (New York: Harper & Row, 1990), 138–260.

73. Painter, *Exodusters*; Jack, *St. Louis African American Community*.

74. "Die Negerwanderung," *Volksstimme des Westens*, March 17, 1879.

75. "Über die Flucht der Farbigen aus dem Süden," *Volksstimme des Westens*, April 21, 1879; "Die Negereinwanderung," *Volksstimme des Westens*, July 15, 1879; "Über Neger-Auswanderung," *Volksstimme des Westens*, September 22, 1879.

76. Socialistic Labor Party, *Platform, Constitution and Resolutions*.

77. Mark A. Lause, *The Civil War's Last Campaign: James B. Weaver, the Greenback-Labor Party, and the Politics of Race and Section* (Lanham: University Press of America, 2001), 3–38; Matthew Hild, *Greenbackers, Knights of Labor, and Populists: Farmer-Labor Insurgency in the Late-Nineteenth-Century South* (Athens: University of Georgia Press, 2007), 22–42. Charles Postel contextualized the GLP in the broader history of late-nineteenth-century egalitarian movements. See Postel, *Equality*, 171–200.

78. Lause, *Civil War's Last Campaign*, 39–42. On St. Louis, see Kanter, "Class, Ethnicity, and Socialist Politics." On New York, see *Irish World*, December 1, 1877.

79. On socialism in the *Irish World* and *Irish World and American Industrial Liberator*, see, for example, "What is Communism?" *Irish World*, June 1, 1878; G. W. H.

Smart, "Socialism in Relation to Government," *Irish World and American Industrial Liberator*, January 11, 18, 1879; G. W. H. Smart, "The Social Labor Movement," *Irish World and American Industrial Liberator*, January 18, 1879; "Individualism v. Communism: Reply of Philip Van Patten to Our Correspondent 'Phillip' of Boston," *Irish World and American Industrial Liberator*, March 1, 1879; Phillip, "The Irish World's Platform: A Socialist Discusses Some of Its Principles," *Irish World and American Industrial Liberator*, January 24, 1880; G. W. H. Smart, "A Socialist's Defense," *Irish World and American Industrial Liberator*, February 7, 1880 (the debate between Smart and Phillip continued for months across 1880 in the following issues: February 28, March 27, April 10, 17, 24); John F. Bray, "Defending Socialism," *Irish World and American Industrial Liberator*, May 15, 1880. On Ford, see James P. Rodechko, "An Irish-American Journalist and Catholicism: Patrick Ford of the Irish World," *Church History* 39, no. 4 (1970): 524–40, https://doi.org/10.2307/3162930.

80. The *Irish World and* American *Industrial Liberator* published daily chronicles of the June 1880 Chicago convention that set the parameters of the presidential coalition (see *Irish World and American Industrial Liberator*, June 19, 26, 1880). The SLP leadership explained its role in the convention to its members in "The Chicago Convention," *Labor Review*, June 1880, 15–20; *Bulletin of the Social Labor Movement*, September 1880. For a critical reconstruction of the event, see Lause, *Civil War's Last Campaign*, 39–60.

81. The text of the socialist resolution was, "We declare that land, air and water are the grand gifts of nature to all mankind, and the law or custom of society that allows any person to monopolize more of these gifts of nature than he has a right to, we earnestly condemn and demand shall be abolished." See Lause, *Civil War's Last Campaign*, 77.

82. The same treatment was accorded to the resolution on women's suffrage: Approved by the assembly, the plank was left out of the printed GLP platforms. A piecemeal reconstruction of the assembly can be found in Lause, *Civil War's Last Campaign*, 61–84.

83. The pro-GLP faction included corresponding secretary Philip Van Patten, Chicago leaders Thomas Morgan and George Schilling, Peter J. McGuire, Adolph Douai, and many other national leaders. Opposing the coalition were in particular the German American groups of Chicago, New York, and St. Louis. The party press reflected this rivalry, with the outlets controlled by the pro-coalition group presenting the alliance as a popular and legitimate move and the opponents describing it as a coup. On the pro-coalition side, see, for example, "Party News" and "The Chicago Muddle," *Labor Review*, July 1880; "What Has Been Accomplished" and "The Duties of Socialists in the Fall Campaign," *Bulletin of the Social Labor Movement*, September 1880. On the anti-coalition side, see the editorials in *Vorbote*, July 7, 1880; "Dissatisfied," *Bulletin of the Social Labor Movement*, September 1880. On the disastrous outcome of the campaign, with pro-coalition SLPers blaming the outcome on the rival faction, see *Bulletin of the Social Labor Movement*, October–November 1880.

84. Albert R. Parsons, *Life of Albert R. Parsons, with Brief History of the Labor Movement in America* (Chicago: Mrs. Lucy E. Parsons Publisher and Proprietor, 1889), 9.

85. This version of Parsons's early biography is taken from Paul Avrich, *The Haymarket Tragedy* (Princeton, NJ: Princeton University Press, 1984), 3–55. It differs in some points from Parsons's own autobiographical account (Parsons, *Life of Albert R. Parsons*, 6–23). I had the chance to confront this information with the preliminary results of an unpublished research on Albert R. Parsons by George N. Green. I would like to thank him for sharing his results with me via private correspondence. See also James Green, *Death in the Haymarket: A Story of Chicago, the First Labor Movement, and the Bombing That Divided Gilded Age America* (New York: Anchor Book, 2006), 55–59; Jones, *Goddess of Anarchy*, 30–89.

86. Parsons, *Life of Albert R. Parsons*, 10.

87. Nelson, *Beyond the Martyrs*, 52–66. See also Green, *Death in the Haymarket*, 85–89; Jones, *Goddess of Anarchy*, 137–66.

88. George Schilling, "History of the Labor Movement in Chicago," in Parsons, *Life of Albert L. Parsons*, XXIX.

89. Mark Erlich, "Peter J. McGuire's Trade Unionism: Socialism of a Trades Union Kind?" *Labor History* 24, no. 2 (1983): 165–97, https://doi.org/10.1080/00236568308584704; Philip Van Patten, "Socialism and the Anarchists," *Bulletin of the Social Labor Movement* (December/January 1881), 3.

90. Richard Oestreicher, *Solidarity and Fragmentation: Working People and Class Consciousness in Detroit, 1875–1900* (Urbana: University of Illinois Press, 1982), 60–96.

91. Avrich, *Haymarket Tragedy*, 68–98; Timothy Messer-Kruse, *The Haymarket Conspiracy: Transatlantic Anarchist Networks* (Urbana: University of Illinois Press, 2012), 69–99; Parsons, *Life of Albert L. Parsons*, XXI; Brad Rockwell, *Secret Lives of Philip Van Patten* in Isabel B. Anthony and Elizabeth Robbins, eds., *The Record 2010: Fifty-First Edition* (Hot Springs, AR: Garland County Historical Society, 2010), 15–31; Jones, *Goddess of Anarchy*, 184–223; *Bulletin of the Social Labor Movement*, June-December 1880; Sozialistische Arbeiter Partei, Officielles Protokoll der National-Convention der S. A. P., abgehalten ab 26, 27, 28 December 1883, in Baltimore, Reel 35, Papers of the Socialist Labor Party of America, Microfilm edition, Hallward Library, Nottingham.

92. "The Negro: Let Him Leave Politics to the Politicians and Prayers to the Preacher," *Alarm*, April 3, 1886. See Jones, *Goddess of Anarchy*, 243–45.

93. "The Negro," *Alarm*, April 4, 1885.

94. Oestreicher, *Solidarity and Fragmentation*, 60–96.

95. Foner, *American Socialism*, 62–68.

96. For a reconstruction of Ferrell's episode in the broader context of the Knights' racial politics, see Postel, *Equality*, 254–66.

97. On Drury, see Robert Weir, "'Here's to the Men WHO Lose!': The Hidden Career of Victor Drury," *Labor History* 36, no. 4 (1995): 530–56.

98. Eleanor Marx and Edward Aveling, *The Working-Class Movement in America* (London: Sonnenschein, 1891), 145–48.

Chapter 5. Savage Capitalists, Civilized Indians

1. T. J. Stiles, *Custer's Trials: A Life on the Frontier of a New America* (New York: Vintage Books, 2015); Richard White, *The Republic for Which It Stands: The United States during Reconstruction and the Gilded Age* (New York: Oxford University Press, 2017), 302–5.

2. *New York Herald*, September 2, 1876.

3. Dee Brown, *Bury My Heart at Wounded Knee: An Indian History of the American West* (New York: Henry Holt, 1991); Jeffrey Ostler, *The Plains Sioux and U.S. Colonialism from Lewis and Clark to Wounded Knee* (Cambridge: Cambridge University Press, 2004); Heather Cox Richardson, *Wounded Knee: Party Politics and the Road to an American Massacre* (New York: Basic Books, 2010); White, *Republic for Which It Stands*.

4. Frederick Jackson Turner, "The Significance of the Frontier in American History," *Proceedings of the State Historical Society of Wisconsin*, December 14, 1893. On the significance of Turner's thesis to interpret U.S. history, see Greg Grandin, *The End of the Myth: From the Frontier to the Border Wall in the Mind of America* (New York: Metropolitan Books, 2019).

5. Richard White, "Frederick Jackson Turner and Buffalo Bill," in *The Frontier in American Culture: An Exhibition at the Newberry Library, August 26, 1994-January 7, 1995*, ed. James R. Grossman (Chicago: Newberry Library, 1994), 7–65. For an analysis of the importance of evolutionism in Turner's work, see Tiziano Bonazzi, "Frederick Jackson Turner's Frontier Thesis and the Self-Consciousness of America," *Journal of American Studies* 27, no. 2 (1993): 149–71, https://doi.org/10.1017/S0021875800031509.

6. Steven Conn, *History's Shadow: Native Americans and Historical Consciousness in the Nineteenth Century* (Chicago: University of Chicago Press, 2004), 179; Francisco Bethencourt, *Racisms: From the Crusades to the Twentieth Century* (Princeton, NJ: Princeton University Press, 2013), 253–306.

7. Marcello Musto, *The Last Years of Karl Marx: An Intellectual Biography* (Stanford: Stanford University Press, 2020).

8. Marx died in 1883, when his anthropological studies were nothing more than a bunch of notes. Friedrich Engels took this material and turned it into *The Origins of the Family, Private Property, and the State*, a short work that broke new ground on many aspects but did not capture many aspects of Marx's thinking. Only the publication of Marx's notes in 1971 shed light on its full complexity. See Lawrence Krader, ed., *The Ethnological Notebooks of Karl Marx (Studies of Morgan, Phear, Maine, Lubbock)* (Assen: Van Gorcum, 1972).

9. Étienne Balibar used a Marxist framework to develop a non-biological definition of racism in "Is there a 'Neo-Racism?'" in *Étienne Balibar* and Immanuel Wallerstein, *Race, Nation, Class: Ambiguous Identities* (London: Verson, 1991), 17–28.

10. Roxanne Dunbar-Ortiz, *An Indigenous Peoples' History of the United States* (Boston: Beacon Press, 2014), 135–53; Walter L. Hixson, *American Settler Colonialism:*

A History (London: Palgrave Macmillan, 2013), 113–40. For a broad conceptualization of settler colonialism, I found useful Patrick Wolfe, "Land, Labor, and Difference: Elementary Structures of Race," *The American Historical Review* 106 (2001): 866–905, https://doi.org/10.2307/2692330; Lorenzo Veracini, "'Settler Colonialism': The Career of a Concept," *The Journal of Imperial and Commonwealth History* 41 (2013): 313–33. On Indian-U.S. policy, I consulted the still valuable Francis Paul Prucha, *The Great Father: The United States Government and the American Indians* (Lincoln: University of Nebraska Press, 1984); and the more recent C. Joseph Genetin-Pilawa, *Crooked Paths to Allotment: The Fight over Federal Indian Policy after the Civil War* (Chapel Hill: University of North Carolina Press, 2012).

11. Richard White, *Railroaded: The Transcontinentals and the Making of Modern America* (New York: W. W. Norton and Co., 2011).

12. H. Glenn Penny, *Kindred by Choice: Germans and American Indians since 1800* (Chapel Hill: University of North Carolina Press, 2013).

13. Penny, *Kindred by Choice*, 30–39.

14. Penny, *Kindred by Choice*, 40–48; infra chapter 2.

15. Jens-Uwe Guettel, *German Expansionism, Imperial Liberalism, and the United States, 1776–1945* (Cambridge: Cambridge University Press, 2012), 44.

16. Guettel, *German Expansionism*, 42–69. Guettel corrected Penny's analysis on Humboldt as well, saying that while he hated slavery, "His rejection of forced labor was inconsistent with his uncritical acceptance of the 'vanishing native' topos." See Guettel, *German Expansionism*, 58. See also infra chapter 2.

17. Penny, *Kindred by Choice*, 69–95.

18. On the *Arbeiter Union*, see Stan Nadel, "The German Immigrant Left in the United States," in *The Immigrant Left in the United States*, eds. Paul Buhle and Dan Georgakas (Albany: State University of New York Press, 1996), 53–54; Justine Davis Randers-Pehrson, *Adolf Douai, 1819–88: The Turbulent Life of a German Forty-Eighter in the Homeland and in the United States* (New York: Peter Lang, 2000), 289; infra chapter 1.

19. As noted by Julian Go, in 1868, there were more U.S. soldiers on the frontier than in the entire South, which was still occupied after the end of the Civil War. See Julian Go, *Patterns of Empire: The British and American Empires, 1688 to the Present* (Cambridge: Cambridge University Press, 2011), 38.

20. "Die Indianerfrage," *Arbeiter Union*, June 27, 1869.

21. "Die Indianerfrage," *Arbeiter Union*.

22. On the situation of Plain Indians in these years, see William T. Hagan, "How the West Was Lost," in *Indians in American History: An Introduction*, eds. Frederick E. Hoxie and Peter Iverson (Wheeling, IL: Harlan Davidson, 1998), 157–61; Richard White, "The Winning of the West: The Expansion of the Western Sioux in the Eighteenth and Nineteenth Centuries," *Journal of American History* 65 (1978): 319–43, https://doi.org/10.2307/1894083.

23. "Die Indianer-Politik," *Arbeiter Union*, March 14, 1870.

24. "Die Indianer-Politik," *Arbeiter Union*.

25. On Grant's policies, see Prucha, *The Great Father*, 152–80; Edmund J. Danziger Jr., "Native American Resistance and Accommodation During the Late Nineteenth Century," in *The Gilded Age: Perspectives on the Origins of Modern America*, ed. Charles W. Calhoun (Lanham: Rowman and Littlefield Publishers, 2007), 167–86.

26. On the programs for the education of American Indians, see Michael C. Coleman, *American Indian Children at School, 1850–1930* (Jackson: University Press of Mississippi, 1993); David Wallace Adams, *Education for Extinction: American Indians and the Boarding School Experience, 1875–1928* (Lawrence: University Press of Kansas, 1995); Jacqueline Fear-Segal, *White Man's Club: Schools, Race, and the Struggle of Indian Acculturation* (Lincoln: University of Nebraska Press, 2007).

27. Prucha, *The Great Father*, 183–93; Paul Stuart, *The Indian Office: Growth and Development of an American Institution, 1865–1900* (Ann Arbor: UMI Research, 1979); White, *Republic for Which It Stands*, 288–304.

28. "A Disgrace to the Nation. The Indian Bureau Investigated," *New York Times*, January 8, 1878.

29. Donald L. Fixico, *Bureau of Indian Affairs* (Santa Barbara: Greenwood, 2012), 53–55.

30. See infra chapter 4; Hans L. Trefousse, *Carl Schurz: A Biography* (New York: Fordham University Press, 1998); Alison Clark Efford, *German Immigrants, Race, and Citizenship in the Civil War Era* (Cambridge: Cambridge University Press, 2014); Walter Johnson, *The Broken Heart of America: St. Louis and the Violent History of the United States* (New York: Basic Books, 2020), 265–87.

31. "Die Spitzbubenwirtschaft im Indianer Department," *Volksstimme des Westens*, June 6, 1878.

32. "Wie die Indianer beraubt und betrogen worden," *Volksstimme des Westens*, July 24, 1878.

33. "Die Ursache der Indianer-Kriege," *Volksstimme des Westens*, November 14, 1878.

34. "Der neueste Indianerkrieg," *New Yorker Volkszteitung*, May 13, 1882.

35. On the clashes involving the Nez Perce in the summer of 1877, see White, *Republic for Which It Stands*, 337–42.

36. "Wie man Indianer civilisiert," *Volksstimme des Westens*, August 23, 1878.

37. "Wie man Indianer civilisiert," *Volksstimme des Westens*.

38. "Die armen Indianer," *Volksstimme des Westens*, May 10, 1878.

39. "Die armen Indianer," *Volksstimme des Westens*.

40. "Die Zivilisierung der Indianer," *Sozialist*, July 18, 1885.

41. "Die Zivilisierung der Indianer," *Sozialist*.

42. Carl Schurz, "Present Aspects of the Indian Problem," *North American Review* 258, no. 4 (1881; repr. Winter 1973): 45. For a critique of Schurz's policies, see Johnson, *Broken Heart of America*, 282–87.

43. Schurz, "Indian Problem."

44. Schurz, "Indian Problem."

45. "Die Zivilisierung der Indianer," *Sozialist*. Emphasis added.

46. Bethencourt, *Racisms*, 290–305. The progressive academization of the study of Native Americans was described in Curtis M. Hinsley, *The Smithsonian and the American Indian: Making a Moral Anthropology in Victorian America* (Washington: Smithsonian Institution Press, 1981).

47. Lewis Henry Morgan, *Ancient Society, or Researches in the Lines of Human Progress from Savagery, through Barbarism to Civilization* (1877; repr. New York: Henry Holt, 1907); Daniel Noah Moses, *The Promise of Progress: The Life and Work of Lewis Henry Morgan* (Columbia: University of Missouri Press, 2009); Robert F. Berkhofer, *The White Man's Indian: Images of the American Indian from Columbus to the Present* (New York: Vintage Books, 1979), 53; Frederick E. Hoxie, *A Final Promise: The Campaign to Assimilate the Indians, 1880–1920* (Lincoln: University of Nebraska Press, 1984), 14–21; Conn, *History's Shadow*, 139.

48. Conn, *History's Shadow*, 179.

49. Musto, *Last Years of Karl Marx*, 25–35. Marx's notes on Morgan's book were published in 1971. See Krader, *Ethnological Notebooks of Karl Marx*.

50. Franklin Rosemont, "Karl Marx and the Iroquois," libcom.org, accessed June 23, 2015, https://libcom.org/library/karl-marx-iroquois-franklin-rosemont (emphasis in the original).

51. Franz Boas, *Race, Language and Culture* (Chicago: University of Chicago Press, 1965), 243–59; Berkhofer, *White Man's Indian*, 62–64; Martha Hodes, "Utter Confusion and Contradiction: Franz Boas and the Problem of Human Complexion," in *Indigenous Visions: Rediscovering the World of Franz Boas*, eds. Ned Blackhawk and Isaiah Lorado Wilner (New Haven, CT: Yale University Press, 2018), 185–208; Maria Baghramian and Adam Carter, "Relativism," *The Stanford Encyclopedia of Philosophy* (Fall 2015 edition), accessed September 10, 2015, http://plato.stanford.edu/archives/fall2015/entries/relativism/.

52. Rosemont, "Karl Marx and the Iroquois"; Moses, *Promise of Progress*, 281.

53. Moses, *Promise of Progress*, 278.

54. Krader, *Ethnological Notebooks of Karl Marx*; Raya Dunayevskaya, *Rosa Luxemburg, Women's Liberation, and Marx's Philosophy of Revolution* (Atlantic Highlands: Humanities Press, 1982); Kevin B. Anderson, *Marx at the Margins: On Nationalism, Ethnicity, and Non-Western Societies* (Chicago: University of Chicago Press, 2010), 199–208. Other contributions favoring a multilinear interpretation of Marx's thinking include Lucia Pradella, "Marx and the Global South: Connecting History and Value Theory," *Sociology* 51, no. 1 (2016): 146–61, https://doi.org/10.1177/0038038516661267; Sandro Mezzadra and Ranabir Samaddar, "Colonialism," in *The Marx Revival: Key Concepts and New Interpretations*, ed. Marcello Musto (Cambridge: Cambridge University Press, 2020), 247–65.

55. As chapter six will clarify, the SLP leader Daniel De Leon was a great supporter of Morgan's theories. On the debate on evolutionism in the Second International, see Lorenzo Costaguta, "Before Baku: The Second International and the Debate on Colonialism (1900–1920)," in *The Comintern and the Global South: Global Designs/Local Encounters*, eds. Anne Garland Mahler and Paolo Capuzzo (London: Routledge, 2022).

56. "Über die Zivilisationsfähigkeit der Indianer," *Chicagoer Vorbote*, March 4, 1882.

57. "Über die Zivilisationsfähigkeit," *Chicagoer Vorbote*. On Morton and phrenology, see Stephen Jay Gould, "American Polygeny and Craniometry before Darwin: Blacks and Indians as Separate, Inferior Species," in *The "Racial" Economy of Science: Toward a Democratic Future*, ed. Sandra Harding (Bloomington: Indiana University Press, 1993), 84–115.

58. "Indianer Politik," *New Yorker Volkszeitung*, January 28, 1882.

59. James T. King, "George Crook: Indian Fighter and Humanitarian," *Arizona and the West* 9, no. 4 (Winter 1967): 333–48.

60. "Zur Indianerfrage," *New Yorker Volkszeitung*, October 4, 1884.

61. "Sollen die Indianer Kommunisten bleiben oder zu Individualisten gemacht werden?" *Sozialist*, November 28, 1885.

62. "Sollen die Indianer," *Sozialist*.

63. "Die Indianer Frage," *New Yorker Volkszeitung*, January 10, 1891.

64. White, *Republic for Which It Stands*.

Chapter 6. The SLP in the 1890s

1. *People*, May 1, 1899. An engraved image of the slave Gordon was published for the first time in 1863. See "A Typical Negro," *Harper's Weekly*, July 4, 1863.

2. Frank Girard and Ben Perry, *The Socialist Labor Party: A Short History, 1876–1991* (Philadelphia: Livra Books, 1993), 17–22; Rudolph Katz, "With De Leon since '89," in *Daniel De Leon, the Man and His Work: A Symposium* (New York: New York Labor News Company, 1919), 32, 48.

3. B. F. Keinard, "The 'Color Line' Develops into the 'Class Struggle,'" *People*, May 1, 1899.

4. The phrase "prudential unionism" comes from Bruce Laurie, *Artisans into Workers: Labor in Nineteenth-Century America* (New York: Hill and Wang, 1989), 211–20. For this period, I also refer to Rosanne Currarino, *The Labor Question in America: Economic Democracy in the Gilded Age* (Urbana: University of Illinois Press, 2011), 86–113. Historians discuss three main attempts made by socialists to influence American organized labor: the attempts to "bore from within" both the American Federation of the Labor and the Knights of Labor in the early 1890s, and the foundation of the Socialist Trade and Labor Alliance in 1895. These attempts are discussed and referenced below in this chapter.

5. See, for example, Theodore Draper, *The Roots of American Communism* (New York: Viking, 1963), 31; Seymour Martin Lipset and Gary Marks, *It Didn't Happen Here: Why Socialism Failed in the United States* (New York: W. W. Norton, 2000), 138; Michael Kazin, *American Dreamers: How the Left Changed a Nation* (New York: Alfred Knopf, 2011), 85–90. An exception that stresses the dynamic interconnection between immigrant and American socialism is Paul Buhle, *Marxism in the United States: A History of the American Left* (London: Verso, 2013), 19–57.

6. An example of this trend with regards to Edward Bellamy can be found in Kazin, *American Dreamers*, 77–85.

7. I further articulated this idea in the introduction of the article Lorenzo Costaguta, "'Geographies of Peoples': Scientific Racialism and Labor Internationalism in Gilded Age American Socialism," *Journal of the Gilded Age and Progressive Era* 2 (2019): 199–220, https://doi.org/10.1017/S1537781418000701. For examples of how ethnic radicalism shaped American radicalism during the Gilded Age, see James R. Barrett, *History from the Bottom Up and the Inside Out: Ethnicity, Race, and Identity in Working-Class History* (Durham: Duke University Press, 2017), 122–43; Tony Michels, *A Fire in Their Hearts: Yiddish Socialists in New York* (Cambridge, MA: Harvard University Press, 2005); Tom Goyens, *Beer and Revolution: The German Anarchist Movement in New York City, 1880–1914* (Urbana: University of Illinois Press, 2007); Bruce Nelson, *Beyond the Martyrs: A Social History of Chicago's Anarchists, 1870–1900* (New Brunswick, NJ: Rutgers University Press, 1988); Jacqueline Jones, *Goddess of Anarchy: The Life and Times of Lucy Parsons, American Radical* (New York: Basic Books, 2017).

8. Louis C. Fraina, a collaborator and long-time admirer of Daniel De Leon, first emphasized De Leon's attempt to "Americanize" the American socialist movement. See Louis C. Fraina, "Daniel De Leon," *The New Review* 2, no. 7 (July 1914): 391.

9. Howard H. Quint, *The Forging of American Socialism: Origins of the Modern Movement* (Columbia: University of South Carolina Press, 1953), 28. See also P. E. Maher, "Laurence Gronlund: Contributions to American Socialism," *The Western Political Quarterly* 15 (1962): 618–24, https://doi.org/10.1177/106591296201500403.

10. Laurence Gronlund, *The Cooperative Commonwealth in Its Outlines: An Exposition of Modern Socialism* (Cambridge, MA: Harvard University Press, 1965), 6–7.

11. See Mark Pittenger, *American Socialists and Evolutionary Thought, 1870–1920* (Madison: University of Wisconsin Press, 1993), 44–46; "Selection from the Autobiography of Peter Anderson Lofgreen," in Benjamin E. Lofgren, *A Simple Faith: Anders Persson Löfgren. Swedish Son—Mormon Immigrant* (Salt Lake City: Andres Lofgren Family Organization, 1996), 110. I am indebted to David R. Roediger for sharing this information relative to this curious (and unsolved) Gronlund/Lofgreen controversy.

12. The pamphlet was advertised in the SLP press across the late 1870s and early 1880s. See *Labor Review*, March, April 1880.

13. Gronlund started speaking on behalf of the SLP in 1887, in the period following Henry George's defeat and the painful separation between the United Labor Party and the socialists. See "Socialism Pure and Undefiled," *Sun*, June 26, 1887. The *Workmen's Advocate*, the English-language paper published in New Haven and New York, published extracts from *The Cooperative Commonwealth*, followed Gronlund's public events closely, and advertised his works in the 1887–1891 period. See, for example, "White Slavery," *Workmen's Advocate*, July 18, 1886; "Lesson on Trusts," *Workmen's Advocate*, July 16, 1887.

14. Gronlund, *Cooperative Commonwealth*, 4.

15. Samuel Haber, "The Nightmare and the Dream: Edward Bellamy and the Travails of Socialist Thought," *Journal of American Studies* 36, no. 3 (2002): 417–40, 420,

https://doi.org/10.1017/S0021875802006898; Philipp Reick, "If *That* Is Socialism, We Won't Help Its Advent": The Impact of Edward Bellamy's Utopian Novel *Looking Backward* on Socialist Thought in Late-Nineteenth-Century Western Europe," in *Socialist Imaginations: Utopias, Myths, and the Masses*, eds. Stefan Arvidsson, Jakub Beneš, and Anja Kirsch (London: Routledge, 2019).

16. Quint, *Forging of American Socialism*, 30.

17. See the following issues of the *Workmen's Advocate*: February 2, 1889; December 28, 1889; January 11, 1890; February 14 and 22, 1890; June 7, 1890; September 13, 20, and 27, 1890.

18. *Workmen's Advocate*, November 8, 1890; *Workmen's Advocate*, March 17, 1891.

19. "The Ticket," *Workmen's Advocate*, October 4, 1890.

20. On the internecine fighting in the SLP in the late 1880s, see Morris Hillquit, *History of Socialism in the United States* (New York: Funk and Wagnall Company, 1903), 243–50; Daniel Bell, *Marxian Socialism in the United States* (Ithaca: Cornell University Press, 1953), 30–32; Michels, *Fire in Their Hearts*, 42–46.

21. The most exhaustive analysis of Daniel De Leon's background and his conversion to Marxian socialism is L. Glen Seretan, *Daniel De Leon: The Odyssey of an American Marxist* (Cambridge, MA: Harvard University Press, 1979), 5–46.

22. On De Leon in New York in the 1880s, see Thomas Bender, *Intellect and Public Life: Essays on the Social History of Academic Intellectuals in the United States* (Baltimore: Johns Hopkins University Press, 1993), 54–57.

23. Seretan, *Daniel De Leon*, 47–80.

24. Abraham Cahan, *From 'Bletter fun Mein Leben' by Abraham Cahan*, trans. and ed. Louis Lazarus, 1979, unpublished, Socialist Labor Party Papers, Tamiment Institute, New York. The Jewish American community was the second most important ethnic constituency of the SLP (after the German American). Cahan went on to become the editor of the *Jewish Daily Forward*, which he contributed to found in 1897, and a leading realist novelist. See Michels, *Fire in their Hearts*, 79–83, 91–115; Jules Chametzky, *From the Ghetto: The Fiction of Abraham Cahan* (Amherst: University of Massachusetts Press, 1977); Moses Rischin, ed., *Grandma Never Lived in America: The New Journalism of Abraham Cahan* (Bloomington: Indiana University Press, 1985).

25. Quoted in Paul Buhle, "Daniel DeLeon: Enigmatic Giant of the Left," *Reviews in American History* 8, no. 2 (1980): 264, https://doi.org/10.2307/2701128.

26. "Socialist Labor Party of the United States of America. National Platform adopted by the Seventh National Convention, at Chicago, Ill, October 12–15, 1889," marxists.org, accessed February 10, 2021, https://www.marxists.org/history/usa/eam/slp/slpdownloads.html.

27. Girard and Perry, *Socialist Labor Party*, 18; Socialist Labor Party, Proceedings of the Ninth Annual Convention of the Socialist Labor Party, held at Grand Central Palace, 43 st. and Lexington Ave., N.Y. City. July 4th to July 10th, 1896, ed. Robert Bills, accessed October 27, 2015, http://www.slp.org/pdf/slphist/nc_1896.pdf; Socialist Labor Party, Proceedings of the Tenth National Convention of the Socialist Labor

Party held in New York City, June 2 to June 8, 1900 (New York: New York Labor News Company, 1901).

28. Hillquit, *History of Socialism*, 285–301; Seretan, *Daniel De Leon*, 82–115; Laurie, *Artisans into Workers*, 187–90.

29. Among the works translated by De Leon were Engels's *Socialism: Utopian and Scientific*, Marx's *Eighteenth Brumaire of Louis Bonaparte* and *The Critique of the Gotha Programme*, Bebel's *Women and Socialism*, and several short works by Karl Kautsky. See Seretan, *Daniel De Leon*, 83.

30. Daniel De Leon, "Uncle Sam and Brother Jonathan," *People*, 1891–1899.

31. Geoff Eley, *Forging Democracy: The History of the Left in Europe, 1850–2000* (New York: Oxford University Press, 2002), 33–46; Michaels, *Fire in Their Hearts*; Marcella Bencivenni, *Italian Immigrant Radical Culture: The Idealism of the Sovversivi in the United States, 1890–1940* (New York: New York University Press, 2016), 7–32.

32. Pittenger, *American Socialists*, 48.

33. Gronlund, *Cooperative Commonwealth*, 8. Emphasis in the original.

34. Daniel De Leon, Reform or Revolution: An Address Delivered by Daniel De Leon under the Auspices of the People's Union, at Wells' Memorial Hall, Boston, January 26, 1896, marxists.org, accessed June 8, 2016, https://www.marxists.org/archive/deleon/pdf/1896/RefRev.pdf, 7; for a critical analysis of this aspect, see the important revisionist article: Don McKee, "Daniel De Leon: A Reappraisal," *Labor History* 1, no. 3 (1960): 264–97, https://doi.org/10.1080/00236566008583855.

35. Daniel De Leon, "Reform or Revolution," 8.

36. Herbert Spencer attacked British socialism in an 1884 article in the *Contemporary Review* titled "The Coming Slavery." This article was later reprinted in the collection *The Man versus the State, with Six Essays on Government, Society and Freedom* (Indianapolis: Liberty Fund, 1982). In March 1890, the *New York World* reproduced articles in which Spencer attacked socialism. The *Workmen's Advocate* responded to those articles. See "Herbert Spencer on Socialism," *Sunday World*, March 21, 1891.

37. "Herbert Spencer," *People*, April 5, 1891.

38. For examples of mentions of Morgan in De Leon's speeches, see De Leon, "Reform and Revolution"; Daniel De Leon, *Socialism versus Anarchism: A Lecture Delivered at Boston, October 13, 1901* (New York: Socialist Labor Party, 1919); Buhle, *Marxism in the United States*, 54–55; Pittenger, *American Socialists*, 103; on Morgan in the *People*, H. S. Sley, "Literary Notice," *People*, February 7, 1897.

39. Daniel De Leon, "The Philosophy of the History of Political Parties," *People*, April 21, 1895.

40. Matthew Maguire and Lucien Sanial, "American Report to the International Socialist and Trade Union Congress," *People*, August 16, 1896; *People*, May 1, 1899.

41. Daniel De Leon, "Restiveness among Colored Workingmen," *People*, May 9, 1897.

42. Richard White, *The Republic for Which It Stands: The United States during Reconstruction and the Gilded Age* (New York: Oxford University Press, 2017), 836–54.

43. David W. Blight, *Frederick Douglass: Prophet of Freedom* (New York: Simon and Schuster, 2018), 691–744.

44. Daniel De Leon, "Stone-Blind Douglass," *People*, October 19, 1894.

45. De Leon, "Stone-Blind Douglass."

46. Daniel De Leon, *Flashlights of the Amsterdam International Socialist Congress, 1904* (1904; repr. New York: New York Labor News Company, 1923).

47. De Leon, *Flashlights of the Amsterdam International Socialist Congress*; David R. Roediger and Elizabeth D. Esch, *The Production of Difference: Race and the Management of Labor in U.S. History* (New York: Oxford University Press, 2012).

48. Daniel De Leon, "Good for the Negroes!" *Daily People*, December 31, 1903.

49. S. M. White, "Georgia: The SLP at Work," *People*, May 1, 1899.

50. S. H. D. McTier, "Virginia: The Proud Mother of Presidents," *People*, May 1, 1899.

51. Harry R. Engel, "Alabama: Cimerian Conditions of Backwardness," *People*, May 1, 1899.

52. *People*, November 3, 1895; April 5, 1896.

53. Engel, "Alabama."

54. Frank Lellner, "Texas: Progress in the Lone Star State," *People*, May 1, 1899.

55. Henry McAnarney, "Maryland: The Movement Purging Itself Clean," *People*, May 1, 1899.

56. J. Howard Sharp, "The Negro Question in America," *People*, August 29, 1897.

57. Sharp, "Negro Question."

58. Sharp, "Negro Question."

59. The Blair education bill, a proposal put forward by the Republican Congressman Henry W. Blair in 1891, advocated the use of federal funds to favor programs of education and prevent exclusion from the franchise based in illiteracy. See Gordon B. McKinney, *Henry W. Blair's Campaign to Reform America: From the Civil War to the U.S. Senate* (Lexington: University of Kentucky Press, 2013).

60. *People*, April 24, 1898.

61. Robert Windon, "What Will Socialism Do for the Negro?" *People*, December 4, 1898.

62. Daniel De Leon, "Is there a 'Woman Question'?" *People*, January 14, 1900.

63. James Stevenson, "Daniel De Leon: The Relationship of Socialism Party and European Marxism, 1890–1914" (unpublished Ph.D. dissertation, University of Wisconsin-Madison, 1977), 120. Stalvey has a full breakdown of the SLP's electoral results in the 1890s. James Stalvey, "Daniel De Leon: A Study of Marxian Orthodoxy in the United States" (unpublished Ph.D. dissertation, University of Illinois, 1946), appendix 1, 270–72.

64. Katz, *Daniel De Leon*, 32.

65. Philip S. Foner, *History of the Labor Movement in the United States, Vol. II: From the Founding of the American Federation of Labor to the Emergence of American Imperialism* (New York: International Publishers, 1956), 279–300; David Herreshoff, *American Disciples of Marx: From the Age of Jackson to the Progressive Era* (Detroit:

Wayne State University Press, 1967), 120–29; Laurie, *Artisans into Workers*, 187–91; Buhle, *Marxism in the United States*, 49–55.

66. Hillquit offers his own side of the story in *History of Socialism*, 307–30. See also Bell, *Marxian Socialism*, 44–45; Ira Kipnis, *American Socialist Movement 1897-1912* (New York: Columbia University Press, 1952), 7–42.

67. Socialist Labor Party, Proceedings of the Ninth Annual Convention, 52.

68. Michels, *Fire in Their Hearts*, 95–107.

69. Daniel De Leon, "Signposts That Will Have to Guide the Party for the Safe-Keeping of a 'Daily People,'" *People*, April 2, 1899.

70. Daniel De Leon, "The Class Struggle within the Party," *People*, July 16, 1899.

71. "'American' Socialism," *People*, November 12, 1899.

72. Buhle, "Daniel DeLeon," 270.

Conclusion

1. Quoted in Philip S. Foner, *American Socialism and Black Americans: From the Age of Jackson to World War II* (Westport, CT: Greenwood Press, 1977), 95.

2. Foner, *American Socialism*, 95–96.

3. Foner, *American Socialism*, 97.

4. Foner, *American Socialism*, 98.

5. For the SLP resolution, see infra chapter four. For the SPA resolution, see Paul Heideman, "Introduction," in *Class Struggle and the Color Line: American Socialism and the Race Question, 1900–1930*, ed. Heideman (Chicago: Haymarket Books, 2018), 18–19.

6. Jack Ross, *The Socialist Party of America: A Complete History* (Minion: Potomac Books, 2015).

7. On the SPA and race, see Sally M. Miller, *Race, Ethnicity, and Gender in Early Twentieth-Century American Socialism* (London: Garland, 1996); Heideman, *Class Struggle*; Michael C. Dawson, *Blacks in and Out of the Left* (Cambridge, MA: Harvard University Press, 2013). On Ameringer and Oklahoma, see James R. Green, *Grass-Roots Socialism; Radical Movements in the Southwest, 1895–1943* (Baton Rouge: LSU Press, 1978); on Harrison and Du Bois, see Jeffrey B. Perry, *Hubert Harrison: The Voice of Harlem Radicalism, 1883–1918* (New York: Columbia University Press, 2009); David Leverling Lewis, *W. E. B. Du Bois: Biography of a Race, 1868–1919* (New York: Henry Holt, 1993); Dan S. Green and Earl Smith, "W. E. B. Du Bois and the Concepts of Race and Class," *Phylon* 44, no. 4 (1983): 262–72; on Berger, Sally M. Miller, *Victor Berger and the Promise of Constructive Socialism, 1910–1920* (Westport, CT: Greenwood, 1973); on O'Hara, Sally M. Miller, *From Prairie to Prison: The Life of Social Activist Kate Richards O'Hare* (Columbia: University of Missouri Press, 1993).

8. Heideman, *Class Struggle*, 24.

9. Quoted in Heideman, *Class Struggle*, 48–55.

10. Jacob A. Zumoff, *The Communist International and U.S. Communism, 1919–1929* (Leiden: Brill, 2014); Mark Solomon, *The Cry Was Unity: Communists

and African Americans, 1917–1936 (Jackson: University Press of Mississippi, 1998); Michael Denning, *The Cultural Front: The Laboring of American Culture in the Twentieth Century* (London: Verso, 1996); Eric Arnesen, "A. Philip Randolph: Emerging Socialist Radical," in *Reframing Randolph: Labor, Black Freedom, and the Legacies of A. Philip Randolph*, eds. Andrew E. Kersten and Clarence Lang (New York: New York University Press, 2015), 45–76.

11. Jacquelyn Dowd Hall, "The Long Civil Rights Movement and the Political Uses of the Past," *The Journal of American History* (2005), 1233–63, https://doi.org/10.2307/3660172; Glenda Elizabeth Gilmore, *Defying Dixie: The Radical Roots of Civil Rights, 1919–1950* (New York: W. W. Norton Company, 2008); Barbara Ransby, *Ella Baker and the Black Freedom Movement: A Radical Democratic Vision* (Chapel Hill: University of North Carolina Press, 2004); John D'Emilio, *Lost Prophet: The Life and Times of Bayard Rustin* (Chicago: University of Chicago Press, 2003).

12. On women's activism in the SLP and the SPA, see Mari Jo Buhle, *Women and American Socialism: 1870–1920* (Urbana: University of Illinois Press, 1983). On the SPA, the CPUSA, and the Left between the 1920s and the 1950s, Beth Slutsky, *Gendering Radicalism: Women and Communism in Twentieth-Century California* (Lincoln: University of Nebraska Press, 2015); Kate Weigand, *Red Feminism: American Communism and the Making of Women's Liberation* (Baltimore: Johns Hopkins University Press, 2001); Carole Boyce Davies, *Left of Karl Marx: The Political Life of Black Communist Claudia Jones* (Durham: Duke University Press, 2007). On the 1960s, see Sharon Monteith and Peter Ling, *Gender and the Civil Rights Movement* (London: Garland, 1999); Ashley D. Farmer, *Remaking Black Power: How Black Women Transformed an Era* (Chapel Hill: University of North Carolina Press, 2017).

13. Quoted in Keeanga-Yamahtta Taylor, ed., *How We Get Free: Black Feminism and the Combahee River Collective* (Chicago: Haymarket Books, 2017), 19.

14. Taylor, *How We Get Free*, 7.

15. Robin Archer suggested that animosity against racial minority was a key fact in the creation of a labor party in Australia. See Robin Archer, *Why Is There No Labor Party in the United States?* (Princeton, NJ: Princeton University Press, 2008), 55–58. Allison Drew indicated that a similar dynamic took place in South Africa. See Allison Drew, *Discordant Comrades: Identities and Loyalties on the South African Left* (2000, repr. London: Routledge, 2019). On the AFL, see Philip S. Foner, *The Black Worker during the Era of the American Federation of Labor and the Railroad Brotherhoods* (Philadelphia: Temple University Press, 1979).

16. Geoff Eley, *Forging Democracy: The History of the Left in Europe, 1850–2000* (New York: Oxford University Press, 2002), 45.

17. Richard Iton, *Solidarity Blues: Race, Culture, and the American Left* (Chapel Hill: University of North Carolina Press, 2000), 13–22.

Index

Page numbers in italics refer to figures.

LORENZO COSTAGUTA is a lecturer in US history at the University of Bristol.

The Working Class in American History

Worker City, Company Town: Iron and Cotton-Worker Protest in Troy and Cohoes, New York, 1855–84 *Daniel J. Walkowitz*
Life, Work, and Rebellion in the Coal Fields: The Southern West Virginia Miners, 1880–1922 *David Alan Corbin*
Women and American Socialism, 1870–1920 *Mari Jo Buhle*
Lives of Their Own: Blacks, Italians, and Poles in Pittsburgh, 1900–1960 *John Bodnar, Roger Simon, and Michael P. Weber*
Working-Class America: Essays on Labor, Community, and American Society *Edited by Michael H. Frisch and Daniel J. Walkowitz*
Eugene V. Debs: Citizen and Socialist *Nick Salvatore*
American Labor and Immigration History, 1877–1920s: Recent European Research *Edited by Dirk Hoerder*
Workingmen's Democracy: The Knights of Labor and American Politics *Leon Fink*
The Electrical Workers: A History of Labor at General Electric and Westinghouse, 1923–60 *Ronald W. Schatz*
The Mechanics of Baltimore: Workers and Politics in the Age of Revolution, 1763–1812 *Charles G. Steffen*
The Practice of Solidarity: American Hat Finishers in the Nineteenth Century *David Bensman*
The Labor History Reader *Edited by Daniel J. Leab*
Solidarity and Fragmentation: Working People and Class Consciousness in Detroit, 1875–1900 *Richard Oestreicher*
Counter Cultures: Saleswomen, Managers, and Customers in American Department Stores, 1890–1940 *Susan Porter Benson*
The New England Working Class and the New Labor History *Edited by Herbert G. Gutman and Donald H. Bell*
Labor Leaders in America *Edited by Melvyn Dubofsky and Warren Van Tine*
Barons of Labor: The San Francisco Building Trades and Union Power in the Progressive Era *Michael Kazin*
Gender at Work: The Dynamics of Job Segregation by Sex during World War II *Ruth Milkman*
Once a Cigar Maker: Men, Women, and Work Culture in American Cigar Factories, 1900–1919 *Patricia A. Cooper*
A Generation of Boomers: The Pattern of Railroad Labor Conflict in Nineteenth-Century America *Shelton Stromquist*
Work and Community in the Jungle: Chicago's Packinghouse Workers, 1894–1922 *James R. Barrett*
Workers, Managers, and Welfare Capitalism: The Shoeworkers and Tanners of Endicott Johnson, 1890–1950 *Gerald Zahavi*
Men, Women, and Work: Class, Gender, and Protest in the New England Shoe Industry, 1780–1910 *Mary Blewett*

Workers on the Waterfront: Seamen, Longshoremen, and Unionism in the 1930s
Bruce Nelson
German Workers in Chicago: A Documentary History of Working-Class Culture from 1850 to World War I *Edited by Hartmut Keil and John B. Jentz*
On the Line: Essays in the History of Auto Work *Edited by Nelson Lichtenstein and Stephen Meyer III*
Labor's Flaming Youth: Telephone Operators and Worker Militancy, 1878–1923
Stephen H. Norwood
Another Civil War: Labor, Capital, and the State in the Anthracite Regions of Pennsylvania, 1840–68 *Grace Palladino*
Coal, Class, and Color: Blacks in Southern West Virginia, 1915–32
Joe William Trotter Jr.
For Democracy, Workers, and God: Labor Song-Poems and Labor Protest, 1865–95 *Clark D. Halker*
Dishing It Out: Waitresses and Their Unions in the Twentieth Century
Dorothy Sue Cobble
The Spirit of 1848: German Immigrants, Labor Conflict, and the Coming of the Civil War *Bruce Levine*
Working Women of Collar City: Gender, Class, and Community in Troy, New York, 1864–86 *Carole Turbin*
Southern Labor and Black Civil Rights: Organizing Memphis Workers
Michael K. Honey
Radicals of the Worst Sort: Laboring Women in Lawrence, Massachusetts, 1860–1912 *Ardis Cameron*
Producers, Proletarians, and Politicians: Workers and Party Politics in Evansville and New Albany, Indiana, 1850–87 *Lawrence M. Lipin*
The New Left and Labor in the 1960s *Peter B. Levy*
The Making of Western Labor Radicalism: Denver's Organized Workers, 1878–1905 *David Brundage*
In Search of the Working Class: Essays in American Labor History and Political Culture *Leon Fink*
Lawyers against Labor: From Individual Rights to Corporate Liberalism
Daniel R. Ernst
"We Are All Leaders": The Alternative Unionism of the Early 1930s
Edited by Staughton Lynd
The Female Economy: The Millinery and Dressmaking Trades, 1860–1930
Wendy Gamber
"Negro and White, Unite and Fight!": A Social History of Industrial Unionism in Meatpacking, 1930–90 *Roger Horowitz*
Power at Odds: The 1922 National Railroad Shopmen's Strike *Colin J. Davis*
The Common Ground of Womanhood: Class, Gender, and Working Girls' Clubs, 1884–1928 *Priscilla Murolo*
Marching Together: Women of the Brotherhood of Sleeping Car Porters
Melinda Chateauvert

Down on the Killing Floor: Black and White Workers in Chicago's Packinghouses, 1904–54 *Rick Halpern*
Labor and Urban Politics: Class Conflict and the Origins of Modern Liberalism in Chicago, 1864–97 *Richard Schneirov*
All That Glitters: Class, Conflict, and Community in Cripple Creek *Elizabeth Jameson*
Waterfront Workers: New Perspectives on Race and Class *Edited by Calvin Winslow*
Labor Histories: Class, Politics, and the Working-Class Experience *Edited by Eric Arnesen, Julie Greene, and Bruce Laurie*
The Pullman Strike and the Crisis of the 1890s: Essays on Labor and Politics *Edited by Richard Schneirov, Shelton Stromquist, and Nick Salvatore*
AlabamaNorth: African-American Migrants, Community, and Working-Class Activism in Cleveland, 1914–45 *Kimberley L. Phillips*
Imagining Internationalism in American and British Labor, 1939–49 *Victor Silverman*
William Z. Foster and the Tragedy of American Radicalism *James R. Barrett*
Colliers across the Sea: A Comparative Study of Class Formation in Scotland and the American Midwest, 1830–1924 *John H. M. Laslett*
"Rights, Not Roses": Unions and the Rise of Working-Class Feminism, 1945–80 *Dennis A. Deslippe*
Testing the New Deal: The General Textile Strike of 1934 in the American South *Janet Irons*
Hard Work: The Making of Labor History *Melvyn Dubofsky*
Southern Workers and the Search for Community: Spartanburg County, South Carolina *G. C. Waldrep III*
We Shall Be All: A History of the Industrial Workers of the World (abridged edition) *Melvyn Dubofsky, ed. Joseph A. McCartin*
Race, Class, and Power in the Alabama Coalfields, 1908–21 *Brian Kelly*
Duquesne and the Rise of Steel Unionism *James D. Rose*
Anaconda: Labor, Community, and Culture in Montana's Smelter City *Laurie Mercier*
Bridgeport's Socialist New Deal, 1915–36 *Cecelia Bucki*
Indispensable Outcasts: Hobo Workers and Community in the American Midwest, 1880–1930 *Frank Tobias Higbie*
After the Strike: A Century of Labor Struggle at Pullman *Susan Eleanor Hirsch*
Corruption and Reform in the Teamsters Union *David Witwer*
Waterfront Revolts: New York and London Dockworkers, 1946–61 *Colin J. Davis*
Black Workers' Struggle for Equality in Birmingham *Horace Huntley and David Montgomery*
The Tribe of Black Ulysses: African American Men in the Industrial South *William P. Jones*
City of Clerks: Office and Sales Workers in Philadelphia, 1870–1920 *Jerome P. Bjelopera*

Reinventing "The People": The Progressive Movement, the Class Problem,
and the Origins of Modern Liberalism *Shelton Stromquist*
Radical Unionism in the Midwest, 1900–1950 *Rosemary Feurer*
Gendering Labor History *Alice Kessler-Harris*
James P. Cannon and the Origins of the American Revolutionary Left, 1890–1928
Bryan D. Palmer
Glass Towns: Industry, Labor, and Political Economy in Appalachia, 1890–1930s
Ken Fones-Wolf
Workers and the Wild: Conservation, Consumerism, and Labor
in Oregon, 1910–30 *Lawrence M. Lipin*
Wobblies on the Waterfront: Interracial Unionism in Progressive-Era Philadelphia
Peter Cole
Red Chicago: American Communism at Its Grassroots, 1928–35 *Randi Storch*
Labor's Cold War: Local Politics in a Global Context
Edited by Shelton Stromquist
Bessie Abramowitz Hillman and the Making of the Amalgamated Clothing
Workers of America *Karen Pastorello*
The Great Strikes of 1877 *Edited by David O. Stowell*
Union-Free America: Workers and Antiunion Culture *Lawrence Richards*
Race against Liberalism: Black Workers and the UAW in Detroit
David M. Lewis-Colman
Teachers and Reform: Chicago Public Education, 1929–70 *John F. Lyons*
Upheaval in the Quiet Zone: 1199/SEIU and the Politics of Healthcare Unionism
Leon Fink and Brian Greenberg
Shadow of the Racketeer: Scandal in Organized Labor *David Witwer*
Sweet Tyranny: Migrant Labor, Industrial Agriculture, and Imperial Politics
Kathleen Mapes
Staley: The Fight for a New American Labor Movement *Steven K. Ashby and
C. J. Hawking*
On the Ground: Labor Struggles in the American Airline Industry
Liesl Miller Orenic
NAFTA and Labor in North America *Norman Caulfield*
Making Capitalism Safe: Work Safety and Health Regulation
in America, 1880–1940 *Donald W. Rogers*
Good, Reliable, White Men: Railroad Brotherhoods, 1877–1917
Paul Michel Taillon
Spirit of Rebellion: Labor and Religion in the New Cotton South *Jarod Roll*
The Labor Question in America: Economic Democracy in the Gilded Age
Rosanne Currarino
Banded Together: Economic Democratization in the Brass Valley
Jeremy Brecher
The Gospel of the Working Class: Labor's Southern Prophets
in New Deal America *Erik Gellman and Jarod Roll*
Guest Workers and Resistance to U.S. Corporate Despotism *Immanuel Ness*

Gleanings of Freedom: Free and Slave Labor along the Mason-Dixon Line, 1790–1860 *Max Grivno*
Chicago in the Age of Capital: Class, Politics, and Democracy during the Civil War and Reconstruction *John B. Jentz and Richard Schneirov*
Child Care in Black and White: Working Parents and the History of Orphanages *Jessie B. Ramey*
The Haymarket Conspiracy: Transatlantic Anarchist Networks *Timothy Messer-Kruse*
Detroit's Cold War: The Origins of Postwar Conservatism *Colleen Doody*
A Renegade Union: Interracial Organizing and Labor Radicalism *Lisa Phillips*
Palomino: Clinton Jencks and Mexican-American Unionism in the American Southwest *James J. Lorence*
Latin American Migrations to the U.S. Heartland: Changing Cultural Landscapes in Middle America *Edited by Linda Allegro and Andrew Grant Wood*
Man of Fire: Selected Writings *Ernesto Galarza, ed. Armando Ibarra and Rodolfo D. Torres*
A Contest of Ideas: Capital, Politics, and Labor *Nelson Lichtenstein*
Making the World Safe for Workers: Labor, the Left, and Wilsonian Internationalism *Elizabeth McKillen*
The Rise of the Chicago Police Department: Class and Conflict, 1850–1894 *Sam Mitrani*
Workers in Hard Times: A Long View of Economic Crises *Edited by Leon Fink, Joseph A. McCartin, and Joan Sangster*
Redeeming Time: Protestantism and Chicago's Eight-Hour Movement, 1866–1912 *William A. Mirola*
Struggle for the Soul of the Postwar South: White Evangelical Protestants and Operation Dixie *Elizabeth Fones-Wolf and Ken Fones-Wolf*
Free Labor: The Civil War and the Making of an American Working Class *Mark A. Lause*
Death and Dying in the Working Class, 1865–1920 *Michael K. Rosenow*
Immigrants against the State: Yiddish and Italian Anarchism in America *Kenyon Zimmer*
Fighting for Total Person Unionism: Harold Gibbons, Ernest Calloway, and Working-Class Citizenship *Robert Bussel*
Smokestacks in the Hills: Rural-Industrial Workers in West Virginia *Louis Martin*
Disaster Citizenship: Survivors, Solidarity, and Power in the Progressive Era *Jacob A. C. Remes*
The Pew and the Picket Line: Christianity and the American Working Class *Edited by Christopher D. Cantwell, Heath W. Carter, and Janine Giordano Drake*
Conservative Counterrevolution: Challenging Liberalism in 1950s Milwaukee *Tula A. Connell*
Manhood on the Line: Working-Class Masculinities in the American Heartland *Steve Meyer*

On Gender, Labor, and Inequality *Ruth Milkman*
The Making of Working-Class Religion *Matthew Pehl*
Civic Labors: Scholar Activism and Working-Class Studies
Edited by Dennis Deslippe, Eric Fure-Slocum, and John W. McKerley
Victor Arnautoff and the Politics of Art *Robert W. Cherny*
Against Labor: How U.S. Employers Organized to Defeat Union Activism
Edited by Rosemary Feurer and Chad Pearson
Teacher Strike! Public Education and the Making of a New American Political Order *Jon Shelton*
Hillbilly Hellraisers: Federal Power and Populist Defiance in the Ozarks
J. Blake Perkins
Sewing the Fabric of Statehood: Garment Unions, American Labor, and the Establishment of the State of Israel *Adam Howard*
Labor and Justice across the America *Edited by Leon Fink and Juan Manuel Palacio*
Frontiers of Labor: Comparative Histories of the United States and Australia
Edited by Greg Patmore and Shelton Stromquist
Women Have Always Worked: A Concise History, Second Edition
Alice Kessler-Harris
Remembering Lattimer: Labor, Migration, and Race in Pennsylvania Anthracite Country *Paul A. Shackel*
Disruption in Detroit: Autoworkers and the Elusive Postwar Boom
Daniel J. Clark
To Live Here, You Have to Fight: How Women Led Appalachian Movements for Social Justice *Jessica Wilkerson*
Dockworker Power: Race and Activism in Durban and the San Francisco Bay Area *Peter Cole*
Labor's Mind: A History of Working-Class Intellectual Life *Tobias Higbie*
The World in a City: Multiethnic Radicalism in Early Twentieth-Century Los Angeles *David M. Struthers*
Death to Fascism: Louis Adamic's Fight for Democracy *John P. Enyeart*
Upon the Altar of Work: Child Labor and the Rise of a New American Sectionalism *Betsy Wood*
Workers against the City: The Fight for Free Speech in *Hague v. CIO*
Donald W. Rogers
Union Renegades: Capitalism, Miners, and Organizing in the Gilded Age
Dana M. Caldemeyer
The Labor Board Crew: Remaking Worker-Employer Relations from Pearl Harbor to the Reagan Era *Ronald W. Schatz*
Grand Army of Labor: Workers, Veterans, and the Meaning of the Civil War
Matthew E. Stanley
A Matter of Moral Justice: Black Women Laundry Workers and the Fight for Justice *Jenny Carson*
Labor's End: How the Promise of Automation Degraded Work *Jason Resnikoff*

Toward a Cooperative Commonwealth: The Transplanted Roots of Farmer-Labor Radicalism in Texas *Thomas Alter II*

Working in the Magic City: Moral Economy in Early Twentieth-Century Miami *Thomas A. Castillo*

Where Are the Workers? Labor's Stories at Museums and Historic Sites *Edited by Robert Forrant and Mary Anne Trasciatti*

Labor's Outcasts: Migrant Farmworkers and Unions in North America, 1934–1966 *Andrew J. Hazelton*

Fraying Fabric: How Trade Policy and Industrial Decline Transformed America *James C. Benton*

Harry Bridges: Labor Radical, Labor Legend *Robert W. Cherny*

Strong Winds and Widow Makers: Workers, Nature, and Environmental Conflict in Pacific Northwest Timber Country *Steven C. Beda*

Purple Power: The History and Global Impact of SEIU *Edited by Luís LM Aguiar and Joseph A. McCartin*

The Bosses' Union: How Employers Organized to Fight Labor before the New Deal *Vilja Hulden*

Workers of All Colors Unite: Race and the Origins of American Socialism *Lorenzo Costaguta*

The University of Illinois Press
is a founding member of the
Association of University Presses.

University of Illinois Press
1325 South Oak Street
Champaign, IL 61820-6903
www.press.uillinois.edu